The Composition of Worlds

Philippe Descola

The Composition of Worlds

Interviews with Pierre Charbonnier

Translated by Ninon Vinsonneau and Jonathan Magidoff

polity

Originally published in French as *La composition des mondes. Entretiens avec Pierre Charbonnier* © Flammarion, Paris, 2014

This English edition © Polity Press, 2024

Polity Press
65 Bridge Street
Cambridge CB2 1UR, UK

Polity Press
111 River Street
Hoboken, NJ 07030, USA

All rights reserved. Except for the quotation of short passages for the purpose of criticism and review, no part of this publication may be reproduced, stored in a retrieval system or transmitted, in any form or by any means, electronic, mechanical, photocopying, recording or otherwise, without the prior permission of the publisher.

ISBN-13: 978-1-5095-5547-5 – hardback
ISBN-13: 978-1-5095-5548-2 – paperback

A catalogue record for this book is available from the British Library.

Library of Congress Control Number: 2023932762

Typeset in 10.5 on 12.5 pt Times New Roman
by Fakenham Prepress Solutions, Fakenham, Norfolk NR21 8NL

Printed and bound in the UK by TJ Books Limited

The publisher has used its best endeavours to ensure that the URLs for external websites referred to in this book are correct and active at the time of going to press. However, the publisher has no responsibility for the websites and can make no guarantee that a site will remain live or that the content is or will remain appropriate.

Every effort has been made to trace all copyright holders, but if any have been overlooked the publisher will be pleased to include any necessary credits in any subsequent reprint or edition.

For further information on Polity, visit our website:
politybooks.com

Contents

Foreword to the English edition	vii
1 A Taste for Inquiry	**1**
Philosophical journeys	1
Discovering the mind, discovering the world	7
Among the tribe of anthropologists	23
Entering the pantheon	36
2 An Amazonian Sojourn and the Challenges of Ethnography	**49**
The world of the forest	49
Living and working among the Achuar	66
The trial of return	78
3 The Diversity of Natures	**86**
The four corners of the world	86
Methodological questions	98
Conceptual reform	108
Forms of figuration	125
4 The Contemporary World in the Light of Anthropology	**133**
We moderns	133
From anthropology to ecology	154
The politics of anthropology	167
The museum	176
Notes	189
References	191
Index	195

Foreword to the English edition

Intellectual autobiography is a rather banal genre in the anglophone world, though less so in the dialogical form that it takes here. This calls for a few words of explanation to introduce this book, first published in French in 2014, to its new anglophone readership. When I agreed to engage in a book-long series of interviews with Pierre Charbonnier, as initially suggested by my publisher Flammarion, I had in mind an illustrious predecessor: the interviews of Claude Lévi-Strauss with Georges Charbonnier (no relation to Pierre!), recorded in 1959 for a radio broadcast and published two years later in book form. In these conversations, Lévi-Strauss candidly discussed both classic themes from his work—the status of anthropologists in their own society, the origins of language, the shift from nature to culture—and more contemporary topics of general interest such as modern art, the political responsibility of the scholar, and the ambiguity of progress. Without drawing too strong a parallel between the present book and those earlier interviews of Lévi-Strauss, his example convinced me that this format offered an ideal way to reach beyond the usual readership of scholarly books and to address, in an easy conversational style, both aspects of my contributions to anthropology that I had in mind to clarify and more general reflections on our present that are inspired by the theoretical positions I have taken over the years.

In contrast with the Lévi-Strauss interviews, however, these are more autobiographical. This is not due to any particular inclination to confide, but rather to the desire, shared by Pierre Charbonnier, to locate my anthropological arguments within a broader genealogy, namely within the intellectual, social, and political landscape in which they took shape. This kind of contextualization is often neglected in social science writing. Despite the concern for reflexivity that viii *Foreword to the English edition*

characterizes these disciplines, despite the recognized need to indicate the historical conditions that inform their conceptual orientations, despite the care taken by scholars to position their work in relation to that of predecessors and contemporaries, it is often the case that readers give in to the illusion of presentism, taking books and articles that were conceived and written decades earlier as if they were works of the current moment. So it is in order to dispel this kind of amnesia, to which even the most gifted students are not always immune, that I agreed to engage in this series of interviews. I have nonetheless removed from the English version all the lengthy passages on the academic institutions with which I have been affiliated throughout my career and on figures who have supported and influenced me at various points in my life, yet are little known outside France. I am confident that any anglophone readers who are interested in these more detailed aspects of the history of ideas will be able to find the relevant information in the French edition.

But this interview between a middle-aged anthropologist and a young philosopher does not deal with a bygone moment of anthropology— far from it. On the contrary, its intention is to show anthropology in the making, and especially that anthropology to which I have contributed during the past few decades. Under the paradoxical rubric "anthropology of nature"—paradoxical because it has resulted in the provincialization of the concept of nature itself—it seeks to incorporate nonhumans into the analysis of social life: not as productive forces, ecological constraints, foundations of symbolic systems, or backdrops to human action but as autonomous agents that provide greater depth and diversity to the kinds of relations that develop between humans and the various elements that compose their worlds. Countless non-European civilizations have invited us to perform such a decentering, and yet it took a long time for anthropology, and for the social sciences as a whole, to draw the full conclusions. This book seeks to highlight the circumstances that gave rise to the intuitions that allowed nonhumans to be brought back into the study of human praxis. Those intuitions were born of the intellectual and political tumult of 1970s and 1980s France, further kindled by ethnographic fieldwork—which was every bit as stimulating—in native Amazonia, whose enigmatic character our generation of anthropologists was just discovering, even while trying to give it intelligible form.

It is a tragic paradox that the very civilization that invented the idea of nature also became, as its values spread across a large part of the world, the instrument of the destruction of what that idea is meant

Foreword to the English edition   ix

to represent. For it is in the West, around the Mediterranean basin to begin with, and then in Western Europe, that this extraordinary idea first emerges: that all living beings and the inorganic surroundings in which their existence takes shape form an autonomous whole, from which humans have removed themselves. This idea did not emerge all at once. Ancient Greek sages, philosophers, and physicians had already developed the notion that the cosmos could be explained separately from the decrees of the gods and the effects of human action. They had objectivized, with Aristotle, a field that is made up of all beings that display an order and obey laws. Yet their version of nature was not as comprehensive as that of the moderns. For the advent of modern nature, there had to be a second separation, humans had to become external and superior to nature. It was Christianity that performed this second mutation, imposing, as it spread across Europe, the dual idea of the transcendence of the human being and of a universe extracted from nothingness by divine will. From this, humans derive the right and duty to administer the earth, God having formed them in order to exert control over creation, to organize and arrange it according to his needs. The final stage in the invention of nature took place in seventeenth-century Europe, resulting from a complex process that combined changes in aesthetic sensibilities and pictorial techniques, the discovery of other continents, progress in the mechanical arts, and the greater mastery it afforded over certain environments. The transformations in geometry, mathematical physics, optics, taxonomy, and the theory of the sign emerged from a reorganization of human-kind's relationship with the world and the tools that made it possible, rather than from accumulated discoveries and improved skills. The scientific revolution of the age of reason thus legitimized the idea of a mechanical nature, in which laws accounted both for the behavior of each element in a whole considered to be the sum of its parts and for the interactions between these elements.

The rest is well known. The withdrawal of humans from the world of which they had hitherto been part, and the transformation of that deserted world into a field of investigation and experimentation, into a system of resources and—later and only for a part of it—into a site of aesthetic delectation, all this only consolidated the initial divorce between the human and the nonhuman. The form that this divorce took was a very particular cosmology, naturalism, which has developed in Europe over the past three centuries and, characteristically, affirms the absolute singularity of humans as regards their cognitive and moral attributes—they alone have a soul—and connects them to

x

Foreword to the English edition

other beings only where physical attributes are concerned: they are subject to the same material laws. This gave rise to an unprecedented expansion of science and technical know-how, to the pageant of progress that it engendered, and to the unbridled exploitation of nature whose catastrophic consequences are now plain for all to see. This double movement was made possible by the external position that humans had acquired in relation to plants, animals, minerals, rivers, and mountains—now considered soulless objects and factors of production to be exploited. Other civilizations did not experience the same history; and it has been less than a century since some of them adopted the unrestrained mode of development induced by naturalism. It is not that these other cultures had been unaware of the fact that there may be differences and resemblances between the human and the nonhuman, but they did not locate them in the same way as westerners and went on thinking of nature, to borrow the poet Fernando Pessoa's formulation, as "parts without a whole."[1] A large part of my life as an anthropologist has been devoted to studying and trying to understand forms of worlding that are based on schemas through which certain peoples have identified and systematized continuities and disconti-nuities between the human and the nonhuman and have thus sought to compose distinct worlds. This book offers a glimpse into the results of these endeavors and the circumstances that have enabled them.

Hence it also has a political dimension. It would surely be absurd to claim that naturalist ontology alone is responsible for global warming, for the massive extinction of species, for the pollution of land, air, and sea—in short, for the accelerated degradation of that portion of the world whose autonomous existence it promoted. Yet it must be admitted that other civilizations, which did not imagine that the fate of humans was separate from that of nonhumans, have a lot to teach us about how we might extricate ourselves from our exorbitant anthropo-centrism and mend our severed ties with the many kinds of inhabitants our planet hosts. Joined by the lucid minds who, from within the West itself, perceived the tragic consequences of the withdrawal of humans from nature, these civilizations offer us an opportunity to meditate on mistakes made and on the way forward in attempting to mitigate their consequences. For a true cosmopolitics—one that associates all the world's occupants—can arise only from the construction of vast

---

[1] From poem XLVII, originally published in 1925, in Fernando Pessoa, 1997. *The Keeper of Sheep*, translated by Edwin Honig and Susan M. Brown, New York: Sheep Meadow Press.

Foreword to the English edition xi

networks that bring together human and nonhuman agents, mobilized in anticapitalist struggle at all the geographical levels at which their solidarity can be expressed, in the manner of the diverse beings that native populations have assembled into collectives in order to defend their territories and conditions of life. The "ontological turn" that the present author has contributed to promoting, far from being an escape into a metaphysics of abstraction, offers the possibility of a renewal of political action that makes imaginable hitherto inconceivable alliances between subjects far more diversified than those whose emergence was encouraged by nineteenth and twentieth-century political movements, reformist and revolutionary alike.

1

A Taste for Inquiry

Philosophical journeys

PIERRE CHARBONNIER *One often imagines that the lives of anthropologists must be filled with adventure and that, before becoming an anthropologist, one would need to have developed a strong taste for travel and for the other. What in your background might have led you on to this path?*

PHILIPPE DESCOLA I have sometimes said that anthropologists are 'professional onlookers' insofar as they turn a spontaneous curiosity for the spectacle of the world and for observing their fellow creatures into a form of knowledge; such curiosity is a part of their character long before they consider embracing this line of work. Claude Lévi-Strauss has rightly pointed out that, together with mathematics and music, ethnography is one of the few genuine vocations. In my case, this curiosity developed rather early on. It prompted me to travel, of course—and I'll come back to that—but it was also related to a sneaking feeling I had from childhood of being, in a sense, ill adapted to the world into which the contingency of birth had cast me. Having discussed it with colleagues, I believe that this sense of gentle incongruity is common among anthropologists, and perhaps even among social scientists and philosophers more broadly. In the end, it brings us to doubt that the world in which we live is a given; even if we find a place in it and lead a rather normal life in other respects, we never feel entirely at ease, for we have the feeling that one part of ourselves is always observing another part playing a role on the social stage, with more or less grace and conviction.

2   *A Taste for Inquiry*

This disposition creates a kind of reflexive distance from the scene of our activity that may follow either of two distinct paths. One is that of the writer and novelist and consists in making one's relationship with others the stuff of fiction; the other is that of the social scientist and entails a permanent questioning of the state of the social world and environment in which one happens to find oneself, of the values it upholds, and of the behavioral norms it deems acceptable—as well as of the part one plays in it as a subject, and as a political subject in particular. This habit of deliberate distancing from oneself and others is an important dimension of the vocation I was referring to; and it is sometimes encouraged by one's social environment. As has often been pointed out, minorities, for instance, are over-represented in anthropology. Lévi-Strauss, who was otherwise very discreet about his Jewishness, remarked what a paradoxical position he had been put in the first time he was called a "dirty Jew" at the local school, finding himself suddenly excluded from the national community to which he thought he belonged, and thus being made to consider it both from the inside, where he felt he was, and from the outside, where he had been placed. In the United Kingdom, anthropology drew Catholics in higher numbers than average, and the same goes for Protestants in France. There may thus be, owing to the social context in which one grows up, an ingrained habit of considering oneself marginal that hones one's faculties of observation vis-à-vis the society by which one is not fully accepted. However, this was not at all the case for me, as I happen to come from a bourgeois Catholic family that had been settled in Paris for several generations and from a long line of writers, doctors, and high-level civil servants typical of the French intellectual elite. From this perspective, I have never had the feeling of being apart from the dominant social world, especially not as I was growing up or during my studies, even if in my family we cultivated a suspicion of, and indeed contempt for, money and all those who attached excessive importance to it—probably the legacy of a Jansenist inflection in the family religious tradition. I was thus never put in a position of otherness of any kind and so, in my case, the choice to turn to the study of social realities likely stemmed rather from this aspect of my personal disposition that I have already invoked, of feeling withdrawn, yet also receptive.

The other appeal of this distancing from the common world stemmed from a taste for travel and for manifest difference, which I developed also early on. As a child, I had—and still have—bound

Philosophical journeys 3

volumes of issues of the *Le Tour du monde,* a kind of French *National Geographic* of the latter half of the nineteenth century that reported on discoveries and explorations and had been very popular among families like mine. The volumes enjoyed worldwide success at a time when the French language was widely spoken and read. They featured the travel narratives of erudite explorers, geographers, and proto-ethnographers, covering all corners of the world. Prominent illustrators contributed to the magazine, including Gustave Doré and Édouard Riou. The latter had drawn the illustrations for the novels of Jules Verne in the Hetzel collection, which I was fortunate enough to read as a child, the hefty volumes opened wide on the carpet. In the end, there was, to my mind, no major difference between the travel narratives of the likes of Jules Crevaux, who voyaged up the Maroni and Oyapock rivers in Guyana, or Darwin's journal in the Galapagos, and novels such as Théophile Gautier's *Captain Fracasse* or Jules Verne's *In Search of the Castaways.* They all belonged to a world of adventure profoundly informed by nineteenth-century travel culture, the images it produced, and the maps that oriented it, still dotted as they were with bits of *terra incognita.* However seemingly odd for a child growing up in the 1950s and early 1960s, my early years were marked by a rather quaint relish for the discoveries and explorations of the end of the previous century; this sentiment was no doubt given further impetus by the absence of television in our home—a fact born not so much of conviction as of indifference. I also had a pronounced fondness for picaresque novels and I remember as a child passionately reading and re-reading Lesage's *Gil Blas* over the course of several months; I was delighted with the constant twists in the plot, the complex embedded narrative structure, and the striking portraits of characters from all walks of life who meet in improbable ways. Later I practically lived inside the world of *Don Quixote,* thanks to a beautiful edition in Spanish illustrated by Doré that my grandfather had given me, and I believe this was how I managed to learn the rudiments of the language even before studying it at school.

Very early on, these books ignited in me a desire to enter, so to speak, into the world of these illustrations, to find myself inside a picture of Samarkand, or of the Amazonian rainforest, or of an inn on the English Channel. I thus began traveling at an early age. This was facilitated by my father, Jean Descola, who was a historian of Spain and Latin America. On several occasions he took me with him on professional trips, and I began accompanying my parents abroad

4 *A Taste for Inquiry*

rather early—especially to Spain, but also to the United Kingdom and Canada. I probably travelled more often than most young people of my age at the time. And as my father was a Hispanist, Spanish was often spoken in my family, in a slightly playful manner. I should add that my grandfather was a humanist doctor of the old school, an austere and cultivated man, who read half a dozen modern languages and three or four dead ones, and who was also an amateur botanist and avid hiker, as was my father. My father's family was from the Pyrenees, and we thus regularly walked in the mountains. During these rambles, my grandfather would move seamlessly between identifying plants we found along the path and narrating Greek myths that featured them. At night he taught me constellations and their history. Thus, from very early on, I was imbued with a combination of classical knowledge and taste for the spectacle of the world and, more precisely, for the beauty of nature. I must admit that I grew up in a family that venerated knowledge and I was always surrounded by books and paintings, my grandmother and her father being both artists. My father was a brilliant conversationalist and wit, as well as a workaholic, and I remember him spending most of his time writing or correcting manuscripts and proofs when he was at home or on holiday. Indeed, my parents let me read more or less anything I wanted, and I devoured the entire family library indiscriminately, from Virgil's *Aeneid* to the novels of Victor Margueritte. There was a forbidden section, of course, which included Pierre Louÿs together with Brantôme's *Book of the Ladies*; but it was not very difficult to access. I quickly developed a lively interest in writing, which remained my only academic talent for a long time. In short, there was little doubt in my mind that I was going to inhabit a world that straddled the pleasure of language and curiosity for unknown places and practices.

My first real childhood experience of travel was rather particular: my parents had had the brilliant idea of sending me to a boarding school in England for the final quarter of each school year. It was my English teacher at Lycée Condorcet who had suggested the idea, probably finding my accent appalling. Since the English school year ended later than the French one, I would spend the months of May, June and July in what was known in England as a minor public school. It was housed in a medieval manor in Gloucestershire, which was somewhat rundown but not lacking in majesty. Come to think of it, this was my first direct confrontation with exoticism. For a young French boy aged twelve, finding himself at a British

Philosophical journeys

boarding school—which was in every way the polar opposite of a school in the French system—required a not inconsiderable capacity for adaptation. My schoolmates were for the most part children of British expatriates—in the waning years of the British Empire—as well as children of British subjects from the colonies, that is to say, primarily of Kenyan and Indian merchants. Amid this rather motley mix I learned to speak English and to play cricket, and I even became a rather ardent Anglophile.

All this led me to take off. I had learned life in novels; I unlearned it in travels. I thought I knew all there was to know about the roar of passion, the nobility of the soul, and the calculations of interest and I discovered the pulsing beat of the world and sweet surprise. My first big trip, when I was about seventeen, took me to Canada and the United States; I arrived via the Great Lakes, working on a small cargo ship. The following year I went to Turkey and northern Syria. A bit later I visited Iran. It was rather common in my generation to go backpacking in the East. Even in the most remote villages of Anatolia and the Fars Plateau, a few words of Turkish or Farsi earned one a warm welcome. And you could go far on very little money. It may also have been true that we unconsciously reproduced a bit of the colonial mindset, which made it quite natural to feel at home anywhere in the world. It was on those excursions that I saw the *Tour du monde* illustrations come to life. In those days you would still come across dromedary caravans and mud-brick caravanserais, nomadic horsemen kitted out with antique rifles, and country wedding feasts spread out on carpets in the shade of a willow tree. This is how, little by little, I formed the idea that observing the habits, mores, and practices of the world could be more than a pleasant pastime that required merely letting go of a part of yourself and drifting into the lives of other people; it might also become a genuine occupation. I knew what an anthropologist was because I had read *Tristes tropiques* very early on, at the age of sixteen or seventeen. But it was the figure of Lévi-Strauss himself, more than his profession, that had struck me most and elicited my admiration, and in any case the latter seemed to be something that emanated from him rather than something he had embraced. At that age, how could I not identify with this refined and discerning savant, who wrote, in turns, like Rousseau and Chateaubriand, led a life of adventure while being well versed in Rabelais and Debussy, and had brought the scraps of humanity he found in the depths of Brazilian forests to the pinnacle

6   *A Taste for Inquiry*

of literature and philosophy? Surely, this was the kind of man one should aspire to be. And, since he was an anthropologist, that must be a worthy occupation!

PC *One of the essential aspects of your work is the question of the relationship to nature. Can this interest be explained by anything in your biography? What elements in your background led you to this issue?*

PD I have already mentioned the mountain hikes I went on with my parents and my grandfather. This is probably how my taste for landscapes developed, as well as my liking for the kind of solitude that only large, unpopulated areas can provide. I do not remember my grandfather's botanical lessons very well, but I am always awestruck when I come across a marten running along the edge of a wood or a heron pecking at a frog, calmly ignoring my presence as if I were the last human being. In these moments I feel a sense of plenitude, as if I had become a minute drop of water in the great flow of nature, losing all sense of self. Yet it is in the most isolated places—in the desert, as we used to say—that this sentiment is best expressed. I remember, for instance, the exaltation that came over me one day in Amazonia, as I was floating on a pirogue with some Achuar. We had to go over rapids and then push the canoe across some shallows. It was a very beautiful afternoon, the river was broad and littered with sand shoals on which white egrets paced ceremoniously, and I realized that we were about fifty kilometers from the closest Achuar settlements in either direction, upstream or downstream. I then felt fully like a particle of the world, but on its outer fringes, in a universe that had hardly been touched by humans. This is a sentiment that is, of course, nourished by romantic literature and art, and I would have had a very difficult time explaining it to my Achuar companions. But I have experienced this sense of plenitude on several occasions, in different corners of the planet, where it is still possible to feel like a very small particle in an immense macrocosm. My taste for nature developed in this way, drawn to the sublime, so to speak, rather than to the agrestic.

And yet I also appreciate the ordered landscapes of our temperate regions—the patina of integrated layers, burnished over generations of economic and social history, a technical system, and a particular ecosystem. It was in fact while doing fieldwork in Amazonia that I came to understand this, that I felt vividly what I missed most in my own culture, what really mattered to me. Until then, I saw myself as a citizen of the world, footloose, a cosmopolitan taking advantage of everything the planet had to offer. And then, suddenly, I found myself profoundly nostalgic for the apparently trivial things I no longer had; chief among them were the rural landscapes of Europe, especially those of Southern France, which had been periodic settings of happy childhood memories. But there was just nothing sublime about these landscapes; they were not "nature" in the ordinary meaning of the word. I appreciated them for other reasons, namely because they made glaringly visible a very ancient and comforting alliance between human and natural history, multiplying the diversity of one by the diversity of the other and thus enabling the identification of something familiar in ever renewing novelty. In fact I have always been attuned to my environment in a broad sense. In adolescence I explored every corner of Paris before taking to walking in the countryside, drawn to new scenes and landscapes, my gaze always alert to the rich happenings of everyday life. This is why the question of nature, before becoming an intellectual matter, was a central element in the formation of my power of discernment and my sensibility. And it is for this reason that, noting the social sciences' relative lack of interest in this question, I realized that it deserved more attention than it was receiving at the time.

Discovering the mind, discovering the world

PC *So, it was a combination of experiences and a particular relationship with knowledge that determined your path. How did this inclination for travel turn into a scholarly vocation?*

PD In the last two years of secondary school I developed an interest in politics, especially through the Student Action Committees that were protesting the war in Vietnam; for many of my generation, this was the starting point of political awareness. Indeed, opposition to that war was for us the catalyst of a broader movement, which combined loathing for the moral order and its hypocrisy, a rejection of political structures that seemed fossilized in an antiquated conservatism, struggle against imperialism and neocolonialism, and—perhaps especially—an enthusiasm for the counterculture, mostly the American counterculture, in its most exuberant forms, from music to cinema to comics. In its spirited, disorderly, and

8   *A Taste for Inquiry*

relatively under-politicized variant, this tendency culminated in the May '68 movement, in which I readily took part, with a touch of dandyism.

This situation elicited a paradoxical reaction, from me as well as from many of my comrades at the time: rather than moving into the factories and trying to convert workers to the revolution, as renowned intellectuals encouraged us to do from the perch of their university chairs, we convinced ourselves that it was essential to continue to pursue the path of knowledge, for it was absolutely clear to us that we needed to acquire the intellectual tools necessary for thinking through the contemporary political situation. And, given the complexity of the moral and political crisis we were going through, these tools could be acquired only through long and arduous study. We thought that, to be effectively engaged in politics, we needed to master critical discourse; and these tools could be acquired only through the discipline of knowledge. This was reinforced by our attraction to a form of intellectual challenge that could be met only by undertaking demanding academic research. Unlike in the populist myth, which sees "68ers" as lazy pleasure-seekers, many of us were stimulated by a somewhat grandiose sense of the need to demonstrate an intelligence equal to the situation. Hence my decision to prepare for the selective entrance exams to the École Normale Supérieure, where I was admitted in 1970 with the intention of studying philosophy.

Our generation had a voracious appetite for new ideas and, in retrospect, I feel—probably erroneously—that there were many more to be had then than now. Our relish for new ideas, our drive to explore the world of thought went hand in hand with our discovery of the real world. We read everything we could lay our hands on, without necessarily always having the tools to understand it, but at least we read, and we had a penchant for what seemed to us the most difficult texts. In other words, the intellectual baggage of the young man of that time was a total hybrid; it had great diversity even if Marxism held a preeminent place within it, given the project of reform, if not revolution, that we all had. In a sense, we simply accepted the contradictions that we found between the great authors we read, for example between Husserl and Marx. We thought deep down that there were points of agreement between them, which was probably very naïve on our part. We convinced ourselves for instance that Husserl's *Krisis* was a profoundly political text, because it recast the progress of the West as a descent into the abyss. Husserl indeed

Discovering the mind, discovering the world 9

showed in that book that the 1930s political crisis in Europe had been first and foremost a crisis of reason, except that, unlike Marx, he did not base this analysis on social and economic considerations.

My interest in anthropology began at the École Normale Supérieure, where I attended the seminar of Maurice Godelier, himself an alumnus of the École fifteen years earlier. Initially also a student of philosophy, Godelier became Lévi-Strauss' assistant, and subsequently decided to do anthropological fieldwork himself, with the Baruyas of New Guinea. Not long before that, he had published *Rationality and Irrationality in Economics*, simultaneously offering a critique of the concepts and methods of classical political economy and a reading of Marx's *Capital*; and his seminar was on that theme. We were very engrossed in the reading of Marx's economic texts at the time, especially *Capital,* which provided one of the major intellectual reference points for my whole generation. Godelier's interpretation was rather distinct from the one offered earlier by Althusser and Balibar in *Reading Capital*, especially insofar as it contrasted political economy with "primitive" and "pre-capitalist" economic forms, in which production and exchange did not obey market principles. This dimension caught my attention, as it offered an opening onto non-modern societies while retaining some of the tools Marx had developed to analyze the capitalist system.

It was Godelier who convinced me that I could make something of my somewhat abstract interest in anthropology. In the meantime, that interest had grown, nourished by reading Lévi-Strauss, and especially some of his more technical works, which philosophy students hardly ever read, such as *The Elementary Structures of Kinship*. Philosophers would often take an interest in the first chapters of the book, which are the most philosophical, but rarely in what follows these general considerations on the nature–culture divide and the incest taboo, namely the discussions of the Australian and Chinese matrimonial rules, which were less accessible. I had of course read *The Savage Mind*—one of the great works of philosophy of the twentieth century, since it tackled, in a novel and very concrete way, the central question of the transition from sensibility to intelligibility. But I had also learned to appreciate classic anthropological monographs, especially those of the English tradition, for example Evans-Pritchard on the Nuer and the Azande, or Leach on the Kachin. These works showed me the ways in which concepts can emerge from the fabric of things and from observing them, without forcing it, so to speak. I have always found that dimension

10 *A Taste for Inquiry*

of ethnographic work quite compelling: to bring out a form of native thought that is radically different from our own and to do so by small strokes, simply through description, without injecting a philosophy that is foreign to it. This is how anthropology gradually impressed itself upon me, even while I was still in my early twenties.

During his seminar at the École Normale, Maurice Godelier helped me see that it was possible to do anthropology, that this was not the reserve of a few exceptional figures, but also that it was necessary to do fieldwork. This is when I decided—it must have been sometime in late 1971—to pursue a degree in anthropology at the University of Nanterre, then the best undergraduate program in the discipline, at the same time as a master's in philosophy, which was in fact a master's in anthropology in disguise. My work on the Incas was supervised nominally by Georges Labica, who was then professor at Nanterre, but in actual fact by Godelier. The project focused on the nature of Inca ideology and was itself a hybrid; it used the notion of ideology, as Althusser had developed it in his analysis of the state ideological apparatuses; and it also drew on Pierre Bourdieu's work, in particular *Reproduction in Education, Society and Culture*, and structural anthropology, for that was the moment of the first structuralist studies on the Andes. I have in mind texts such as Nathan Wachtel's *The Vision of the Vanquished* and Tom Zuidema's writings on *ceques*, a highly complex sociospatial organizational system of the Inca Empire. The result was thus a rather strange combination of neo-Marxist and neo-structuralist interpretations of a social reality I knew only through the ethno-historical documents on which I had worked. In short, this master's thesis marked the decisive tipping point toward anthropology.

PC *How did your transition from philosophy to anthropology come about? What were its initial stages, and how did it resonate with your political concerns?*

PD First of all, I decided to do fieldwork that combined political and environmental anthropology. I thus enrolled as a doctoral student at the École Pratique des Hautes Études and, in the summer of 1973, together with my partner Anne-Christine Taylor, who was herself also an anthropology student, I went to southern Chiapas in Mexico to conduct preliminary fieldwork research. I was interested in interethnic relations between two native populations, the Lacandon and the Tzeltal, and in the differences between their

Discovering the mind, discovering the world 11

respective relationships with the common environment—the tropical rainforest. We thus settled for three months in the Lacandon rainforest, in Taniperla, a small settler colony of the Tzeltal that had fled its traditional highland habitat years earlier, pushed out by large landowners. The two populations spoke Mayan languages and had a few common traits, but the Lacandon had long inhabited the forest ecosystem, whereas the Tzeltal had only recently begun trying to adapt to it. The situation was rather tense and, in retrospect, one might even say prerevolutionary, since it was in that lowland region that the Zapatista movement began mobilizing Amerindians only a decade and a half later. The Tzeltal seemed to suffer as a result of having been uprooted, even though they had had earlier experience of migration to the lowlands, going there on a regular basis to work for the lumber companies. In the 1930s Bruno Traven had written *March to Caobaland*, an extraordinary novel about this grim saga. However, if the Tzeltal were used to going down to the forest, it was only as peons, forced through a form of indenture to work under inhuman conditions, not as permanent residents among the communities already present.

Compelled to leave the highlands, the Tzeltal had tried to rebuild a world that closely resembled the one they had left, but in a radically different environment; and this proved most difficult. First of all, for ecological reasons: apart from a few residual pine stands on the mountainsides, the highlands are already divided up into hedged fields, interspersed with ceremonial sites related to social and cosmic segments that combined humans and nonhumans. These hierarchized units, called *kalpul*, functioned as legal entities that controlled the distribution of farmland and the rites each segment performed for the sacred places and the divinities they host. When there were only two sections, which was the most common occurrence, their division followed a line perpendicular to the slope of the terrain shared by the community, at the level of the village, generally across its central square, sometimes running the length of the church nave. In the forest ecosystem into which they were displaced, the Tzeltal no longer found any such bearings and obsessively sought to re-create the physical and symbolic landscape they had lost, as well as the social logic that went with it.

At the time, Taniperla could be reached only by foot, after a week-long trek from the highlands, or by a single-engine plane that landed on a small strip. The Tzeltal had turned this strip into the axis of separation between the two moieties of the village, but in

12   *A Taste for Inquiry*

the end this did not work very well. Indeed, in the highlands, the moiety that had ritual, symbolic, and demographic preeminence was located in the upper part, being associated with the mountains and the deities that inhabit them, so that its patron saint was that of the community as a whole, whereas the lower moiety was linked to warm lands, agricultural abundance, and the world of demons and non-Indians. Now it was the entire village that was de facto in the lowlands. I thus witnessed the permanent struggle of the inhabitants against an environment that was unfamiliar to them and the strategies they deployed as they tried to tame it. One of these, for example, was to envelope the village in a permanent "civilized" soundscape in order to keep the disquieting otherness of the forest and its inhabitants at bay. There was a small shop selling next to nothing—rice, black beans, tins of tuna, candles—that had a loudspeaker mounted on a pole. All day long it played *rancheras* and Mexican popular music. Between songs, the shopkeeper would announce that such and such family had requested this song to be played for some other family, as if to re-create the reciprocal relations between social segments; and this music would be constantly blaring until the middle of the night, when the electric generator ran out of fuel. It was also as if they were trying to create a proper Mexican environment, perhaps so as to make a new start, at an equal distance from the traditionalism of highland Indians and the strange ways of forest Indians. This appeared obvious to me when we went with a few village men to visit a Lacandon who lived three or four hours away by foot, and I was struck by how different their worlds were. This was also my first foray into the depth of the forest, and I was immediately seduced by the staggering hustle and bustle of the tropical forest, that overflow of life that is often not very agreeable but always endlessly diverse. In short, I was not in tune with the Tzeltal. Little by little, their difficulties in re-creating an acceptable living environment insidiously contaminated my mood and I thought to myself that it would be preferable to "do my fieldwork" among people who felt at ease in the forest. This is how I came to Amazonia.

That experience was thus a detour, but probably a necessary one. While not fully admitting it to myself, I had long been drawn to Amazonia, but I thought that going there for fieldwork was impossibly romantic and petit bourgeois. It would probably have been my spontaneous choice, influenced as I was by both Lévi-Strauss and my childhood reading. But spending time with the Amazonian

Discovering the mind, discovering the world   13

Amerindians was to give in to a form of consumerism of the exotic, to an outdated love of mystery and adventure, entirely disconnected from my politics, whereas going to Chiapas, the heart of colonial domination, was a worthy challenge. Those few months in Taniperla convinced me that I needed to let go of these qualms and head for Amazonia. It so happened that, at that time, the situation in Amazonia was not a particularly happy one either. At a conference held in Barbados in 1971, a group of mostly Latin American anthropologists issued a solemn declaration that publicly denounced the massacre of Amerindian populations, the invasion of their territories, the violation of their rights, and their effective "lobotomization" by missionaries—all of which was little known at the time. The Amazonian peoples were high up on that somber list of dispossessed and abused indigenous populations, which served to permanently orient Americanist anthropology toward a more critical and politically engaged position. It was indeed at this moment that Robert Jaulin introduced the concept of "ethnocide" in France. As a result, Amazonia became a new front of political resistance, and to conduct one's anthropological fieldwork there no longer necessarily implied giving in to nostalgia for a paradise lost. This was more or less how gradual adjustments led me to choose Amazonia for my fieldwork.

PC *What was the transition period like between your status as a philosophy professor-to-be and your aspiration to become an anthropologist?*

PD You would think that such a situation might induce a kind of schizophrenia, but I did not experience anything of the sort. Following the abortive ethnographic work in Mexico, I successfully passed the exam for the philosophy professorate and even taught philosophy for a year, at secondary school level. At the same time, I decided to ask Claude Lévi-Strauss if he would agree to supervise my work on an Amazonian society, and I managed to obtain a leave of absence from the Ministry of Education that allowed me to return to fieldwork. I proposed to Lévi-Strauss a study of the Achuar Jivaros, who live in the Ecuadorian Amazon and on whom I had begun to do a bit of research. Much to my surprise, he agreed to supervise my doctoral thesis, which led me away from the teaching of philosophy for good, since my entire career followed from that second and, this time, successful ethnographic venture.

14 *A Taste for Inquiry*

PC   *The circumstances that determine the choice of site of one's anthropological fieldwork are very complex, various factors coming into play. Could you describe how all this happened in your case?*

PD   It was a combination of chance and personal inclination. I very much admire anthropologists, and I know quite a few, who conduct their fieldwork under extremely difficult conditions—among utterly destitute populations, sometimes dealing with highly precarious situations, profoundly degraded environments, or intense violence—which make the pursuit of scholarly objectives and the attempt to make sense of these situations very complicated. Some anthropologists work in refugee camps, with homeless people or urban gangs, in regions where civil war is raging. Fieldwork under such conditions, in my view, amounts to a form of heroism. While I would not want to champion anything like an ethnographic hedonism, it seems to me that we must be able to identify with the people we observe in other ways than through compassion or a desire to lend assistance. To fully share the flavor of daily life, to enjoy the thousands of small discoveries offered by a new world, to appreciate the wisdom or humor of one's interlocutor—all this is made easier if one is not constantly having to assess the chances of survival of one's hosts. Even if fieldwork in Amazonia was not without its difficulties, to which I shall return later, it remained a very different experience from work with communities subjected to unbearably oppressive conditions, plunged into distress and despair.

    The choice of site for one's fieldwork is also influenced by the affinities one may or may not feel with the various ways of life already described in the ethnographic literature. As a result, at least for those of my generation, the choice of fieldwork site was often informed by a prior attraction for the region. To the contrary, I never had any spontaneous affinity with Asia, for instance, especially not the Asia of the great civilizations, which is a very complex world as a result of its multiple cultural layers, languages, religions, and exchanges among neighboring civilizations. All these great movements that crisscrossed that immense continent, and the resulting sediments, make Asia the exact opposite of Amazonia, where, given the lack of written records, one may entertain the fantasy of an archipelago of isolated peoples. This is of course an illusion, as we know, and in fact a process of interethnic mixing and exchange unfolded there over tens of millennia, crowned by the cataclysm of the conquest. As Lévi-Strauss put it, Amazonia confronts the observer with a "a kind

Discovering the mind, discovering the world 15

of Middle Ages which lacked a Rome,"[1] a Rome that, even with the remarkable recent developments in Amazonian archaeology, we still struggle to reconstitute in all its complexity. It was therefore possible to imagine that pre-Columbian history did not exist, since one could have only a highly incomplete understanding of it. By contrast, the study of the great empires and historically complex formations of Asia demanded typical orientalist erudition—a command of a great many living and dead languages, a solid foundation in philology and even in paleography, as well as considerable knowledge of the history of religions—such that an immediate grasp of the ethnographic object there seemed vastly more difficult and constantly mediated by other forms of knowledge. I loved the Near East—the Arab world, and even Iran—for its landscapes, its architecture, and its ways of life, but I also saw this world as obsessively dominated by religion in its daily life, which made me uncomfortable. And then there are other regions of the world that also did not spontaneously appeal to me, although for different reasons. In Africa, for instance, relations of domination seemed to me to exert considerable force, whether between castes, generations, elder and younger siblings or between ancestors and the living—all of which the ethnographic literature on lineage societies of the time had dealt with extensively. The general impression was that these were societies in which customary authority governed most dimensions of everyday life. I could not see myself doing fieldwork in a society in which, in the end, everyone's fate was set from birth on the basis of their position within a segmentary system. It was one of the reasons why Africa did not really appeal—together with the fact that there seemed to be less mystery there, and perhaps also in Asia, by comparison with South America, with Amazonia. In Africa and Asia the anthropologist dealt with very complex mechanisms, magnificent clockworks with intricate inner workings, highly codified behaviors, and clearly defined statuses. Reading the works of some of the French and British Africanists who painted a picture of extremely hierarchized court societies, I sometimes felt as if I were in a world enthralled by social distinction, as described by Saint-Simon. And I had the impression that, once these complex mechanisms, their genesis and evolution, were analyzed, there would be nothing left to pique our curiosity—since in that case a history was possible. Amazonia, from that perspective, was far more enigmatic.

Indeed, except for the societies of central Brazil and, to a lesser extent, those of the Amazonian northwest, the situation in

16   *A Taste for Inquiry*

Amazonia in the last third of the twentieth century was not very different from that described by the chroniclers of the sixteenth century. We were still dealing with peoples "without faith, law, or king," in other words peoples who had none of the conventional institutions by which we have come to recognize an organized society in Europe—a "polity," as they used to say in the eighteenth century: no state, of course, but also no chiefs, big or small, no cult, gods, clergy, clans, lineage or ancestors, no system of assembly, and no conflict resolution mechanisms. Added to this was a clear lack of interest in village life and a distinct taste for war and vendetta, an open indifference to the historicization of the past and projection into the future in the form of a common destiny. In short, at first sight, something that resembled Hobbes's state of nature: a sociological scandal, societies that had more to do with teratology than anthropology, as Georges Balandier once put it to me. This was the mystery that needed to be penetrated: these tribes, which by all appearances were entirely anomic and constantly engaged in bloody conflict, still exhibited a very high degree of resilience in the face of four centuries of massacres, territorial spoliation and demographic collapse triggered by infectious disease. Where did this resilience come from? How can we define what, for them, constituted society? How did they differ, other than by default, from the Nuer, the Trobriand, or the Kachin? None of the traditional concepts of social anthropology, informed as they were by the study of segmentary societies in Africa, Asia, and Polynesia, seemed to supply an adequate compass for navigating this anarchic fog. Everything remained to be done, nothing stood to reason, and this is what was so exciting.

PC   *So, you would agree with the idea of Lévi-Strauss, who sometimes said that the regions of the world have personalities that resonate to a greater or lesser degree with one's own?*

PD   I believe this to be profoundly true. It is further confirmed in informal discussions among colleagues about our respective ethnographic experiences. We have internalized the cultural styles specific to the communities in which we did our fieldwork to such a degree that the practices of other places appear spontaneously bizarre, even outrageous, not by comparison with how things are done in Europe, but in relation to the customs of the people with whom we are familiar. And this identification of each of us with a specific

Discovering the mind, discovering the world

ethnographic continent is so strong that it must in fact preexist our fieldwork experience and speak to idiosyncratic character traits. Sometimes these differences in sensibility lead to misunderstandings, and even to disputes. This was the case in France in the 1970s and 1980s, when Africanists accused Americanists, in turn or all at once, of idealizing the noble savage, of being indifferent to the movement of history, of confusing anthropology with metaphysics, of being contemptuous of peasant struggle or hostile to *métissage*, and so on. This was a very apt illustration of the differences, both in our relationships with the anthropological object and in our personalities, that further down the line would bring us to turn to a certain type of questioning rather than another.

It seems to me that controversies that appear to be theoretical in fact often reflect differences in our ways of doing fieldwork and, hence, in short, in our relationships with the populations we spend time with. When Africanists accused the anthropologists of Amazonia of a certain Rousseauism—and it is true that some obligingly put on a show of "going native"—they ignored the fact that it was nearly impossible in Amazonia not to fully adopt the way of life of one's hosts. There were almost no bilingual interlocutors, and therefore no guides or interpreters; in consequence, one had to learn the vernacular language to get by. There were no huts reserved for visitors or any local administration, which forced one to share the Indians' home life in its entirety; there were no roads, which made it impossible to bring more than the bare necessities that could fit in a backpack. Living half naked, hunting with a blowpipe, and eating ants were not affectatious ways of playing the native, they were simply the normal conditions of life. Conversely, the conditions under which Africanist anthropology developed at the end of the war in francophone colonial Africa have strongly marked the generations of anthropologists—all nonetheless impeccably anticolonial—that followed. It was generally necessary to proceed through official institutions, either formally French or under French patronage, or through local development and foreign aid organizations. The situation was radically different from that of Amazonia, given that, since Africa was still largely under French influence, there were material, institutional and logistical frameworks at the disposal of researchers to assist them in their research and logistics. Thus their style of research could only have been radically different from that of other anthropologists, who were operating, sometimes in a semi-clandestine manner, among Amazonian populations that were very difficult to access and often subjected to persecution by the authorities.

But, beyond these conjunctural factors, I believe that the choice of fieldwork site is also revealing of a taste for a certain way of being and experiencing the human condition that one senses long before having tried it out. The Amazonian Indians are "peoples of solitude," to borrow Chateaubriand's phrase about North America, not just because the shock of infectious diseases diluted their numbers in the vast forest—which they used to inhabit much more densely before the catastrophe of the conquest—but also because they can still afford to live in relative isolation from their human neighbors, as stowaways of a chaotic globalization whose brutality they have endeavored to evade for five centuries. Averse to authority and hierarchy, often uncomfortable with the congestion of village life, appreciative of the society of plants and animals well beyond what the necessities of subsistence demand, these jaunty individualists can appeal only to visitors who resemble them.

There was yet another reason why I was drawn to Amazonia, and that was the obvious importance of nature in social life. The theme constantly resurfaces in the writings of observers, from the first chroniclers of the sixteenth century to contemporary documentaries, either in a positive vein—celebrating the "naked philosophers" of Montaigne, who live effortlessly on the generous bounty bestowed by the forest—or in a negative light—condemning the savagery of these beings governed by their bellicose natures, cannibals who are barely worthy of the name man. Either way, Indians were perceived in the West as appendages of nature, incapable of truly dissociating themselves from it or transforming it, perhaps as a result of an overly successful adaptation to their tropical environment. The anthropologists who had set this caricatural vision right, starting with Lévi-Strauss, also insisted on the scope and ingenuity of the ecological knowledge and techniques for using the environment that forest peoples possessed. It thus appeared to me that all these observers could not have been consistently wrong, that they had probably sensed something essential when they identified the Amazonian Indians as peoples of nature. Not because they were, as in the garden of Eden, freed from work and the vagaries of subsistence or condemned to a rough and brutal life in a state of nature, but because they had granted the nonhuman a singular place in their social life. The apparent lack of structuring institutions, the political anarchy, may be the flipside of an attitude that stretches

Discovering the mind, discovering the world 19

sociability well beyond the boundaries of the human species. It was with this still vague intuition that I went to Ecuadorian Amazonia to study the relationship of the Achuar with the environment. The Achuar were a great tribe in what was then called the "Jivaro" (and now the "Aénts Chicham") linguistic group, and the last one that had not yet been the object of an in-depth ethnographic study.

PC *You have briefly described the political tumult of the 1960s and 1970s, while also invoking the resulting deadlocks. How did this atmosphere, and the ideals that were formulated within it, resonate with the objectives of anthropology?*

PD When I try to recall the state of mind that my classmates and I were in at the time, I believe we were divided between two rather distinct aspirations. On the one hand, there was a more or less organized project of political revolution, in Europe, based on the idea that the present situation was intolerable. We could no longer bear the weight of the moral and political order—the prevailing racism, the arrogance of ruling elites, the subservience of much of the media to a lethargic and vulgar conservatism. And our reaction consisted in saying: "Everything must change, everything must be overturned and transformed." The primary path we had available to us was the revolutionary path, the Leninist path. It must be said that very few of us had a politics that went much beyond a kind of zeal to see off the old world. Like many of the bourgeois students of my generation, with whom I shared a guilty conscience stemming from our status as "heirs," I threw myself into a revolutionary political movement, but without any clear-eyed analysis of the situation, which was anything but pre-revolutionary. The heroic model of Leninism—the alliance of intellectuals and workers, who came together in the revolution of 1917 and in the Spanish Civil War—still exerted considerable influence, which we did not interrogate in any rigorous way. And then there was anthropology, which held the key to understanding social and political realities that were vastly different from our own. But the two rarely intersected. Despite proclaimed internationalism, an abyss still separated industrial democracies with their problems from third-world peasantries. At least as far as I was concerned, the conjunction only came about little by little, during fieldwork, then on my return from fieldwork, and, finally, very gradually until my most recent work, which is marked by the idea that human beings as a species are accountable

20 *A Taste for Inquiry*

for the planet but their degree of responsibility for its devastation is far from being the same for all. My decision to conduct fieldwork in Latin America surely reflected a desire to stand in solidarity with oppressed peoples, but no fully developed broader political project.

And this was probably because the thinking in political anthropology was rather weak at the time, torn as it was between a sociology of social change and unequal development on the one hand and, on the other, an essentially typological analysis of the forms of political organization that had come out of the work on African segmentary systems. The only scholar who had produced truly original thought in political anthropology, thought that contrasted with the neo-Leninist tradition, was Pierre Clastres. And he exerted an unquestionable influence over the anthropologists of my generation, especially Americanists. I must confess, however, that I for one was not fully convinced by the central idea articulated in *Society against the State*. Clastres's thesis was that "the savages"—in fact the Amerindians of Amazonia—had invented the institution of the "chief without power" as a mechanism designed to prevent the emergence of the state. This form of chiefdom, to which Robert Lowie had already called our attention a few decades earlier, consisted in conferring on an individual the title of chief, along with the prestige attached to the function, while depriving that individual of the coercive means to effectively issue orders to others. In this way power had a name and a face, but was paralyzed and even somewhat ridiculous. According to Clastres, this exorcism prevented any future development of effective power, any domination of one over the many, any separation between society and the state.

It was a powerful idea, simple and appealing, but I was uncomfortable with its implicit functionalism—the powerless chief had no other purpose than to prevent the rise of the state—and even more so with the paralogism of its explicitly teleological dimension: the institution both prefigured and warded off something that had not yet happened. There were certainly historical circumstances in which "powerless chief" societies opposed the imposition of the state, as was the case in the Andean foothills, for instance, where Amazonian populations devoid of internal political differentiation successfully resisted all attempts at annexation by Andean imperial formations. As a result of geographical proximity, they knew about domination exerted by a state system and the despotism of absolute power, and they learned to fight against it. These are established facts, but they only concern one fringe of the Andean foothills. And it

Discovering the mind, discovering the world

seemed to me excessive to turn this successful resistance into a kind of prescience about the ravages of the state, of which all "savage" societies would have been vaguely aware. In addition, it was difficult to engage with Clastres about this, and I remember him as being a rather curt interlocutor, who was little inclined to discuss his ideas with the rebellious students we were at the time.

Having said that, whether or not one agrees with Clastres's positions, the effort to draw from ethnographic data, as he sought to do, intellectually stimulating elements for reworking the categories of political thought was in itself an exciting project. For the first time in a long period, perhaps since Montaigne, it was not institutions and concepts of European history that were being used as models for thinking the political in its most general form, but organizational modes of living together that had no equivalent in the West and whose philosophical and moral dignity was thus restored. Very few people had dared to make such a lateral move. The weight of Leninism was considerable then, even if we coyly preferred to blame Stalinism; and, in a way, it was indeed against all this that Clastres fought.

Still to this day, we are only at the very early stages of a renewal of political thought that would be free of both Leninism and liberal thought, two branches of Enlightenment philosophy that are apparently opposed but in fact rest on the same anthropocentric premises. The indigenous struggles of today, against both the large planning projects of the developmental left and the predatory policies of multinational companies, point to a third way, which is suggestive of how the long-strained ties between humans and nonhumans can be rewoven in terms of the forms of sovereignty they each exert over themselves. But it takes a long time to sort out the intellectual frameworks through which we have become used to think both the interactions between beings and the worlds they build together. It takes time for new political categories that are not simply counter-models to take shape. It is a very long operation into which our generation has thrown itself with passion, even if it took longer than planned to get there.

PC *Did your interest in relationships with nature find much support in the political culture of the 1970s? Was ecology already a discernible critical preoccupation?*

PD In the political organizations I knew, not at all. And I must say that this was the start of my own disenchantment with political activism. It was indeed a period of high ferment within ultraleft groups, but two elements were conspicuously absent: political ecology did not spark much debate, and neither did feminism. We were always told that these were "secondary contradictions," which meant that revolution in the ordinary sense of the term had to happen first, and transformations in those domains would occur by themselves, without ever becoming a terrain of critical thought. That idea always seemed to me absurd, since any reform of our modes of life presupposed a profound reform of our ways of using nature and of the relations between the sexes. It was a dimension of Leninism that already seemed very old-fashioned. Despite the exuberant and sometimes rather joyous character of these political movements, it was a rather dated way of conceiving of political emancipation. And this is one of the factors that led me to leave the world of political activism.

This conviction was then further confirmed by my fieldwork experience, where it quickly became very clear that nature was a central political concern in South American countries, and not only as part of a competition over resources between divergent interests. Safeguarding the autonomy of native populations, and in particular the continuance of their conditions of life, clearly involved reflecting on the intimate link between the preservation of certain kinds of environments and the capacity of local populations to maintain, if they so wished, a way of life within them that was very different from that of productivist consumption, which was already the norm at the time. I remember trying to defend this perspective with the Ecuadorian authorities when, after my stay in Amazonia, I was teaching at the Catholic University of Quito in the late 1970s, in what was then the only anthropology department in the country. I suggested that they create in Amazonia mixed reserves that would be protected against both environmental damage and the pressure exerted on renewable resources, zones in which native populations could continue to lead their chosen way of life. They would thus not need to limit all kinds of activity that were transformative of nature, or all kinds of hunting, and yet they would still protect the primary equilibria of the environment. At the time I was completely ignored. I have been comforted by the fact that some of my former Ecuadorian students gradually took up these ideas and became activists, creating for example NGOs that defend the principles we had discussed back then.

In Europe, a form of ecological thought had begun to develop, with people like André Gorz and Hans Jonas, but it remained rather theoretical. When I returned to France, in the early 1980s, there was little truly political reflection on this front, and the sentiment I had—which has not changed much since—was that political ecology as it gradually developed in French politics was of a managerial and planning variety, more preoccupied with bicycle lanes and waste recycling than animated by a desire to imagine a world in which interactions between humans and nonhumans would be radically different from what they are today. I think anthropology played a major role in the recent resurgence of more radical ecological demands, even if it has so far had little political impact. And, to return to the issue of politics, it is worth asking why, given my interest in ecology, I did not pursue it with one or the other of the ecologist parties that emerged then. In a way, this gives me the same sense I had when I was a young activist: that of an inadequacy between the activist groups and the ideals they purported to serve. The political structures that support ecology today in the French system do not seem up to the challenge, and I am left with the feeling that I would not achieve much by engaging with this kind of political party, even if on occasion I may have interesting exchanges with this or that politician.

Among the tribe of anthropologists

PC *Let us now return to your academic career, leaving aside for the moment your stay in Amazonia, to which we shall of course return. How were you introduced to the world of anthropologists and who were your mentors in the early stages of your career?*

PD I have already recalled my first, abortive ethnographic experience with the Tzeltal Indians of Chiapas, in Mexico; and I have explained why I initially chose that fieldwork site and why I gave up on it. I then decided to turn to Amazonia. As for a supervisor, Claude Lévi-Strauss stood as the obvious choice for several reasons. First, he was probably the most renowned specialist in the world on that cultural area, whose study was not yet very developed in France; at least he was the only one in a position to supervise doctoral work in that field at the École Pratique des Hautes Études, where I was enrolled. But, needless to say, I also had an immense admiration for him as a person and for his body of work, as much of it as I was able to discern from what I had read and from the lectures I

24 *A Taste for Inquiry*

had attended at the Collège de France. I was still quite ignorant of anthropology, but no one seemed to match his theoretical intelligence and his breadth of perspective and knowledge. I was already convinced that he was the most important anthropologist of the twentieth century. And I thought to myself that I might as well deal directly with God rather than with one of his saints. Yet it was not without some trepidation that I requested an appointment to meet with him. I think it was in late 1973 or early 1974. For me, it was like going to see Kant in Königsberg! He received me very affably in his office at the Laboratory of Social Anthropology, directing me to take a seat in a beat-up leather armchair that was inordinately low, while he assumed a dominant perch next to me, on a high wooden chair that was clearly very uncomfortable. Slumped as I was under his impassive gaze, I presented my project for an ethnographic study in Amazonia, growing less and less confident as I spoke, and more and more convinced that I was disturbing the great man and distracting him from no doubt more important tasks. To my great surprise, he not only very kindly paid careful attention to what I was saying but agreed to supervise my dissertation. The leather armchair where I sat so uncomfortably that day is now in my office, as part of the furniture I inherited when I was appointed to the anthropology chair at the Collège de France. Every day it reminds me of how my career began.

Among the lectures that made an impression on me at the time, those of Maurice Godelier remain particularly vivid in my mind. His seminar at the EPHE drew crowds, especially among students and researchers of Latin America, where his reputation was formidable. With an inimitable combination of analytic virtuosity, conceptual rigor, and cheeky energy, he would develop before our eyes the material that was to become his great books, adding in each session corrections and clarifications, in a kind of long inspired trance, as it appeared to us. I have rarely had the sensation, as I did with him, of seeing a thought in the making, as it clears a path through words, then becomes tighter, rises up, and takes off. From his intimate familiarity with Marxism, his interest in economic anthropology and history, his voracious ethnographic curiosity, Godelier had drawn a maniacal interest in the apparently most insignificant details of material life and their integration into dynamic systems. But he was also familiar with Lévi-Strauss and the theorists of symbolic anthropology, especially British, from Edmund Leach to Mary Douglas. He would navigate the tangle of relations between the ideal

Among the tribe of anthropologists 25

and the material with such ardor—keen as he was to account for all phenomena—that he blew his listeners away.

Another figure played an essential role for many of us: the very discreet yet endearing André-Georges Haudricourt. He was an unconventional researcher, simultaneously linguist, ethnologist, agronomist, botanist, technologist, and geographer, and by far the most learned man I have ever met; he had an extraordinary knowledge of the plant world. He expressed himself laconically and with biting irony, both in speech and in writing, but exerted a veritable fascination over people of very diverse intellectual interests. His work has been disseminated through numerous articles—generally brief and technical, some of them republished posthumously as a book—and through a few collective works he co-authored with colleagues; in consequence he remains largely unknown to the wider public.

But some of his articles have nevertheless played an important role, especially the most famous one, translated into English as "Domestication of Animals, Cultivation of Plants and Human Relations" and initially published in 1962 in one of the first issues of the journal *L'Homme*, alongside Lévi-Strauss and Roman Jakobson's analysis of Baudelaire's "Les Chats" and an article by Clastres on Indian chieftainship. It is a dazzling reflection on the connections between techniques of nature management and political forms and it had a profound influence on me, though I am far from being the only one to have tried to make use of it.

I was thus influenced at the time by the intellectual ferment in France around phenomena of technical and ecological interaction between humans and nonhumans and by the controversy—which came from the United States—between relativists and universalists on the question of ethnobiological classifications. This had shifted the lines of debate between structuralism and Marxism; and Godelier had offered a synthesis of this debate or an intellectual compromise in which he emphasized that both were vigorously opposed to empiricism, to the idea that the visible order of facts, just in itself, revealed their reason, since, unlike empiricism, both structuralism and Marxism located the key to social phenomena in principles and orders that are concealed from the consciousness of subjects. The Marxist dimension of Godelier's approach rested mostly on the strategic character assigned to "relations of production," that is, on the links that humans formed among themselves in the appropriation and transformation of natural resources. According to him, these relations, which determined the form of society, did

26 *A Taste for Inquiry*

not themselves have a predetermined form: in some societies it was kinship relations that served as relations of production, because it was through them that access to resources was determined; in others, it was religious organization into castes, for instance, that played this role. But that approach had its limits: given all the classless societies in which anthropology is interested, how was one to make distinctions between the thousands of societies in which kinship relations functioned as relations of production, when these societies obeyed neither the same social dynamics nor the same institutional logic? We were then compelled to return to superficial sociocultural differentiations or to specific historical evolutions, thereby losing the benefit of the original hypothesis about causal hierarchies.

These debates on ethnoscience, technical systems, and types of environmental adaptation showed me the beginning of an alternative approach, the need to pay more attention to what was called—again, in Marxist parlance—"productive forces," in other words the ways in which people make use of their relationships with the natural world to draw their means of existence from it: the organization of work, the technical system, the understanding of nature, and the symbolic representations through which it is apprehended. But this required not falling into a kind of technical determinism, a fault to which Marxism has often succumbed. At the time, it was indeed environmental determinism that served as a foil, especially in the form of "cultural ecology," which then dominated the anthropology of Amazonia in the United States. This was a simplistic and reductive form of materialism whose herald was Marvin Harris: it claimed to explain away all cultural institutions—from witchcraft in Europe to the tapir taboo in Amazonia—by presenting them as mechanisms of adaptation to ecosystem constraints. This trend never really took off in France, where, from very early on, the nineteenth-century tradition of human geography pioneered by Vidal de la Blache had conceived of material conditions as mere potentialities, which social systems might actualize or not. Thus, in those years of preparation for fieldwork, I learned to compose with Marxist principles on the one hand and with the lessons of ethnoscience and environmental anthropology on the other. This supplied part of the intellectual framework within which I developed the research question I tackled in my doctoral thesis, *In the Society of Nature*.

PC *In this intellectual configuration, Lévi-Strauss stands out as a personality and researcher of decisive importance. What did he represent in the intellectual world of the time, and what was your relationship with him like?*

PD   To be honest, I was not immediately aware of the influence Lévi-Strauss exerted over me. I realized it only later, after my doctorate, when I began to present my research outside France. Among the questions I was asked at the end of a talk there was almost always one that referred to my "structural analysis" of the data I had just presented. This came as a surprise, since I did not see myself particularly as a structuralist at the time. I was trying to find my own way, cobbling together concepts and questions from within the intellectual context I just described. Indeed, like others in my generation of anthropologists in France, I was a structuralist without knowing it. And it was through interaction with very different national traditions—in the United Kingdom, Germany, Scandinavia, and the United States—that I realized, through contrast, how profoundly shaped by structuralism my approach indeed was.

As I tried, while avoiding anachronism, to put my finger on what caused me to realize in the 1970s and 1980s how much I owed that school of thought, I have come up with something very simple—a methodological principle that Jean Pouillon described very well: "Structuralism, properly speaking, begins when we admit that different ensembles can be brought together not in spite of but by virtue of their differences, which we then try to order."[2]

This is what is most characteristic of anthropological structuralism: the idea of a combinatorial analysis that accounts for all the states of an ensemble through the systematic differences that distinguish its elements. I had internalized this principle so much that it seemed to me to hold implicitly, for any pertinent analytical approach in the social sciences. It was by rubbing shoulders with other anthropological traditions outside France that I realized how distinctive the principle was, indeed almost incomprehensible to British and North American anthropologists, who tended to conceive of any comparativist generalization as an inductive method of searching for similarities between already given totalities: societies, cultures, social groups that could be empirically ascertained through ethnographic work. By contrast, in the structuralist approach the totality is never a given: it results from the operation through which collectives, cultural traits, norms, and social positions are constituted as variants of a totality that is constructed analytically. The objects treated in the respective approaches are in no way comparable, and

28   *A Taste for Inquiry*

the misunderstandings with many of our foreign colleagues that this difference creates is as persistent today as it was forty years ago.

Besides, now that Lévi-Strauss has been enthroned as one of the great thinkers of the French nation, we tend to forget that, from the 1960s until the 1980s, he elicited sharp condemnation from a part of the French anthropological community and from the French intellectual world more broadly. Look at the polemics of the time, and not only those between Lévi-Strauss and philosophers such as Sartre, Ricœur, and Derrida, which remained rather mild. He was accused of an abstract intellectualism, of being indifferent to actual living conditions, of being casual with the facts, or else of showing a patronizing contempt for other anthropologists. The number of publications that sought to disprove structural anthropology, a position perceived as being hegemonic, was considerable! This so-called hegemony was largely phantasmatic; other perspectives were commonly expressed, other ways of thinking about anthropology were being developed. The most common of these critiques was articulated by anthropologists who emphasized the historical and political dynamics at work in social decomposition and recomposition, often in connection with colonization and anticolonial struggles, in the wake of Georges Balandier and the "dynamic" anthropology championed by the Manchester school of social conflict theorists, Max Gluckman first among them. And if Marxist thinkers like Althusser and Godelier did engage with Lévi-Strauss, they were a tiny minority. Many anthropologists in Europe and North America who claimed to be Marxist at the time, or at least to be engaged in a progressive political approach, saw Lévi-Strauss as a reactionary idealist, and even a representative of "totalitarian technocracy."[3]

The critiques levelled against Lévi-Strauss could be quite intense. Very early on, books by now forgotten authors came out on *The Elementary Structures of Kinship* that were very virulent in their attacks on Lévi-Strauss and his so-called Structuralist School. This was rather ironic, given that he himself had always abhorred the idea of founding a school. If you look at the people he brought together around him when he created the Laboratory of Social Anthropology, very few were dyed-in-the-wool structuralists. In the end, the only real Lévi-Straussian, who best understood and best explained structuralism in anthropology, was Jean Pouillon, who always held a rather marginal position in Lévi-Strauss's entourage. A philosopher by training, he had begun as the editor

Among the tribe of anthropologists 29

of the journal *Les Temps Modernes* and was thus very close to Sartre. He then discovered structural anthropology, notably through *The Savage Mind*, which fascinated him, and he grew closer to Lévi-Strauss and eventually became editor of *L'Homme*, the anthropology journal that Lévi-Strauss had founded. But Pouillon had this particularity that he never held a university position; his main job was as a parliamentary clerk at the National Assembly. And yet he worked tirelessly to clarify the misunderstandings between existentialism and structuralism, in the hope that the opposition between praxis and structure could one day be overcome and brought into a larger totality, which would make their relationship fully intelligible at last.[4] That project is still relevant today—I would even go so far as to say that it is the only worthwhile project in the social sciences.

Most of the researchers who joined up with Lévi-Strauss have been struck by the intellectual scope of the structuralist project, the brilliance of a powerful and coherent form of thought, and Lévi-Strauss's vast knowledge and penetrating intelligence more than by any attempt to apply structuralist recipes. Even Françoise Héritier turned out to be a heterodox structuralist. Granted, she brilliantly pursued the research program that was outlined in *The Elementary Structures of Kinship*, detailing the semi-complex marital alliance systems in which the choice of partner is based not on a prescription, as in elementary systems, but on a prohibition of marrying into a certain kinship group. In so doing, she displaced structural analysis from a logic of relations to a combinatorial analysis of bodily humors—milk, blood, sperm, and so on—whose rules regarding the compatibility and incompatibility between individuals would account not only for the various forms that the incest prohibition took but also for the principles of filiation and matrimony more broadly; and those rules varied from culture to culture. I think Lévi-Strauss was rather pleased not to be surrounded by disciples, for he had no truck with the parrotry of sycophants. He appreciated the fact that his general anthropological project was shared, of course, but he had no intention of creating a school full of little structuralists who would reproduce to the letter the method he had developed. And, indeed, I believe that most of the members of his group were implicitly convinced that he was the only one who could bring this project to fruition with any chance of success. All in all, the world of anthropology was much more diverse at the time than it sometimes appears in retrospect.

30   *A Taste for Inquiry*

PC *You briefly mentioned the creation and development of the Laboratory of Social Anthropology, which is a major locus of French anthropology and where you have been a member and director. Could you describe the history of that institution? How did Lévi-Strauss negotiate between the Laboratory's need for coherence and the diversity of projects of its members?*

PD The Laboratory of Social Anthropology was unquestionably a very original institution in the French context. When Lévi-Strauss founded it in 1960, he had in mind the great anthropology departments he had seen in the United States during the war: places with extensive resources for conducting fieldwork, with libraries where researchers could find all the materials they needed, and with specialists from very different cultural areas and thematic fields who engaged in a constant dialogue. Nothing of the sort existed in France, where anthropologists were few and far between, dispersed across heterogeneous institutions that did not afford them much opportunity to engage in common reflection. The very choice of the term "laboratory," which was not used in the social sciences at the time, signaled a desire to place anthropological research on an equal footing with the experimental sciences, by emphasizing both fieldwork and what amounts to experimentation in our discipline, namely the development of models that can be compared. If ethnography is a necessarily individual endeavor, anthropology and ethnology require not so much collective work as the existence of a collective of researchers with diverse ethnographic specializations, gathered together in one place where they can engage in a constant exchange of information, hypotheses, and critical assessments and can also get access to the necessary resources and modern systems of data processing. From the very beginning, the Laboratory of Social Anthropology served this role. It was thus the repository of the only copy in Europe of the Human Relations Area Files, a database of more than 11 million records initiated by the North American anthropologist G. P. Murdock that enabled thematic research across several hundred ethnic groups via combinations of keywords. In addition, the Laboratory engaged from the outset in pioneering experiments, which are still being conducted to this day, concerning the application of computer resources to the processing of various kinds of ethnographic corpuses. In short, what Lévi-Strauss had in mind when he created that laboratory was to reactivate Émile Durkheim's and Marcel Mauss's project of achieving a scientific

Among the tribe of anthropologists 31

understanding of the major principles that govern the common existence of human beings by bringing together researchers who, thanks to the diversity of their ethnographic expertise, were in a position to conduct theoretical research on the common rules of social life, their similarities, and especially their differences. The model was tremendously successful and has since been adopted in all large social science research institutions in France.

Lévi-Strauss himself did not impose anything in the way of either a theoretical orthodoxy or a research program. He enabled collective endeavors, supported them, gave his opinion, always very promptly, on this or that idea or text when he was called upon to do so, and encouraged debate among researchers, all of whom shared a boundless admiration for him despite profound differences in their respective approaches—differences that otherwise could have created considerable tension between them. As Isac Chiva once put it, the Laboratory of Social Anthropology was a "community of loners" and, one might add, of loners who all felt that they were taking part in an extraordinary scientific adventure under the aegis of an extraordinary personality. It was on the basis of the respect and admiration that we had for Lévi-Strauss that the authority he exerted was accepted by all—the little authority he exerted, I should say, as the Laboratory was self-managed, according to the principle of participatory democracy. Lévi-Strauss was always very attentive to the members of the Laboratory, whatever their status, but for most of us he was simply the most remarkable mind in twentieth-century social science. Thus, despite his availability, he was not someone we would go to and see casually, in passing, as one might chat with a colleague. There was something monumental about his persona, and no matter how affable and kind he was to us, we never lost sight of the immense stature we quite rightly bestowed on him. Indeed, everyone at the Laboratory referred to him as "Mr. Lévi-Strauss." We never said "Lévi-Strauss," we never said "Claude Lévi-Strauss," and nobody ever dreamed of calling him by his first name. Françoise Héritier once told me that, when she was elected to the Collège de France, he told her: "Now you can call me Claude." But, of course, she never did...

It is sometimes suggested that the legacy of such a figure, beyond the intellectual emulation it elicits, could become a weight on the social sciences in France, and in particular on the immediate successors. As if the essential reference he represented, and still represents today, were like a paternal relationship that one had to

32 *A Taste for Inquiry*

accept or reject. But I do not believe this to be the case, mostly because Lévi-Strauss never demanded adhesion to any doctrine of structural anthropology. He always encouraged originality among those around him and discouraged attempts to do the same things as he was doing. From this standpoint, the only real expectation was that we hold ourselves to the same standard that he imposed on himself. As for me, from the very first presentation I made in his seminar,[5] I have always written for Lévi-Strauss. One always writes with a reader in mind, and the reader I chose for myself from the very start was him. Indeed, in addition to his anthropological expertise and knowledge, his theoretical imagination and incisive judgment, his familiarity with philosophical questions and his talent as a writer, Lévi-Strauss was also highly knowledgeable about nature—botany, zoology, and ecology—and had paid particular attention to the way the human mind draws on the qualities it perceives in natural objects in order to turn them into complex and sometimes very poetic symbolic constructs. I thus felt a profound affinity with his way of thinking, and this is one of the reasons why I chose him as the ideal reader of my work. This was also a way for me to set a certain standard according to which I would choose my intellectual objects and determine the kind of work I would pursue, a standard I believed would satisfy the expectations of a reader such as him. Perhaps this was also a function of our shared proclivities and, not least, of our shared affection for Amazonian Indians, but I did not in any way seek to imitate his approach. He was always remarkably attentive and gracious with me, generous with his time and attention, dispensing laconic advice at just the right moment. Ours was not a relationship of master and disciple; its dynamic was rather what I imagine it would be like between a master artisan and a young apprentice in which the former has detected promise.

PC *How did it go during the years of writing your doctoral dissertation, and then in the initiation ritual of the doctoral defense? What kind of reactions did your work receive at the time, and then a little later, when it was published?*

PD I returned from South America at the end of 1979 and I defended my dissertation in the spring of 1983, so it took me a little over three years to write it. In truth, I had a megalomaniacal project that I did not see through; the thesis I eventually defended under the title *La Nature domestique* was originally only the first part

Among the tribe of anthropologists 33

of it. In that work I sought to describe the relationships that the Achuar had with natural beings by giving equal weight to material and mental realities, to use the vocabulary inspired by Godelier that had informed the way I defined my project at the time. In other words, I made a point of not distinguishing between the uses they made of the environment and their forms of representation, so as to show how the social practice of nature was simultaneously articulated through the idea that a society has of itself, the idea it has of its environment, and the idea it has of its own intervention in that environment. I had thus striven to combine in a single stroke the analysis of objects that in traditional monographs would have been compartmentalized, and I did so by combining in each chapter quantitative analyses—of soil fertility, working hours, and the productivity of cassava gardens—and analyses of ritual practices, myths, and classification systems in order to show how the technical and symbolic dimensions of praxis impacted each other retroactively. In the case at hand, one could indeed speak of a "society of nature"—a "domestic" and not a "domesticated nature," as some commentators have described it—insofar as each household, isolated in the forest, economically and politically autonomous, acted as the hub from which all interactions with plants and animals unfolded, interactions that were themselves governed by the same behavioral principles as those that characterized the relationships between humans within the household.

I was influenced at the time by the work of Nicholas Georgescu-Roegen, and especially by his great book *The Entropy Law and the Economic Process*, which attempted to consider economic phenomena from the perspective of ecological mechanisms, since both obeyed the same principle of thermodynamics. I thus set out to conduct a comprehensive study of the system of energy exchanges that were consciously organized within the Achuar ecosystem by combining an analysis of interactions between humans and nonhumans—which was to become *In the Society of Nature*—with an analysis of the interactions between humans that guaranteed the stability and reproduction of these flows. That prospective second part was to focus on social organization—which was very fluid and under-institutionalized among the Achuar—primarily through a study of the spatial distribution of human settlements that were due to vendettas, kinship networks, and matrimonial policies. It quickly became apparent, however, that such an ambitious program overflowed the boundaries of a regular PhD dissertation, and I thus suggested to Lévi-Strauss that this work take the form of a Doctorat d'État, to which he agreed. But it also became quickly apparent that I was setting myself up for a very long, if not endless, period of doctoral research, while I was subsisting on adjunct teaching at the École des Hautes Études en Sciences Sociales (EHESS) and on occasional grants from the Maison des Sciences de l'Homme. It did not take much for Godelier and Lévi-Strauss to convince me to be reasonable and give up on such a monumental project for the moment, and to quickly complete a more modest PhD dissertation that would allow me to apply for a stable position. I thus defended the first part of that vast research project as a PhD dissertation, and then the circumstances of my life never afforded me an opportunity to write the second part.

On its own, *In the Society of Nature* was enough, however, to attract attention to this novel approach. I had not had much feedback before the defense, as Lévi-Strauss, to whom I had given the manuscript for his opinion, told me that he trusted me and that I could submit the manuscript without his having read it. At the defense, his only comments were on the form: he reproached me in rather strong terms for my affected style and praised the thesis, which he immediately declared I should have submitted as a Doctorat d'État. I could not very well say to him that I would indeed have done so—if only he had read the thesis earlier! He later wrote to me that he appreciated the narrow path I had opened between an idealist approach that was indifferent to material living conditions and a naïve empiricism that took beliefs and representations as simple reflections of modes of life, so as to analyze what he called the interface: the geographical milieu, the environmental conditions "not as one would wrongly imagine they exist independently of humans, but perceived in the manner in which humans grasp them, and already transformed by what these humans make of them." The positive feedback from Lévi-Strauss and the examiners enabled me to publish my dissertation in 1986, under the same title and without many changes, with the publishing house of the Maison des Sciences de l'Homme, then to have it translated soon afterwards into Spanish and a few years later into English. It quickly became a classic of environmental anthropology in the English speaking world, whereas in France the book interested geographers, sociologists, historians, and even philosophers, who identified in it a new and non-Eurocentric way of analyzing the relationships between a society and its environment.

Among the tribe of anthropologists 35

PC *Your status in the world of anthropologists was secured with the publication of* The Spears of Twilight, *in 1993. But that ethnographic study was also your first engagement with a broader, non-specialist readership. What are your memories of that experience?*

PD Indeed, it was *In the Society of Nature* that gained me entry into the world of anthropologists, both in France and abroad. It was a scholarly work written for scholars. *The Spears of Twilight* was my introduction, as an anthropologist, to a readership that had only the vaguest notion of what anthropology was. The two books complement each other, not because *The Spears of Twilight* is the second part of the dissertation that was never written, but because that second book both explained the ethnographic methods I had employed in *In the Society of Nature* and offered a more thorough-going description of aspects of Achuar social life that I had not addressed in my first book. Indeed, I had intended for the book to serve as a complement, from the beginning. While I was still living in Ecuador, I was surprised to receive a letter from Jean Malaurie inviting me, at Lévi-Strauss's suggestion, to write a book for his renowned series Terre Humaine. I felt both very flattered, as I had not yet done anything to be worthy of such faith, and quite embarrassed. For it seemed immediately obvious to me that, if I wanted to become a professional anthropologist, I would need to prove myself to my community of peers by producing novel scholarly work before writing the kind of book that Terre Humaine had made popular with the broader public. Mercifully, Malaurie understood my qualms and waited nearly fifteen years for the manuscript he had commissioned to come to fruition, which is rather remarkable in a publisher. I turned to it as soon as I had finished writing *In the Society of Nature*, with the idea of describing, from within, the daily life of a population that still lived according to its own norms and values. But I also sought to describe something that is very rarely made clear in conventional monographs: the way a culture that is at first completely opaque becomes ethnographically intelligible—the accumulation of fortuitous circumstances, disconnected dialogues, and accidental interactions that allow an observer to generate knowledge of others.

Unlike in my other books, here I did not have Lévi-Strauss in mind as my reader or even as a model, since *Tristes tropiques* is an intellectual autobiography rather than an ethnographic study strictly speaking. In fact my ideal reader was my aunt, now deceased, who

36 *A Taste for Inquiry*

was a highly cultivated doctor, just like my grandfather—with a sharp mind and wide-ranging curiosity; she was well-read but did not know much about anthropology. This was the kind of reader I hoped to speak to. And it worked, in part thanks to Terre Humaine and its loyal and enthusiastic readership, which devours each new title in the collection. I have thus had the pleasure—which continues to the present day—of meeting people of all sorts and in the most unexpected places, such as the metro, who show the greatest appreciation for the Achuar and for the way I wrote about them. My ego was also flattered by the fact that I was treated by the media as a "writer"—an impression that mercifully wore off rather quickly. What did astonish me, however, was the charitable reception the book received from anthropologists, who took it as a legitimate ethnography—especially in the United States, where it has become recommended reading for undergraduates—when I knew that Paul Rivet had refused to receive Lévi-Strauss after the publication of *Tristes tropiques*. And the praise I received from eminent colleagues in other social science disciplines surprised me perhaps even more, since I had not written the book with them in mind at all. Some confessed to me that it was the first work of anthropology they had read in a long time, having previously lost all interest in such books. So here was a book intended for and appreciated by the "wider educated public" that also appealed to historians and sociologists at the École des Hautes Études, who, I thought, would surely find it not scholarly enough. This caused me to reflect on writing in our disciplines, on the balance we need to strike between narrative and argumentation and on the reasons why most books of anthropology do not sell many more than 200 copies, although they describe institutions and communities that are fascinating in their originality.

Entering the pantheon

PC *The next and ultimate stage in your academic career was your arrival at the Collège de France in 2000. What has been your experience of teaching at this prestigious institution?*

PD The challenge of teaching at this institution lies in its demand for constant renewal, since one is obliged to teach an entirely new course each year. So I am pursuing the project I began at the EHESS, which is to explore new domains and thus never to teach things I already

Entering the pantheon 37

know, but rather things I am discovering and learning about. This is in itself a very good thing, as it helps forestall intellectual sclerosis, but it is also somewhat daunting: I am no Renaissance polymath and on every subject I teach there will always be others who know much more about it than I do. And it sometimes happens that these people are in the room—because I have a pretty good idea of who is working on what in whatever field I am tackling. On several occasions I have expounded on a topic in the presence of some of the leading specialists in France. It is a constant challenge and a source of tremendous stimulation to explore new fields rather than stick with those I already know well.

I have colleagues at the Collège de France who are specialists of Indo-Iranian languages, Sanskrit literature, and Greek epigraphy, fields that were established long ago within that institution, and following that model I could very well focus all my teaching exclusively on the comparative anthropology of Amazonian culture, which is really the only scholarly field in which I am truly an expert; most of the doctoral work I supervise still deals with it. Even though research on the anthropology and archaeology of Amazonia has experienced an unprecedented expansion over the past two or three decades, I manage to keep abreast of the many monographs, dissertations, and articles published in Europe and in North and South America, especially in Brazil, which is becoming a major site of scholarly production in the field. I could thus rely on this body of expertise, which is not widely known in France, and confine myself to a limited audience. Yet, on the basis of examples set by my predecessors Marcel Mauss, Claude Lévi-Strauss, and Françoise Héritier, I do not think that this is what is expected of an anthropologist at the Collège de France. And, since I am naturally inclined to adventure, especially of the intellectual kind, I chose to tackle head-on a set of topics for which I had no particular expertise but that I could explore in the spirit of investigation and discovery that is, in my view, the trademark of the Collège de France. As Maurice Merleau-Ponty eloquently put it in his inaugural lecture, what is taught at the Collège is not established truths, but the idea of free research. For instance, I have devoted sessions to the anthropology of the image and of landscape, bringing elements to this research that are unfamiliar to art historians and philosophers of aesthetics. It is of course very demanding, but deep down I am what one might call a frustrated slacker: well aware of my natural indolence, I have always put myself in situations that force me to work.

38 *A Taste for Inquiry*

PC *You mentioned some of the major figures that preceded you at the Collège and we could add others, including Michel Foucault, Bourdieu, and Merleau-Ponty. It is a very French thing to create this kind of pantheon of the humanities, and one can well imagine that it is a heavy mantle to bear. How do you deal with this aspect?*

PD My relationship with these illustrious predecessors is an ambivalent one, both intimidating and stimulating. When I prepare my lectures, I sometimes feel as if these guiding lights were watching me, looking over my shoulder at what I am writing, and encouraging me at the same time. It is no longer for Lévi-Strauss alone that I am teaching, I do it for a cohort of great minds in whose lineage the vagaries of existence have placed me. Having said that, the coming together of the great figures you cited represented a rather unique moment in the history of the institution and of the social sciences in general. It is true that there was a pantheon: Émile Benveniste and Merleau-Ponty were the first to enter, followed a little later by Lévi-Strauss, Roland Barthes, Foucault, André Leroi-Gourhan, Bourdieu, and Jean-Pierre Vernant. The circumstances that made such a convergence of major thinkers possible are still difficult to grasp, and historians of social science may well help us understand it one day. Merleau-Ponty first, then Lévi-Strauss and Vernant surely played major roles, since they were strong personalities and managed to push through candidates, overcoming a certain intellectual conservatism and reluctance to innovate. Let us not forget that Lévi-Strauss himself had to apply three times before he was finally appointed. It is through archival study that we will come to understand what actually happened in that period, during those thirty or forty years of extraordinary influence of the Collège de France in all areas of the human and social sciences. The current situation is rather different. In the necessary balance between erudition and conceptual innovation, I have the feeling that these days the former has won out. I base this sentiment on the fact that candidates whom I have proposed have not received much support, being considered by my colleagues to be too heterodox.

Among the thinkers you mentioned, Foucault and Bourdieu played a very special role in shaping my thinking. These two authors made a deep impression on me from the very start of my academic studies, and their influence is still clear in *Beyond Nature and Culture*. When I was writing my master's thesis on Andean societies, and then my doctoral dissertation, Bourdieu and Foucault

Entering the pantheon

were bedside reading, because they provided me with the means of addressing the questions I was posing just as I was posing them, perhaps more directly than Lévi-Strauss's structural anthropology. I took from Bourdieu the idea of schemas of practice and, from Foucault, an attention to the great historical and epistemological formations. The idea of schema, which I introduced in *In the Society of Nature* and developed in *Beyond Nature and Culture,* was of course originally inspired by Lévi-Strauss and by Piaget's influence over him, which itself goes back to Kant. But I believe that in the way I conceptualized this notion there is a lot of Bourdieu and of his concept of habitus, as developed in *Outline of a Theory of Practice*—a book that I had read as soon as it came out in 1971 and that I deem to be the most fundamental of his works. Rather than historicized habitus—in Bourdieu's usage, ways of doing and thinking that are adjusted to specific social situations—I have tried to highlight practical dispositions that are somewhat more ontologically stable and located upstream from habitus. It was in this sense that I developed the notion of schema.

My relationship with Foucault is similar in that it is, again, the structuralist Foucault whom I admire, the early Foucault of *The Order of Things, Madness and Civilization,* and *The Archeology of Knowledge,* who, much to my surprise, has fallen into relative oblivion, especially in the anglophone world, in favor of the later Foucault of governmentality and biopower. He was steeped in the philosophy of science as well as in a tradition of history of philosophy with which I became familiar very early on, given that Martial Guéroult, one of its major exponents, was my professor at the École Normale Supérieure and we all became avid readers of Gaston Bachelard, Georges Canguilhem, Pierre Duhem, Gilbert Simondon, and Alexandre Koyré. It is easy to see how Foucault gave a more flamboyant and at the same time sharper and more systematic character to tendencies that were already present in the French tradition of the history of philosophy and count among the most precious legacies of French philosophy to the analysis of thought processes.

I was very much inspired by the Foucauldian concept of episteme, that idea of a network of correspondences that govern the various forms of knowledge and practice within a given historical period and whose unity is given definition by this ordering structure. In contrast with the anthropological concept of culture—which, since Franz Boas, has been very tightly bound to spatially circumscribed

40 *A Taste for Inquiry*

languages and social groups—episteme is less descriptive, less empirical, and more analytical. It articulates the conditions of possibility of forms of knowledge and reveals the connections between the various codes that organize the production of norms. This is one of the sources of inspiration for what I called, in *Beyond Nature and Culture*, the modes of identification. But, as with habitus, I de-historicized the concept: the modes of identification are not integrative principles specific to some temporal configuration that gets established by one break and closed by another—as in Foucault's shift from the regime of resemblance in the Renaissance to the regime of representation in the classical age. Rather these schemas generate inferences and actions, modes of composition and of the use of worlds that obey similar principles and, as a result, can be deployed in rather similar ways in very diverse historical contexts. All this to say that, in terms of influences, I am the child of Foucault and Bourdieu as much as the child of Lévi-Strauss.

PC   *The publication of* Beyond Nature and Culture *in 2005 represents a first release of your Collège de France lectures. That book had a considerable impact, which went well beyond the anthropological community. How did you experience that key moment in your intellectual career, and how do you feel today about the book's reception?*

PD   In France at least, *Beyond Nature and Culture* probably had a greater impact outside the world of anthropology than within it. The reception it was given by most anthropologists of my generation was one of polite silence, while some expressed a mix of admiration for the scope of the project and vehement indignation at what they considered the harmful consequences it would have for the future of the discipline. By contrast, the book elicited quite a bit of interest from young scholars and doctoral students, at least among those with a taste for theory, comforted as they were to see that a research agenda that eschewed ethnographism was back on the table. Indeed, the waning of the grand paradigms of the 1970s—structuralism, Marxism, critical sociology, methodological individualism—had led many young scholars to immerse themselves in the minute description of local realities and lose sight of the anthropological project proper, that is, of the ambition to propose models that make sense of the diversity of uses of the world. The current wave of pragmatism in its various forms—from the American school proper to the analysis of language interaction—may have served as the

Entering the pantheon 41

more or less internalized backdrop of this retreat into description. The only standouts were Latour's symmetrical anthropology—with which I share quite a bit—and the cognitive science-based approaches, most of which are so removed from facts and so simplistic in their account of cultural phenomena that they are still rejected by young anthropologists. This may be what drew some of them to the renewed structuralism that I was proposing.

What I did not expect was that a book written by an anthropologist for anthropologists would make such an impact outside the field of anthropology, and first and foremost among historians—especially of the Renaissance, the Middle Ages and antiquity, as well as of the ancient Near East and China—who seem to have found in what I call "analogist ontology" an operational concept for characterizing very diverse civilizations, whose common points were intuited but hard to define. Geographers also became interested in the thesis of the book, which was deeply gratifying to the would-be geographer that I am. They found in it an organizing principle for the interfaces between societies and environments that is both distinct from and complementary to the study of spatial reality at different scales, and this is their preferred approach. Some went so far as to offer cartographic representations of the distribution of ontologies, a project that I view with some skepticism, since it fixes heuristic models within empirical borders. The implications of *Beyond Nature and Culture* for the field of images and spatial organization, aspects that I have myself explored in my teaching in recent years, have also stimulated architects, art historians, prehistorians, and even artists; this provided opportunities for encounters outside my academic milieu, and not without the occasional comical misunderstanding. Even sociologists responded to my ideas regarding economic sociology and the sociology of culture, for instance—or the theory of institutions.

And, finally, the response from philosophers was, one way or the other, intense, reviving a dialogue with the social sciences that had perhaps gone a little dormant. Some were thrilled to discover that philosophy had burgeoned outside its designated turf, lending dignity to forms of thought that deposed European thinkers from their positions of exclusive authority. Others, on the contrary, reproached me for a deterritorialization that ran roughshod over nature, science, reason, and the truth, constituting a dangerous prelude to moral confusion and epistemological uncertainty. More generally, I was attacked by faithfuls on both sides: at one end,

42   *A Taste for Inquiry*

since I place what I call modern naturalism on the same ontological footing as other ways of composing worlds, I am a relativist who undermines the universal principles that western science has bestowed onto other civilizations—and it should legitimately take pride in having done so; at the other end, I am a stealth modernizer who, under the guise of pluralism, in fact reinstates anthropological science in its role as rector, and thus reaffirms the West in its intellectual imperialism. I am not terribly bothered by these reactions, since Lévi-Strauss's work provoked the same turmoil in its day: in the eyes of some he was a totalitarian scientist, while for others he was the gravedigger of the values on which scientific rationality and democracy were erected.

PC   *Looking back on the overall progression of your work, we see first a fieldwork monograph—In the Society of Nature, in 1986—then an ethnographic narrative—The Spears of Twilight, in 1993—and finally, in 2005, a comparative synthesis—Beyond Nature and Culture. These three major stages of your work conform to a classic progression of anthropological scholarship that has rarely been achieved in such a canonical form. Were you aware of embodying, in a certain sense, the ideal anthropological career?*

PD   These are, indeed, the customary three stages of anthropological knowledge. Ethnography is analytical and corresponds to the early stage of research: the fieldwork and the gathering of various kinds of data on a specific society usually leads to a monograph study that is descriptive and circumscribed in time and space. In a second stage, ethnology then expands on ethnography and represents a first pass at generalization, either at a regional level—for a group of neighboring societies with certain affinities—or at a thematic level—when the focus is on a type of phenomenon or practice common to many societies around the world, for instance sacrifice, or a particular form of marriage. Anthropology can be seen as the final moment of synthesis: based as it is on ethnographic and ethnological findings as well as on archeology and history, it strives to generate comprehensive knowledge about humankind by providing principles of intelligibility for the diverse ways of composing and inhabiting worlds. The term "anthropology" encompasses all three approaches, which we can see are quite different. This has been a source of considerable confusion, including within the discipline itself. Indeed, what we call anthropology is most often ethnography. This is

Entering the pantheon 43

especially the case in the anglophone world, which now considers the project once shared by most of the great anthropologists of the twentieth century—shedding light on the formal properties of social life through a comparative approach—to be at best outdated and at worst imperialist and racist. I see this renunciation as arising rather from laziness and pusillanimity, couched in good intentions.

In fact these three levels of approach are entirely complementary. In no way do they imply a hierarchy of modes and objects of knowledge that run with increasing majesty from ethnography to anthropology, from the local to the universal. They are merely different scales; nevertheless they must not be confused, since each has its own logic, method, and internal coherence. It is perfectly normal, indeed necessary, that anthropologists should begin their career with an ethnographic study. It is a form of knowledge whose singularity and spirit of adventure have an immediate appeal, at both the personal and the intellectual level, since, unlike in most other sciences, one is in sole control. But this very special, almost irreplicable experience puts the ethnographer in a position to judge, better than those who have never engaged in this kind of endeavor, the relevance of the ethnographic information collected by others, and hence its value as raw material for generating ethnological syntheses or comparative models. Yet many scholars never make the leap to anthropology and remain ethnographers and ethnologists throughout their careers as a result of having acquired a taste for this kind of work or being attracted to a specific cultural area, sometimes in the hope of achieving a complete mastery of their object, sometimes through lack of affinity with the degree of abstraction required for anthropological theory.

For my part, in any case, I did not follow exactly the steps of an ideal career, even if each of the books you cited takes the same material as a starting point and draws different lessons from my ethnographic fieldwork on the Achuar, who constitute the driving force behind all of them. For my first book, *In the Society of Nature*, can be seen as ethnological, whereas the second, *The Spears of Twilight,* is rather ethnographic. *In the Society of Nature* is the result of long ethnographic fieldwork and comprises minute descriptions that are sometimes very technical, especially when I draw on a series of metrics regarding agricultural production, hunting, soil fertility, and working times: this was not a very common practice in French anthropology at the time. And yet these data have a more general significance than to constitute knowledge about a tribe that

44   *A Taste for Inquiry*

had never been described before. For instance, conventional ethno-ecological wisdom at the time held that Amazonian societies had taken a diverging historical path, in accordance with the kind of environment in which they had evolved: stagnation in the interfluvial areas, where the soil was poor and the fauna sparse; formation of populous chiefdoms in riverside areas characterized by the presence of fertile sediments and abundant fauna. Yet the Achuar were living in both types of ecosystems and had done so for several centuries. In spite of the very real differences in potential between the two milieux, which the Achuar knew very well, there was no noticeable contrast in their use of resources and in their population densities or distribution across the habitat. The only difference was in the possible margins of intensification: these were average in the inter-fluvial region but considerable in the riverside region, which could have sustained a much higher level of human occupation.

These findings invalidated the mechanistic theories of cultural adaptation in the Amazonian basin and raised the more general question of apparent homeostasis in a system of using nature in which the maximization principle had no place. I offered several responses to this question in *In the Society of Nature*. I will cite only one, which is based on the way the Achuar distributed their time: despite considerable individual variation in the productivity of subsistence activities, the amount of time devoted to them remained low and identical for all, variations being accounted for through either increased intensity of effort or greater mastery of some technical skill. This rigid allocation of time to each and every task prevented any increase in their duration, even when an urgent or vital need seemed to call for it. Contrary to the assumptions of marginalist economics, the segmentation and distribution of activities among the Achuar over the course of the day obeyed a system of culturally defined habits that created an effective obstacle to any lengthening of the duration of productive tasks. It is clear that findings of this kind, whose objective is to highlight more general characteristics of the interaction between a society and its environment, are trans-posable to other places, in Amazonia and beyond. In that sense, they have an ethnological reach that transcends ethnographic description and the interpretation of a specific society.

The Spears of Twilight, on the other hand, is a consciously ethno-graphic work. As I have already explained, it originated with a suggestion from the Terre Humaine series that converged with my own desire to renew the ethnographic genre. The project was born of a malaise that I had detected for some time. Why did most anthropologists feel so reticent about addressing a broader audience than that of specialists in the discipline, when their approach is based on an experience that is in theory accessible to all and is expressed for the most part in ordinary language? Historians, who are also practitioners of explanatory narrative and cultural contextualization, generally exhibit no such modesty and the most illustrious among them have appealed to a broader public without compromising the standards of rigor demanded by their discipline. I was thus very keen not only to share the originality of the Achuar with a public beyond the circle of specialists but also to make better known this very particular form of knowledge ethnographers deploy in the field on a daily basis. When Malaurie made his proposal, I had barely begun writing my doctoral dissertation in Quito, and I was struck by the chasm that I perceived between the thick diversity of the still fresh ethnographic experience I had just had and the codified exercise in which I was then engaging to earn my stripes in the profession. Every day I experienced a residue, an excess of meaning and personal involvement for which the orthodoxy of a doctoral dissertation did not provide any outlet.

In those days the rules of monograph writing were still rather strict, forcing any anthropologist who aspired to obtain the recognition of peers into a rather standardized form of expression. These writing conventions remained implicit and resulted quite simply from reading elder scholars, which led novices rather spontaneously to adopt a style and certain rules of composition that they identified with the competence they sought to attain. The process of reproduction of skills gave rise to a sort of standardized form of description, the use of commonly accepted analytical categories, and the erasure of the knowing subject behind the anonymity of scholarly common sense. Such standardization of descriptive procedures was no doubt a necessary step in the maturation of anthropology as a discipline, since it allowed for the informational elements it compares and builds into systems to come pre-packaged in the ethnographic literature in a homogeneous way. Yet, by ruling out any open reference to one's subjectivity, the anthropologist is condemned to exclude everything that characterizes his or her particular approach within the human sciences: this is a form of knowledge founded on a personal and sustained relationship between a particular individual and other particular individuals, a knowledge born out of a combination of circumstances that is different each time and therefore never strictly comparable to any other—not even to the knowledge produced by a previous anthropologist who worked with the very same population.

I have often said that the workshop of anthropologists is their own self and the relationships they have established with a few members of the society in which they have chosen to live. The information they bring back cannot be dissociated from the situations in which chance has placed them, from the role they were made to play in local politics, sometimes unwittingly, and from their possible dependence on the various individuals who become their main sources of information. It also reflects their own character, education, and personal background, all of which have oriented their attention and defined their preferences. In contrast with historians and sociologists, who bring the living and the dead into conversation according to experimental protocols that anyone can repeat and interpret as they wish, anthropologists demand that we give credence to their good faith when they claim to draw from a unique experience a body of knowledge whose validity everyone is asked to accept. Such a privilege becomes exorbitant if it is not tempered by a detailed account of the situations that have given rise to this particularized knowledge. And yet it is precisely on this point that the principles of monograph writing impose silence. I thus wrote *The Spears of Twilight* in an attempt to remedy this state of affairs. It is a book that can be read both as a monument to a culture whose discovery has transformed my life and as a reflexive ethnography that reveals to a broader public how knowledge is formed about a people whose institutions and values are very different from our own.

The third and most recent project is properly anthropological. *Beyond Nature and Culture* offers a synthesis of my thinking on the question of the relations between humans and nonhumans, which has evolved over the many years I taught at the École des Hautes Études and during my early lectures at the Collège de France. It is an anthropological work proper—in that, rather than proceeding through successive generalizations from particular cases, as happens in an ethnological work, it proceeds from hypotheses regarding the dispositions of human nature and explores how these dispositions are actualized in very diverse institutions.

The starting point for this exercise in structural ontology may be worth recalling—namely the thought experiment of a subject. I can identify qualities in an indeterminate other, whether human or nonhuman, only if I can recognize in this other those qualities

Entering the pantheon 47

through which I apprehend my own self. Those qualities pertain to the realm of interiority—one's mental state, intentionality, reflexivity, and so on—and to the realm of physicality—one's physical states and processes, sensorimotor schemas, inner sense of the body, and so on. The original kernel is thus a hypothetical invariant, the relationship between the inner world and the physical world, whose various possible combinations I study. There are four such combinations: either the interiority of nonhumans is of the same kind as mine, but they are distinguished from me and from one another by their physical capacities—and this is what I call animism; or, on the contrary, nonhumans are subject to the same kind of physical determinations as I experience, but are devoid of interiority—this would be naturalism; or else some humans and nonhumans share the same set of physical and moral qualities, while their group differs from other groups of humans and nonhumans, who share other physical and moral qualities—this corresponds to totemism; or, finally, each being is distinguished from others in its specific combination of physical and moral qualities, which must then be related to others through relations of correspondence—and this is what I refer to as analogism. In short, each formula is the hypothetico-deductive expression of all the possible consequences of a kernel that is posited as invariant. And each of them is also the principle of construction of a cosmological type, a regime of temporality, a particular form of collective, and many other social and cultural traits; concrete illustrations of these can be found here and there around the world. One can see that comparison is used here as a mechanism of verification and as the means of confirming the concrete expression of the potentialities contained within the invariant—and not as the starting point, as in the kind of inductive analysis that characterizes the properly ethnological approach.

Yet the fundamental questions that I have tried to address in *Beyond Nature and Culture* were indeed born of my ethnographic experience, and especially of the realization, repeated daily in the course of my fieldwork, that the notions of nature and culture not only made no sense to the Achuar but would be of little help in understanding the way they composed their world. To be honest, one of the things I particularly enjoy about this singular occupation is how it constantly offers opportunities to shift one's attention from the most minute details of everyday life, where it is required in ethnography, to the kind of synthesis and modeling that is proper to anthropology. This discipline may be unique in allowing for

48   *A Taste for Inquiry*

such a wide range of focal lengths and modes of exposition. The back-and-forth between the more particular and the more general was also a way for me to draw on my double training. Like other French anthropologists, I gave up on philosophy out of a very keen appreciation for the infinite complexity of the empirical world, even while retaining a predisposition to abstract thought. And, since the two have never been disconnected for me, having the opportunity to constantly shift registers has been a source of tremendous satisfaction.

I have recently been working on Achuar genealogies as part of a longstanding project with Anne-Christine Taylor on the kinship system of that society—a project that has been slow-going for lack of time. Diving again into material collected quite a while ago and seeing what can be drawn from it has been a real pleasure: each name evokes the texture of a voice, a place, a face. This back-and-forth between empiricism and abstraction is also what lends anthropology an air of complexity from a lay perspective, especially in the eyes of our colleagues in the experimental sciences, because they have difficulty understanding the link between the ethnographic method and anthropology. Even if from a methodological standpoint they are distinct approaches, anthropology is almost impossible to sever from its ethnographic substrate, not only because it provides the original stimulant for raising more general questions but also because it plunges us into a form of experience and contact with social life that no conceptual analysis can replace. If one has not passed through the ethnographic experience, if one does not know what the bricks out of which ethnographic literature and anthropological models are constructed are made of, one is unlikely to select the right bricks or to understand these primary materials for what they are. And it is in this sense, too, that fieldwork is essential: it gives us a more accurate understanding of the conditions of production of the ethnographic knowledge we use to elaborate our anthropological theories.

2

An Amazonian Sojourn and the Challenges of Ethnography

The world of the forest

PC   *Let us now turn to your fieldwork experience, which has played such a central role in your education, your career, and your thought. What went into your decision to go to Amazonia?*

PD   I have already described my short-lived ethnographic experience in southern Chiapas, as well as other factors that had drawn me to Amazonia. First of all, Amazonian tribes do not appear to have any of the classic institutions—chiefdoms, kingdoms, lineages, clans, castes, and so on—through which anthropologists in other regions of the world such as Africa, Southeast Asia, and Oceania have sought to describe and explain how non-European societies work. The ethnographic literature described these human groups, by default, as "fluid," "simple," "loosely structured," "stateless," or, as Lévi-Strauss put it, "without writing." It was thus difficult to say what exactly characterizes collective life in these regions and to describe these groups as anything but aggregates of myth-telling peoples. It is also important to remember that, in the mental representations that have prevailed in Europe since the Renaissance, the Amerindians of Amazonia have been seen as an extension of nature, representing either all that is benevolent and generous about it—an Eden inhabited by philosophers who engage in learned conversation from their hammocks—or its threatening and wild side, to which all those practices long considered abominable pathologies—cannibalism, head shrinking, and permanent war—can testify. Their special relationship with nature, whether negatively or positively assessed, was thus the dominant feature in

50   *An Amazonian Sojourn and the Challenges of Ethnography*

all the descriptions of them that have been made during the past five centuries.

It quickly became apparent to me that, to bring something new to the general understanding of that part of the world and the people who inhabit it, to resolve what appeared to be a kind of anthropological scandal, namely people living more or less without institutions, one had to study their relationships with plants and animals, since it may be just there that we would find the key to understanding their *socius*—the dynamics of their collective existence. To this must be added the appeal (which I have already mentioned) of their amiable, almost libertarian lifestyle, fiercely resistant to status inequalities and submissiveness to authority—all dispositions that align perfectly with my own inclinations, as I believe they do with those of most anthropologists who work on Amazonia.

As for the choice of the particular area where we decided to conduct our research—the upper Amazon, on the Ecuadorian border with Peru—that was the result of chance encounters. I should point out that what anthropologists refer to as "Amazonia" is an immense territory of 6 million square kilometers that stretches well beyond the Amazon basin and falls within the jurisdiction of nine different countries peopled by a mosaic of native societies whose members speak over four hundred languages, some of them further subdivided into numerous dialects. If the generic name "Amazonia" is often used to refer to all of this, the realities subsumed under this name are highly diverse and the choice of studying this or that area is decisive, since one is rarely given an opportunity to change destinations after having set off. When I was doing fieldwork in the Ecuadorian Amazon, I was as far from the Tupi-Guarani of the Brazilian coast as they were from Senegal. I thus tried to get as much information and advice as possible, and it was a friend, Carmen Bernand, who drew my attention to the Jivaros on her return from ethnographic fieldwork in the Ecuadorian Andes. I would not have come up with it spontaneously, since to my mind the Jivaros were the epitome of a sensationalist and kitschy kind of exoticism: it was one of those "primitive tribes" around which the West's vulgar attraction for savage otherness had coalesced in its most morbid form. The shrunken heads—shrunken to the size of a fist, it was customarily said—the Bibaros at war with the Arumbayas of the Tintin cartoons, the Jivaro shaman who reduces uncle Scrooge's pile of gold with his magic potion—I had been steeped in this silly folklore since childhood. Then I began reading the available literature on the Jivaros and realized that, even though a great many books had been published on them, most were unreliable travel narratives that copied from one another. This people, which seemed to live in a permanent state of war of all against all, in fact remained rather enigmatic from a scholarly point of view.

I should add that the term "Jivaro" is a hispanicization of *shiwiar*, which, for a Jivaro, refers to the enemy of another Jivaro group and is an ethnonym now rejected by the Jivaros themselves, on account of its negative connotations in Ecuador and Peru. The term they have adopted for the isolated language they all share is *aénts chicham*, meaning "people's way of speaking." It encompasses in a generic manner a vast ensemble of over 150,000 Amerindians settled throughout the forest of the Amazonian foothills of Ecuador and Peru. This population comprises half a dozen tribes, each with its own dialect, which were for a long time at war with their neighbors. The ethnographic literature on the Shuar of Ecuador, the most studied of the Aénts Chicham, mentions another tribe, a traditional enemy, of which almost nothing was known. This was the Achuar. It is at this point that I went to see Claude Lévi-Strauss and told him that I wanted to work on the Achuar, and he immediately gave his approval.

In fact he gave me more than just approval: he also made it possible for me to obtain funding through the Laboratory of Social Anthropology as well as additional financing from the Collège de France—indispensable support for conducting fieldwork. Then, like all anthropologists in training at that time, I proceeded from the Collège de France across the Rue des Écoles to the camping equipment outfitter Au Vieux Campeur, to acquire the requisite gear for life in the rain forest. Actually the equipment in question was rather rustic by comparison to what one finds today; aside from the mosquito nets and diving flashlights, it consisted for the most part of waterproof boating bags designed to protect our cameras, tape recorders, and field notebooks from the dampness. As the latter were the anthropologist's most essential tool, I bought mine, with heavy weight paper and hard covers, at a high-end stationer that no longer exists. They have not even yellowed in the forty years since. In addition to these items, we acquired several kilos of glass beads, which we had been told to bring and for which the Achuar turned out to have an insatiable desire indeed.

Thus, in the summer of 1976, Anne-Christine Taylor and I set off for Ecuador on board a mixed-cargo ship. This was arguably

52   *An Amazonian Sojourn and the Challenges of Ethnography*

a more convenient mode of travel, since we were going for two or three years and carried quite a bit of baggage with us. But mostly we were just nostalgic for a time when traveling took longer and entailed greater risk, evoking an infinitely expansive world, which I had learned to savor in the volumes of the *Tour du monde* and, more recently, in the novels of Blaise Cendrars and Paul Morand. During that long parenthesis between Europe and America punctuated by legendary ports of call—Maracaibo, Cartagena de Indias, Colón, Buenaventura—we began to learn the rudiments of Aénts Chicham thanks to a missionary grammar book that a linguist friend of ours had dug up.

PC   *In the heroic narrative of anthropology, the start of fieldwork is often described as a key moment. How would you describe your first interactions with Achuar society?*

PD   We arrived at the port of Guayaquil, an experience I recommend to the movie buffs who enjoyed *To Have and Have Not* and *Republic of Sin*. From there we headed for Amazonia. Our first stop was a small town on the colonization frontier called Puyo, in the foothill of the Andes. This was as far as paved roads could take us. It was a collection point for poor settlers of Amerindian or mixed blood, who had been pushed out of the highlands and coastal areas by a system of land ownership that was still largely latifundial, and who had settled on the outskirts of Amerindian territories and cleared a few acres of forest land. There nobody had heard of the Achuar, even though according to our ethnographic information they could not have been more than about 150 kilometers to the east, in the depths of the forest, inaccessible by either road or navigable waterway. We finally met a Dominican who told us that he knew of their existence; but he was rather more interested in getting us to finance his mission than in helping us locate them. The American evangelical missionaries were more forthcoming. They showed us the locations of a few Achuar villages that, at their instigation, had settled around makeshift landing strips, even though they refused to take us to those villages in their small single-engine planes.

We eventually turned to the army, since the entire region was then under military control, and managed to get them to take us to Montalvo, a small garrison in the middle of the forest. There we were introduced to Quichua-speaking guides, members of the Sacha Runa tribe, whose population is spread throughout the territory

The world of the forest　　　53

north of the Achuar; and they agreed to take us to an Achuar village. We walked for two days, carrying with us a small bag of rice and a cooking pot, and finally reached the village where we first set to work, on the Kapawientza River. Things got off to a good start, probably because evangelical missionaries had already been through there and the inhabitants had had periodic contact with Whites over the previous five or six years. To call it a "village" is in fact overstating things: it was just a half-dozen large houses without walls and with roofs made of palm fronds, all scattered among manioc gardens. The village was not far from Montalvo; and the Quichua, who provided support for the garrison, regularly came to trade with the Achuar. This was an occasion for sporadic contact with the outside world. Indeed, there was a young man in that village who spoke a few words of Spanish, having worked as a tracker for oil companies further north, in the Ecuadorian Amazon, and his presence helped us communicate at the beginning.

This was how our nearly three-year adventure began. Over its course we moved away from that first village, little by little, into regions that had not yet been visited by missionaries, where the Achuar maintained a lifestyle that probably rather resembled the one they had led in the previous centuries. Their techniques, skills, and habitat did not differ much, on the whole, from what they had been in the past, even though metal tools had been introduced— machetes, axes, and of course rifles. This aspect was important for me, since I wanted to study the relationship of that society to its environment. So, first, I conducted the kind of research that was necessary to anyone interested in these questions: I studied their various work modes and forms of access to resources, I sampled the soil to measure pH levels, I collected plants, trying to identify the main species, and I regularly measured, over many months, the quantities of cultivated plants and game that went into households so as to assess their intake of protein, calories, vitamins, and so on. Since my goal was to produce a critique of ecological determinism that did not limit itself to epistemological arguments but also rested on factual elements that invalidated the theory, I had to collect these elements in a methodical and precise manner.

From that standpoint, we quickly realized the advantage that Anne-Christine Taylor and I had in the field as a couple. Each of us adopted the expected role in the gender division of labor, Anne-Christine by gardening or making manioc beer in the women's company while I took part as best I could in the slashing and

54   *An Amazonian Sojourn and the Challenges of Ethnography*

hunting sessions. The Achuar of the upper Kapawi thus became accustomed to seeing us collecting plants, weighing the haunches of peccaries, mapping gardens with a topographic plane table, drawing plans of house interiors, and taking a keen interest in local artisanal techniques, from basket weaving through blowpipe making to pottery. The initial amazement at our presence, or even the suspicion that they may have harbored toward us, quickly gave way as they realized that we were harmless, probably a new kind of missionary that, oddly, eschewed all proselytizing.

PC   *In the popular imagination, the Jivaros have a reputation for being very bellicose. Did you confirm this? Was your work on the notion of "predation" intended to displace the traditional discourse?*

PD   During the few months we spent in that first village, the Achuar seemed, on the contrary, to be peaceful, a far cry from the usual clichés of deceitful and bloodthirsty Jivaros. To be sure, the men always carried their rifles with them, especially for visits, and this was a habit I myself eventually adopted. I quickly realized that the man who was now my ritual friend had abducted his first wife a few years earlier, in the course of a raid against the southern Achuar during which the woman's first husband was killed, yet none of it seemed to show in the evident affection the two had for each other. It was also clear that the men were prone to flying off the handle and that the slightest hint of a conflict between distant relatives in the Achuar country could cause bellicose bluster; but it was difficult to tell whether it would lead to actual warfare. On the whole, however, daily life in that first village was peaceful and it was only later and in more remote areas that I was confronted to situations of armed conflict. It was also only later, after careful cross-checking, that I realized that most of these good-humored Achuar, who had welcomed us with such generosity when we arrived in the upper Kapawi, had killed a man on at least one occasion.

Upon my return from fieldwork, I developed the notion of predation when trying to understand this warring ethos, which even the women shared, since they were the first to encourage men to take revenge for an assassination, a death attributed to witchcraft, or even an affront. Against the prevalent interpretation at the time— which treated war in Amazonia as an exchange of dead persons comparable to an exchange of goods, and thus posited a symbolic

The world of the forest 55

continuity between commerce and vendetta—I operated on the premise that the Achuar's attitude to enemies and to hunting game was based on the same rejection of reciprocity. This rejection was not intended to annihilate the other, be it human or animal, or to express supremacy or contempt. Quite the opposite: the hunts, abductions, and murders, as well as the rituals that accompanied them, expressed a conception of predation that took the other, which is materially or symbolically consumed, to be indispensable to the perpetuation of one's own existence. The other that is absorbed in war or hunting is thus not an object, as in the mass slaughter of the twentieth century, but indeed a person like me and, as such, a condition of my own life—which corresponds to the biological definition of predation. But I realized this only much later.

PC *Upon arrival, then, you already had a well-defined research plan, along with the idea of critiquing received theories?*

PD The ethnoecological work on Amazonia at the time was premised on an implacable environmental determinism. The constraints of the particular ecosystems to which societies had to adapt were seen to account for the development of certain institutions, which supposedly responded to these constraints in an adequate manner. For the adherents of "cultural materialism" in the United States, these constraints resulted mostly from the scarcity of protein available for human consumption, since the plants cultivated by the Amazonian populations, primarily manioc, are rich in calories but poor in protein. Hence the crucial role attributed to hunting and fishing for obtaining essential animal protein. Since the species hunted in Amazonia are rather mobile and dispersed, maximizing access to protein through hunting was deemed to have induced a form of human settlement pattern adapted to the configuration of these animal populations: dispersed and low-density settlements. According to Marvin Harris,[1] for instance, war was the social response that Amazonian societies had found to that limiting factor, as it regularly caused villages to split into subgroups on opposite sides, in conflict. From the moment these villages reached a certain size, war was the mechanism through which the population was redistributed more homogeneously over a given territory. According to this model, war also allowed for the culling of the male population through homicide, and thus for a reduction of the pressure on protein resources.

56   *An Amazonian Sojourn and the Challenges of Ethnography*

This last point was not very convincing, because a society's demographics are determined more by the number of breeding females than by the number of breeding males. If the homicide rate among women is low—which is the case in Amazonia as a whole—institutions such as polygamy and levirate—that is, a woman's obligation to marry the brother of her deceased husband—would create the opposite situation, where a reduced number of men can have a large number of children with several women. This was indeed the case among the Achuar. In fact the main factor of demographic regulation among the Achuar was not war but a very high infant mortality rate.

To respond to the challenges posed by these theories and to offer more convincing explanations, I had to carry out the kinds of studies of the resources and their use that I learned to conduct while I was at the Museum of Natural History in Paris and by specializing in economic anthropology with Godelier; and I did so even while remaining attentive to the more specifically social and cultural dimensions of Achuar life. I include in this category kinship and matrimonial alliance relationships, the barter system, the factional and vendetta policy, rites and ceremonies, the domestic organization of space, drinking celebrations, myths and ethnobiological classifications, in short, everything that makes up daily life and arouses the ethnographer's interest. All this took me quite a lot of time, because the Achuar language, even if it is not the most difficult one among those spoken in Amazonia, is still structurally very different from the Indo-European languages with which I am familiar. Mercifully, neighboring dialects, especially Shuar, had been described by the Salesian missionaries in a lexicon and grammar book based on the structure of Latin that we had crammed before our arrival. This proved sufficient for initial exchanges.

Over time, I began acquiring a clearer sense of the way the Achuar inhabited their environment. Two findings emerged out of that initial ethnographic study. On the one hand, as was my initial intention, I managed to successfully demonstrate that technical and environmental determinism, as expounded by the American materialist school, did not hold. For the Achuar, in fact, very efficiently exploit two rather different biotopes: the first is that of the alluvial valleys of the great rivers, characterized by their fertile soil and abundant resources in animal protein; the second is that of the area described as interfluvial, a landscape of small hills, whose rugged terrain consists of poor soil and highly dispersed, mostly

The world of the forest 57

arboreal fauna. On the basis of the scant ethnohistorical data and life stories that we collected, it seems that the Achuar have inhabited these two distinct environments for a long time and, if we apply the theses of cultural ecology, they should have developed, over time, different institutions, each one adapted to the constraints specific to its respective environment. But, as I have already observed, this was absolutely not the case: the social patterns were in every way the same, whether the communities lived in the wide valleys or on the hills. One of the reasons why there were no significant differences is that the resources available to all these communities far surpassed their needs. By taking into account garden outputs, hunting and fishing yields, and the human effort these activities required, I was able to show that in principle the Achuar could have fed two or three times their present population, perhaps even more. They were thus in no way enslaved to their environment. We were quite clearly dealing with an example of what Marshall Sahlins has called "the original affluent society."[2] Rather than putting in the same amount of working time as we do in industrial societies, and thus exploiting the ecological and economic potential of their environment to the fullest, the Achuar worked three to four hours a day to be able to abundantly fulfill their needs, and thus remained well below their development potential. They lived very well in this manner and, with a population that otherwise remained constant, it would be difficult to see what could have induced them to increase their working time and intensify their production. Thus reasoning in terms of adaptation to the environment seemed absurd to me, because the Achuar were not determined in their social existence by environmental constraints or technical limitations, but rather by an ideal of existence that was culturally defined and called in their language *shiir waras*, "the good life." After having shared for a time their use of the world, I can only pay tribute to their wisdom.

The other finding that questions the relevance of the notion of adaptation as an automatic response to environmental constraints emerged out of my study of their practice of clearing horticulture. Like other Amazonian Indians, the Achuar practice slash-and-burn horticulture, whose impact on the forest was profoundly transformative. To create a garden, they clear a plot in the forest, burn the cut vegetation and plant in the ashes around sixty different species of plant—some, like manioc, in over thirty varieties. But they also transplant into their gardens an almost equal number of woodland species, generally fruit trees, palm trees, and plants with

58   *An Amazonian Sojourn and the Challenges of Ethnography*

pharmaceutical properties, or else they spare them in the slashing phase. In addition, many small predators come to these gardens and help themselves—*agoutis, acouchis, pacas*, and a huge number of bird species—leaving behind, in their droppings, the seeds of woodland plants they have eaten. Once these seeds begin to sprout, the women recognize and carefully protect them. After three or four years of use, the garden's yield diminishes because the soil is exhausted. The Achuar then abandon it and open a new one farther afield. The forest quickly reclaims the plot, the cultivated species disappear, but the woodland ones that were transplanted or protected remain and have much higher density than would have existed naturally. And, if we consider that this process has been going on since the beginning of plant domestication in Amazonia about 8,000 years ago, this means that the structure of the forest and the plant combinations that compose it have been profoundly altered by human presence.

My work, together with that of William Balée among the Ka'apor,[3] has thus revealed that the Amazonian forest is, in part, the unintentional result of these plant management techniques. For this reason, it is absurd to envision the forest as a wild world, as our imagination intuitively has it. It is in fact a kind of macrogarden. The Amerindians do not deliberately seek to alter the vegetal structure, yet they are fully aware of the fact that their horticultural techniques have an impact on it and that garden and forest are part of a structural continuum. This continuum can be explained by the fact that, in the thousands of years in which horticulturists domesticated the main Amazonian cultivars, they gradually perfected their plant management techniques, which did not differ much in principle from those they used to manage woodland resources—especially the selective maintenance of certain seedlings, whose proliferation in the forest undergrowth they encouraged. Slash-and-burn horticulture and agroforestry are thus two sides of the same process of plant manipulation.

Insofar as this anthropization, while visible, is not the outcome of planned activity, the Achuar acknowledge it only indirectly, at one remove, so to speak: according to them, the forest had indeed been planted, but by a spirit. This spirit answers to the name of Shakaim and its chief function is to guide humans through the work of clearing. In its role as guardian of forest vegetation, Shakaim visits humans in their dreams and shows them the best spots for opening new garden clearings, since it is best placed to know which grounds are fertile and where the plants it nurtures have flourished and become lush. What is more, the garden plants are all mixed together

The world of the forest 59

in seeming chaos, the taller ones protecting the shorter—a configuration that reproduces on a small scale the layered structure of forest vegetation and contributes to reducing the destructive impact of torrential rains and strong solar irradiation on the often mediocre soil. It then becomes clear that it makes no sense to turn the contrast between garden and forest into an opposition between the domestic and the wild. When the Achuar open a clearing, they replace a spirit's plantings that imitate a garden with human plantings that imitate the forest. It is thus difficult in this case to speak of a human society determined by the limiting factors of an ecosystem, as if the two existed separately, since the ecosystem itself is shaped and maintained by the society, which makes good use of it and is one of its component parts.

PC *But the relationship with nature does not consist only of technical and economic mediations. How did you incorporate the symbolic dimension of that relationship?*

PD It is fundamental, as we have seen with the role that the Achuar assigned to Shakaim. Indeed, as my command of the language progressed alongside this meticulous research on the use of gardens and economic practices, I became aware that the Achuar maintained very particular relationships with the plants and animals of the forest and rivers as well as with those of the gardens. Of course, these things only become noticeable once one understands what people say about them—and this is why having a good command of the language marks a new threshold in ethnographic work. There were two types of clues that revealed to us how the Achuar conceive of their relationships with nonhumans. The first came from discussions about their dreams that the Achuar engage in every day, upon waking up. Let us recall that the Achuar live in vast houses without internal partitions that generally host an entire polygamous family, that is, up to a dozen adults and twenty-five or thirty children, if we count the sons-in-law who must reside with their spouses' parents. In times of war, that number may increase even more, as several families congregate into a single large house surrounded by fortifications for purposes of defense. In these houses, well before dawn, they gather around the fire and offer commentary on their dreams, in order to determine what the latter portend for the coming day.

Some of these dream narratives appear to be very simple and are perfect illustrations of the principle of structural inversion:

60   *An Amazonian Sojourn and the Challenges of Ethnography*

dreaming that one goes blowpipe hunting is interpreted as a good omen for fishing, and the other way round; dreaming that one comes across a herd of peccaries could mean that one is to encounter a troop of enemy warriors, and the other way round; for a woman, dreaming that she is stringing glass beads on a thread heralds that she will have to empty the intestines of a game animal her husband has hunted. It is thus an elementary grammar that prevails here: the almost automatic interpretation of dream visions according to a chiastic relation between activities, locations, movements, and the objects of an action, according to the logical principles of homology and inversion. In this case, dreams are considered metaphors.

Then there are other dreams, which lend themselves to more literal interpretation. Very often they feature nocturnal visits: during sleep, the soul of the dreamer is known to move through space without physical constraints, leaving the body behind, and to encounter all sorts of interlocutors who are themselves in the same situation and appear in human form. Thus dreams are also occasions to come into contact with the spirits of plants, animals, and game, with the heroes of myths, and sometimes with the spirits of the dead, who come to address the dreamer and send him a message. For example, an Achuar once told me that he had dreamt of a man covered in blood who reproached him for having shot him; it was the soul of a recently deceased man who had been incarnated as a small stag he had shot, in violation of the widely respected prohibition on hunting deer. In another example, a woman explained that a girl had come to her to complain that someone was trying to poison her; it was the soul of a manioc seedling that had been planted too close to a barbasco plant, a very toxic plant poison used in fishing. Discussing these dreamlike apparitions with the Achuar, I came to understand that, in their eyes, animals and plants see themselves as human and, since the Achuar see them as such in their dreams when their souls travel, the dreamer grasps them in their human dimension as well, which is what enables communication between humans and nonhumans. Sometimes these spirits provide indications as to the places where they may be found; sometimes they complain about the bad treatment they have been subjected to.

Another lead I followed was the magic cantilenas, called *anent* in Achuar. These chants, generally recited silently or in a very low voice, are incantations that humans direct to the soul of their human or nonhuman addressees. The word *anent* comes from *inintai*, "the heart," which indicates that the chants come from

The world of the forest 61

deep inside. They speak from the soul directly to the soul of the addressee. This is why *anents* can be chanted silently, with the melody sometimes whistled or played on a flute or mouth harp. Important above all are the lyrics, which are often poetic and always allusive. The injunctions can be directed at all manner of addressees. It might be distant humans, whom one seeks to influence via a message. For instance, when two brothers-in-law have quarreled, a very common and potentially dangerous situation, an *anent* is chanted to conciliate the parties. Or, when one's spouse has gone off on an expedition, be it for bartering or for war, the chants can serve to keep the flame of love alive. But many of these chants are addressed to plants and animals, being intended to give instruction, to charm, or to ward off. Here is an example; the *anent* is chanted by a woman who addresses her plantings as she poses as Nunkui, the garden spirit:

As a Nunkui woman, walking only in my own small garden
I go by the great river (*bis*)
I go filling to the brim (*bis*)
What might you be?
Where the Nunkui woman goes, what might there not be?
Come all, my edibles, in my small garden! (bis)
The Shakaim man (*bis*), the little Nunkui woman, the one who says "I am the woman of the edibles,"
"There you will plant," they say (*bis*)
As a Nunkui woman, I go by the great river (*bis*).

Examining the *anent* repertoire, one notices that there are chants for all circumstances of life and for all forms of interaction both among humans and between humans and nonhumans. A competent Achuar is able to summon dozens of chants suited to any situation— as many as one hundred. These chants are not improvised but obey rather strict rules, both in their melody and in their content, and are always transmitted by one's forebears. Of course, since they are most often performed silently, it took us some time to become aware of their existence. But once we did, we had no difficulty collecting a large number of them. Indeed, people were ready to have them recorded, on the simple condition that they be circulated. This seems paradoxical, because the *anents* are cherished goods, jealously guarded, and a large proportion of an Achuar's powers resides in their ability to influence the future of others, human and

62   *An Amazonian Sojourn and the Challenges of Ethnography*

nonhuman, through these instruments. But, by circulating them via the tape recorder, people were divesting the Achuar of some of their *anents* in the hope of acquiring others, and thus we quickly became traffickers in magical chants. Listening to Achuar's commentary on these chants, we realized that, just like dreams, the *anents* established person-to-person dialogues with the souls of nonhumans and through them messages were addressed to plants and animals, who were treated as persons and enticed to follow certain courses of action.

The stability of the system of resource use, which my ethnoecological analyses were beginning to bring to light, was also based on the conception that the Achuar had of their relationships with plants and animals. Even though they had considerable knowledge of and expertise in botany, agronomy, and animal ethology, members of this community did not dissociate their technical skills from the ability to establish, through all kinds of conciliatory mechanisms such as the two we have just discussed, harmonious relations with what, at the time, I still called "the beings of nature." These mechanisms were not simply performative tools purported to ensure a favorable outcome to daily activities thanks to some magical efficacy. They were rather considered to be convenient means of establishing communication with a multitude of entities that ordinarily lacked the capacity for linguistic expression, yet seemed otherwise endowed with most of the attributes of humans. In spite of their distinct appearance, then, plants and animals were seen by the Achuar as full-fledged persons whose fundamental humanity was confirmed in all these small and almost indistinguishable rites—whose "implicit mythology," to take up Lévi-Strauss's terminology, I was beginning to analyze; and by this term I mean the cosmological background against which such interactions could play out.

And that background clearly revealed that the Achuar behaved with nonhumans as they would with social partners, in other words they adopted the same attitudes and discourse that they prescribed for relationships between humans. Hence the hypothesis I put forward in *In the Society of Nature*: in such a system of objectivization of the other, the relationship with nonhumans cannot be disrupted without a profound change in the elementary categories of social practice that enable the conceptualization of this relationship. Far from resulting from a kind of technical or ecological determinism, any potential transformation of Achuar's material living conditions would involve a mutation in their way of conceiving of

The world of the forest 63

their relationships with plants and animals, itself determined by the emergence of new forms of social connection.

PC *You had accumulated a host of evidence concerning the Achuar's relationship with nature—and evidence of rather different kinds. Then, I imagine, you had the difficult task of bringing all these pieces together, as parts of a coherent study.*

PD Indeed, when I returned from fieldwork in 1979, I had intended to take the technical systems of construction and use of the environment together with the ideational systems that informed these practices, treating them on an equal footing and thereby escaping the model of the classic monograph, which still limited itself to juxtaposing the various fields—economy, social organization, religion: from the geographic base to the symbolic superstructure, these were placed in as many distinct chapters, as in a layered cake, as if every act of raw material transformation, every hunting ritual, every plant or animal identification were not already thoroughly defined and shaped by ideas, expectations, and ontological inferences. So then: each of my chapters was focused on a site of practice—the house, the garden, the forest, the river—in which I tried to constantly move back and forth between two dimensions: on the one hand, the characteristics of the ecosystems, techniques, organization, and intensity of work and diet, as they are analyzed in western science; on the other, the way the Achuar conceive of all this. I called this a "symbolic ecology": the study of a local system of interactions in which the material dimension and the conceptual one are tightly intertwined. *In the Society of Nature* is ultimately founded on the idea that the forms of interaction that the Achuar have developed in their interhuman relations—in which the household is the stage—also characterize their relations with nonhumans.

Indeed, it very quickly became clear to me not only that the Achuar behaved with plants and animals just as they did with social partners but also that these relationships fell into one of the two main schemas of social interaction: plantings were treated as blood relatives and game animals as relatives by marriage, each being expected to conform to the system of obligations that such relationships involved. As in many other Amazonian societies, they have a kinship system known as "Dravidian," which makes a clear distinction between two categories of relatives, namely consanguineous and affinal. The former contains blood relatives—father,

64 *An Amazonian Sojourn and the Challenges of Ethnography*

mother, brother, sister; the latter, relatives by marriage—spouse, in-laws. In these sparsely populated societies, anyone can calculate and identify their kinship link with anyone else: the consanguineous relative of a consanguineous relative of my consanguineous relative will be a consanguineous relative of mine, even though we may have never met, so long as we can identify a common consanguineous relative. It may be that you're several days' walk away from home, yet everyone you meet will be related to you one way or another, through consanguinity or affinity. This is a key element, in that it determines the rigorously defined system of attitudes one is required to adopt depending on whether one is dealing with a consanguineous or an affinal relative. These two kinship categories play a role similar to the one that occupational categories or social classes have for us: they provide social characteristics and tell us how to behave. In gardens, women, who are tasked with most of the horticultural activities, treat their plantings as children, in other words as consanguineous. As for men, they treat the animals they hunt as brothers-in-law, and behave with the masters of game—the spirits who control the fate of game animals—as they would with fathers-in-law, that is, with affinal relatives. It was thus quite clear that the two central categories of Achuar social life also served them to conceive of their relationships with nonhumans. Their treatment of nature was homologous with their treatment of humans.

But what is one to make of this? At the time, the conceptual tools to think through these kinds of interactions were lacking, since materialist and symbolic approaches enjoyed a shared hegemony over the analysis of social reality. For the former, the humanization of plants and animals was ideological and akin to false consciousness; for the latter, which derived from what we might call Lévi-Straussian intellectualism, these conceptions had an intrinsic value, but only insofar as they revealed properties of the human mind—and not from the perspective of their effect on ordinary life. And having daily social relations with nonhumans as if they were humans lay largely outside the analytical frameworks of anthropology back then—which is rather surprising, if you think about it, because it was precisely by raising this kind of question that anthropology emerged as a discipline. It was difficult for me to return to thinkers such as Lévy-Bruhl, who had tackled this kind of problem head on through the concepts of primitive mentality and participation mystique, since I had thoroughly internalized the structuralist rejection of Lévy-Bruhl on the grounds that he cast doubt on the universality of the human

The world of the forest 65

mind.[4] So I had to grope my way to interpret as best I could, from a theoretical perspective, what I had observed. What Godelier called the mental part of reality[5] could have been a good guide, too, but I always ran up against the problem of what to make of that part once it was more than an abstract dimension of social life, when it was a practical framework that affected all the activities of daily life.

The solution I initially adopted was to consider these phenomena as processes designed to achieve the "socialization of nature"—an expression I subsequently abandoned as overly sociocentric. I had in fact taken up and inverted the totemism model as developed by Lévi-Strauss.[6] He had proceeded to show, starting from an opposition between natural series (animal and plant species) and cultural series (human groups), that totemism could not be defined, as it had previously been, by the relationship that an individual or a group maintains with an animal or a plant; it was defined rather by the homology between the differential gaps that separate the natural species and those that separate social groups. It was not the case that individual A identified with the eagle totem and individual B with the bear totem, but that the contrast between the eagle and the bear enabled a conceptualization of the difference between the eagle clan of individual A and the bear clan of individual B. For Lévi-Strauss, totemism was thus a universal classifying system that used the natural world as a template to organize social differences and discontinuities. It seemed to me at the time that what I was dealing with in the Achuar community stood in an inverse symmetrical relation to Lévi-Strauss's interpretation of totemism: they did not use natural categories to conceptualize social categories, but quite the opposite, they used social categories—in this case, consanguinity and affinity—to conceptualize the relationship with natural objects. And in a rather audacious moment I decided to call this thought pattern "animism."[7] Using this notion was risky, for it had long been discredited, and it harkened back to nineteenth-century British anthropology, Tylor in particular—that is to say, it had associations that contemporary anthropology were rather keen to be rid of.[8] A few years later, Nurit Bird-David used that term again to describe the Nayaka's attitude to the environment. The Nayaka were a group of hunter-gatherers in Tamil Nadu, India, who also treated nonhumans as persons.[9] As a consequence of this new usage, the term "animism" made a comeback in anthropology, so much so that it is now used as a catch-all category, to designate any attitude that is receptive to spirits.

66   *An Amazonian Sojourn and the Challenges of Ethnography*

Animism as I initially defined it, by contradistinction with totemism—that is, as the attribution of social properties to nonhumans as a result of an interiority they share with humans—was thus the first stable hypothesis on which I began working in a comparative manner, especially in my research seminar at the École des Hautes Études, initially at the scale of Amazonia as a whole. This then led me to read the vast body of ethnographic literature on that region that convinced me that what I had noted among the Achuar was also valid elsewhere. The practice of considering plantings as persons related to humans the same way blood kin appeared to be, if not specific to the Jivaros, was at least not readily generalizable. But the relationship of affinity with game animals, and, more specifically, a relationship of affinity that also defined the relationship with enemies, that was everywhere in Amazonia. This was the starting point for the generalizing induction that, after many twists and turns that I will discuss later, led me to the model I subsequently developed.

Living and working among the Achuar

PC   *One of the particularities of ethnographic work is the relative lack of any clear distinction between one's ordinary experience and the need to work. Daily life and fieldwork become one. Yet it is surely necessary to set some time aside for methodical study. How does this happen?*

PD   Having to take measurements, draw garden plans, and do other routine work of this kind was in fact a very good thing for me. Unless you are able to learn the language before setting out—and Aénts Chicham is not taught at universities in Paris—you arrive not being able to understand what is being said. For me, it was like entering a film in its original language without subtitles, leaving aside the young man I mentioned earlier, who knew a few words of Spanish. Communication was minimal for a rather long time, and this despite the fact that, in our case, people were relatively welcoming. During these early months, the situation of the ethnographer resembles that of an ethologist, a specialist in animal behavior: lacking access to the meanings explicitly articulated in language forces one to infer meaning from observed behavior. Gradually fragments of subtitles on people's lives begin to appear in the film, and increasingly so, until one understands almost everything that is being said. One then

Living and working among the Achuar   67

realizes that, most of the time, what is being said is utterly banal. But this is of course normal, since daily life is made of banalities, and this is the stuff of anthropology—normal especially when these banalities do not match those that are familiar from the anthropologist's own background. Singing to strengthen the "soul" of one's blowpipe was something completely ordinary for an Achuar but utterly fascinating to us.

For months, we thus did things that did not require a strong command of the language: village plans, genealogies, plant and animal identifications. I still have in my archives entire folders of topographic maps of gardens, measurements of manioc density (the number of manioc plants per hundred square meters), house floor-plans and elevations, tree identifications along a transect, tables of food weights, and the like. These activities enabled us to take part in daily life, since people would patiently try to explain to us what it was they were doing. Such immersion in a community of practice is a very good starting point for socialization, before one fully understands verbal exchanges and their subtleties.

Then, after about a year, there comes a moment when one can finally express oneself clearly in the language and understand what people say, when one almost never needs to ask questions, when indeed the elementary things one sought information about become known—people's names, their relatives, their genealogical networks, where they come from, who their enemies and allies are. This moment is crucial: it is when we turn into a sponge and absorb everything that is said and done, since our presence in the household is completely normal and our receptivity to everything that is taking place, including the most minute things, has become total. We would of course move quite often from one house to the next within Achuar country, and at each new place where our reputation preceded us we became objects of curiosity again. We then had to answer all the old questions, explain where we came from, who we were, and then, little by little, our presence and integration into the daily life became self-evident and our hosts' questions about what we had come to do would subside. At this point we would, again, become almost invisible to yet another set of Achuar. It was through such immersion into ordinary life, greatly facilitated as it was by our living with them and both observing and being constantly observed, that we could absorb a large amount of information. I always tell my students that real progress in fieldwork begins only when one stops asking questions, when one's presence

68   *An Amazonian Sojourn and the Challenges of Ethnography*

in the house is like that of a piece of furniture and one can soak up what people do and say.

PC   *You have insisted on the passive attitude that the ethnographer must adopt. But isn't it also essential to keep a critical distance, to be attuned to half-truths and misleading elements? How is one to be reflexive when it is perhaps difficult to tell which piece is the most significant one in the mass of information one has to deal with?*

PD   First, I would say that it is rare to be enduringly misled, given the long period of fieldwork. If you share the lives of people on a more or less constant basis for several years, as we did, almost nothing escapes your attention. It may of course happen that you interpret incorrectly a comment or an attitude, just as you may be wrong about what is happening in your own society, but when it comes to the main orientations of social life, the sense you forge over time will be reliable. This has to do with your constantly relying on this social understanding as a handbook, a kind of vade mecum, if only to avoid making a faux pas, to satisfy people's expectations, and to engage in interactions in a natural way. This is why ethnographic knowledge is inextricably bound up with the sort of second socializ-ation that ethnographers experience in fieldwork. And this is also why such knowledge entails a kind of self-analysis: the objective is to convey not abstract knowledge, but skills that one has oneself acquired through contact with another social group, unwittingly, in the moment.

Anthropologists have often drawn a parallel between their learning process and that of children. And indeed, when the Achuar needed to explain something to us, they would use the infinitely patient and somewhat weary ways they adopted with their children. Of course, the form taken by this learning process varies from one society to the next, running from a methodical mode of inculcation to more implicit approaches that discreetly correct errors, as the ones we found in the Achuar. But anthropologists, like children, must become competent participants in the society in which they have chosen to live for a while, and this requires not only the acquisition of practical skills but also an ability to assess the plausibility of certain speech or behavior. And so, if people deliberately attempt to deceive you or to deceive one another, that would be very clear to you. For instance, it may happen that the people you live with instrumentalize you in their interpersonal dealings. But, if you

Living and working among the Achuar 69

are paying attention, you will be aware of it, and then the entire ethnographic observation game will consist in determining how far you are prepared to participate as a consenting accomplice in these strategies. The hackneyed cliché of the anthropologist as a kind of entomologist observing insects through a magnifying glass, armed with notebook and tape recorder, constantly asking questions in order to objectivize a living knowledge—this caricature is pure fantasy; it could sprout only from the minds of people who have no idea what fieldwork is. One's experience and understanding of a social world can be measured on the basis of one's ability to anticipate what others will do or say—which is a bit like how one can predict what someone will do in one's own social context. And you gradually become able to respond adequately to specific situations according to locally expected norms, even though you are of course regularly coming up against ways of doing things that run counter to your habitual ways—and to your moral compass as well.

For instance, violence by men against women was widespread among the Achuar. It was not a generalized disposition, but it was always very shocking to me and my wife, even though it was difficult to react to it in an acceptable way. We would sometimes take care of women who had been beaten by their husbands, but whenever I told a man that one should not commit this act, he would say: "You speak like a missionary." That reaction highlighted a challenge, perhaps even an impasse, in our situation among them. Indeed, the Achuar with whom we lived at the start had been episodically in contact with American evangelists and often asked us questions about our world. Many of their questions concerned God, hell, paradise, the creation of the earth—in other words, things the missionaries had talked to them about. These were questions they were not used to raising in and of themselves, because the origins and the end of the world or the fate of the soul after death were matters to which they were rather indifferent. But the extensive periods of leisure created by their relaxed working schedules afforded them plenty of time to devote to these kinds of issues, alongside more ordinary problems of daily life. And I would make every effort to distinguish my responses from those of missionaries. I would say, for instance, that not everyone thought this way in our society, that there were other theories about the origin of the world. And this is where they would ask me why, if I did not believe the missionaries to be right about everything, I spoke like them where the treatment of women was concerned. It was difficult at that point to make a fuss or engage in endless moral

70   *An Amazonian Sojourn and the Challenges of Ethnography*

debate, which my still embryonic command of the language would have precluded in any case. All I could do was accept that we had reached one of the limits of participant observation.

I found myself in a similar situation for other reasons as well. Before I left for fieldwork I had been given a hunting rifle, which I had brought along even though I was no hunter, thinking that it might prove useful in a society where hunting plays a major role. Once I got there I learned to use it for hunting purposes, of course, whereas for the Achuar a rifle serves mostly as a weapon of war. They use blowpipes for hunting, reserving for armed conflict the use of ammunition, which is rare and difficult to come by. When they got to know me a little better, I became integrated into kinship networks that automatically placed me into factions that were at odds with other factions; and from that moment I became involved in vendettas, which play a major role in Achuar social life. I was thus asked to take part in raids, since I had gained their trust, but also because I owned a gun. Of course I refused, and also refused to lend my rifle—I did not want to become involved in warfare of any kind. But, if I did not want to lose the trust I had painstakingly gained, I had to come up with reasons for my refusal to fight, and I was thus obliged to invent stories that sounded locally plausible. I knew that, when a rifle had been used to kill someone, it became invested with a negative power that rendered it unusable. So I spun a story along these lines, explaining that the rifle had been given to me by my father-in-law—which was indeed true—and that he had made me swear I would never use it to kill someone for fear the rifle might take revenge and cast a spell on him. One is often led to concoct explanations of this sort to get out of embarrassing situations or to avoid being drawn into acts that one does not wish to commit. All this goes to show, once again, that ethnographic work is in no way that of a butterfly collector who gathers facts in the net of objectivity, from a detached distance. The only way to become a really good anthropologist is to immerse yourself in a community of practice, to become involved in its social life, and to let yourself be affected by what people in that community say and do. Indeed, when nothing surprises you anymore, when everything that the people you live with say and do seems banal, it's a sure sign that the time has come for you to return home.

PC   *How far can we take this self-transformation through fieldwork? Does one end up thinking or dreaming in Achuar?*

Living and working among the Achuar

PD I cannot speak in general terms, since each ethnographic context is different. But, with regard to interiorization, I can tell you that I, for one, did end up dreaming in Achuar—and still do, sometimes. The dreams I had were not exactly of the same kind as those whose communal debriefing I described earlier. I was never visited in my dreams by an otter or a yam in human form. But I often dreamt that I would wake up in the middle of the night, lying not in the house where I had fallen asleep but in the depths of the forest, in the middle of a large marsh, and could hear all around me people laughing, shouting, calling one another in Achuar. Sometimes a blurry and mysterious face would appear between the trees. This was probably a dream of repressed anxiety, and my hosts found it very amusing. They all saw in it a sign that my dreamer's soul had wandered into the house of the peccaries: it was their revelry that I had overheard. But there is a big difference between these occasional dreams and the kind of systematization from which one could infer meaning as an anthropologist. We can try to draw lines of explanation from recurring observations, then bring to light generalities regarding the representations on which all seem to agree. This is what I do, for instance, when I infer that the Achuar think of animals as persons in animal guise endowed with human subjectivity, and I do so from the fact that they say that animals perceive themselves as human and that this is why they appear in this form in dreams and chat with us. But I cannot really count my own self as one of these kinds of observed facts. There is a big leap between my dreaming of a somewhat strange man staring at me and coming to me in the night and the systematization that I ascribe to the Achuar in order to analyze their mode of interaction with nonhumans. My dream does not stand as evidence that animals are a kind of humans in disguise. It does, however, help me understand that, in certain circumstances, dreams are a good reservoir of experiences for drawing inferences of this kind.

PC *The ethnographer is thus in a position of irreducible exteriority. And this is further reinforced by the twin fact that Amerindians form an image of the western world and, in some sense, one must conform to it. Have you had that feeling?*

PD We are inevitably perceived as elements of the native cosmology, and the world of the Whites already has a place in local representations, one that is remote yet present. In the end we did get a clear

72   *An Amazonian Sojourn and the Challenges of Ethnography*

sense, through the questions and remarks that were addressed to us, of how the Achuar conceived of our world. What struck me in particular was how attentive they were to sometimes unexpected details. For instance, my wife and I were similarly equipped: same sleeping bags, same hiking boots, same knives, and so on, which gave us a rather similar appearance. And the Achuar interpreted this in the same way as we can identify the unity of an ethnic group through certain ways of styling hair, body painting, or dressing, i.e. attributes that we consider cultural. They thus saw us as the representatives of a certain tribe among the Whites. They did not conceive of the Whites as one undifferentiated whole but as a plurality made up of various groups, each with its own language and customs, since they had noted the distinctive personality traits of those who had visited them. They had seen a Salesian missionary, who was of course unmarried—which had left them perplexed, as they could not understand how a society made only of men could exist. They had also met evangelical missionaries, who sometimes came with women and whom they knew to be married and have children. This, in their view, was yet another tribe. And when an evangelical missionary passed through one of the villages that had a landing strip and we spoke with him in English, they understood that the language we used with him was not the same as the one we used among ourselves. It was the same with soldiers, who in their view formed their own group and were known to have relations with women, since some Quichua women slept with them.

The Achuar did not see the White world as some kind of vast collective entity that surrounded them and threatened to absorb them, but rather as an ensemble of tribes scattered around them; some of the representatives of these tribes came all the way to see them, and each one was endowed with specific and sometimes strange characteristics. What struck me most was that they were not at all aware of living on a kind of island, in the middle of a vast world in which a particular lifestyle, a particular technical system, a particular social system prevailed. This has since changed a lot— what I am describing here dates from forty years ago—but they saw Whites as a sort of neighbor of Achuar or Quichua.

Later on I understood that the way the Achuar conceived of the differences between animal species also applied to humans, and thus to Whites. The different human tribes are thought of as so many animal species, each with its own special body; as a result, this body provides access to a special world, which is the experiential

Living and working among the Achuar   73

continuation of its own organs and habits. This is what Eduardo Viveiros de Castro has described as Amazonian multinaturalism: each class of beings is characterized by dispositions located in the body, not by a particular culture. That there might be a generic "human species" sounded absurd to the Achuar: much to the contrary, all indications suggested that there were many differences between the tribes, each manifesting itself at the natural level—that is, at the level of some of their aptitudes, which were perceived as physical—as was the case with animal species. Language, tools, ornaments, weapons, the shape of houses, all these were seen as intrinsic properties, of the same kind as the sounds, plumage, habitats, claws, and fangs of animal species. Hence the distinctive skills of a human tribe formed a bodily habitus that informed a specific way of engaging with the world, and from this perspective the various tribes of Whites were each endowed with particular characteristics. The hiking boots, sleeping bags, Opinel knives, my rifle, of a kind they had never seen before, the language we spoke were all bodily attributes of the *prancianmaya aénts*, the people of France, and set us apart as a determinate species, distinct from other species of Whites.

PC   *You were lucky enough to work within a society that seems to have preserved its identity, a society that up until then had withstood colonial assaults. Yet most of current anthropology is carried out in very different contexts, characterized by hybridization with the western world or, more tragically, by the disappearance of distinct cultural traits. How has this situation affected your work?*

PD   My goal in going to the Achuar was to study the relationship with the environment in a society whose economic conditions and technical system had not been much affected by contact. The Achuar met that criterion: apart from metal tools, traded cottons, and a few rifles—all still rare among them—they did not own manufactured goods or use money, and had not known cash crops or wage labor. The young man who acted as an intermediary for us when we arrived had worked for an oil company. With his exception, the Achuar, unlike their Quichua neighbors, had not yet started working as seasonal laborers on plantations or working for oil exploration or lumber companies. But the point was not at all to find the most primitive community, some ideal representative of cultural purity, protected from outside influences; it was rather to study a society

74   *An Amazonian Sojourn and the Challenges of Ethnography*

whose relationship with nature and with the fundamental principles that defined it had remained its own.

I must say that sharing in the daily life of a human group that lived by its own rules and was not subjected to, or influenced by, those imposed by some nation-state was an extraordinary privilege. From that perspective, I did not regret my choice. But one must not fall for the absurd idea that some societies are purer than others, for all societies change over time and borrow elements from their neighbors, more or less deliberately and often in indirect ways, sometimes by doing the opposite, in an attempt not to resemble them. What we experienced in the end was a fully functioning society, with its own processes of production and trade, its own solidarity networks and factional groupings, its own kinship and marital systems, its marvelously vivid myths and rites, its language and style of oratory, and its remarkable technical know-how, which ranged from house construction to the making of blowpipes and curare: in short, a society that was autonomous in almost every respect, which is becoming increasingly rare in Amazonia as a result of the depopulation engendered by epidemics and territorial dispossession.

Very often anthropologists find themselves among the vestiges of societies whose demography has plummeted so badly that not much remains that still functions socially. In such cases, then, what lends itself to analysis is mostly the ways in which these residual groups have changed, the relationships they maintain with their neighbors, their manner of incorporating into their representations, rituals, and practices those of other Amerindian cultures, or even of the White world. These are classic hybridization phenomena, linked to these societies' loss of political and social autonomy and need to build new relationships with the outside world. Another possibility is to study language systems, for they are often the only thing that survives: the knowledge, the ritual utterances, and the chants— which constitute vestiges sometimes piously passed on and can be studied as historical monuments. I recently worked with a student who had conducted fieldwork on a Brazilian society made up of only two people, and who therefore had to focus on its myths. The two survivors had been taken in by another Amerindian village, whose residents spoke a different dialect; but the survivors' original group had entirely disappeared. The student thus works on the memory of a vanished society. This is not the case with the Achuar and, to be honest, I am very happy about that, for them as well as for myself.

Living and working among the Achuar 75

The reason why anthropologists are interested in societies that have not been profoundly transformed by contact with either neighboring or national ones and have not lost their language has to do with the specificity of anthropology's comparative project. The discipline is nourished by vast amounts of information about a very large number of societies, and the more diverse the institutions that constitute the material for analysis, the more productive it becomes to study the field of possible variations. Anthropology, like history, is perfectly equipped to deal with questions of subjection, subordination, and subsumption, which are of course important and widespread phenomena in the history of humanity. But the stakes are different from those in play when you describe societies that, as they are observed, represent the outcome of a given historical development at a given moment. For one thing, in many instances it has become impossible to reconstruct that development, in view of the lack of documentary sources. The value of the description resides, then, in the contrast it highlights and in comparative differences with other distinct situations, also treated synchronically and without a necessary reference to the historical background—itself often unknowable. For instance, we have a rough idea of what the Aénts Chicham-speaking groups were like at the time of the conquest in the sixteenth century, because the Spaniards came down from the Andes very early on and established a pioneer frontier on the western fringe of their territory. Shortly afterwards there was a widespread rebellion that scared the invaders off, and the territory remained closed to Whites until the rubber boom in the late nineteenth century. As far as we can tell, there must have been major developments over the course of those several hundred years, but a comparison between the available proto-ethnographic descriptions—the first accounts of exploration, which date from the period of conquest—and what is now known of the Amerindians in the region shows only that, in many respects, things have changed relatively little.

PC *Very often, anthropologists talk about the population they have worked on as "their" society—a phenomenon of identification as well as of appropriation. Does this mean that between them and you something like a contract is concluded, that the anthropologist has a moral responsibility toward the people they are working with?*

PD It is quite clear that one does not emerge from an experience like the one we had with the Achuar without being indelibly marked.

76   *An Amazonian Sojourn and the Challenges of Ethnography*

Even if total identification is impossible—one never becomes completely a native, no matter how much time one spends with a community of this kind—the experience is nonetheless profoundly transformative. Toward the world one comes from and returns to, one develops an attitude that bears the stamp of this experience and is in part shaped by some of the values one has learned to respect during fieldwork. This is in fact an important point: returning from fieldwork is much more difficult than going into it, since the anthropologist now sees his or her own social milieu through different eyes, made more critical and sharp by the experience of transplantation. In any case, I would say that there is indeed a moral contract between us and them. And, first and foremost, that contract takes the form of an obligation to tell the truth—to transcribe with the greatest possible honesty what one has observed, especially by describing the context in which one's observations were conducted and the context in which one speaks and delivers information to the reader. This is one of the reasons why I was happy to contribute a volume to the Terre Humaine series; for it gave me the opportunity to describe, in a reflexive work, the conditions under which I accumulated ethnographic knowledge of the Achuar.

The other obligation, of a more strictly ethical nature, is of course to support as strenuously as possible the people one has lived with when it is subjected to external pressure, as is often the case with ethnic minorities in regions of the world where great-power imperialism and internal colonialism reign. Even if the situation has somewhat changed now for the Achuar and still more for other Amazonian populations, anthropologists have long been the sole advocates defending tribal populations. The *Journal de la Société des Américanistes*—the journal of a venerable and learned society, now more than a century old, of which I am proud to be president—has a regular section devoted to the situation of Amerindians. This is a scholarly journal on the anthropology, archaeology, and linguistics of the native societies of North and South America that for a long time has nevertheless included, in almost every issue, a section devoted to witness accounts presented by researchers of armed conflict, territorial dispossession, and genocidal acts. Something has changed a lot over the past thirty years: Amerindian populations in particular and tribal populations more generally have succeeded in acquiring means of representation at the international level and in making themselves heard in the major global forums where these issues are discussed, especially the United Nations. They therefore

Living and working among the Achuar 77

do not need the anthropologists to act as spokespersons so much as experts of a new kind, such as lawyers, surveyors, cartographers, and radio technicians.

In the forty years I have been going to Amazonia, I have observed major changes in the political engagement of anthropologists, as well as in the way our work is perceived by local populations. When we were doing our fieldwork in the 1970s, and even more so in the two decades that followed, the then incipient native organizations were deeply distrustful of anthropologists, because these groups had only recently developed a sense of their culture as heritage. At the very moment when anthropologists were no longer considering cultures as fixed catalogs of the distinctive characteristics of a given ethnic group, the native populations were starting to present themselves as closed cultures, each one being irreducibly different from its neighbors. The point, of course, was to appear to the outside world as possessing a distinct identity, in order to preserve or claim collective rights from the nation-states in which these communities found themselves. Thus these natives presented themselves strategically, as the bearers of forms of knowledge and practices that needed to be protected in the name of cultural diversity, just like historical monuments or endangered ecosystems. As a result, Amerindians tended to see anthropologists—and sometimes still do—as coming in search of intangible heritage and pilfering a part of the local culture instead of collecting material artifacts and objects for museums, as they used to. This movement lasted for a few years, and I believe it was in part a response to certain anthropologists, who had not bothered to offer any feedback or engage in any work of restitution. They would do their fieldwork and then leave, while their work would have no resonance with the people concerned. For obvious reasons, their publications were not translated into vernacular languages, or even into languages of communication with Amerindians who could read Spanish or Portuguese. But we should not forget that, since the Barbados Conference, anthropologists are the ones who have been at the forefront of defending native populations, creating international organizations and raising public awareness about violations of their rights, territories, and environments. These international forums include the International Work Group on Indigenous Affairs, Cultural Survival, and Survival International—and, in France, the Groupe International de Travail pour les Peuples Autochtones.

78 *An Amazonian Sojourn and the Challenges of Ethnography*

I also think that the situation of defiance that I have just described has largely attenuated over the past fifteen years, at least in South America. The leaders of native organizations now call on anthropologists because they realize that we are not just in the business of collecting facts: we can provide them with an outside perspective on their situation that may help them better assess their own circumstances and their position vis-a-vis the nation-states in which they live. These organizations have now a good understanding of the nature of anthropological work, which does not consist in accumulating information as one would collect butterflies but, on the contrary, in objectivizing the relationship between an observing individual and an observed population. In consequence, this work can enable the population in question to gain a better grasp of how it is perceived by others. This implicit collaboration between anthropologists and native communities is interesting and fruitful and has even given rise to explicit collaborations. One of my former students, Alexandre Surrallés, who is now a renowned scholar in his own right, did his fieldwork in the 1990s with the Candoshi, a tribe in Peruvian Amazonia that adjoins Achuar territory. When he arrived there, he was initially denied access to the villages, because the representatives of the local native organization, who lived in a small town on the colonization frontier, would regularly tell him, when he visited them, that they did not want to be part of any ethnographic colonialism. This went on for a few months but, being a stubborn person, he managed not only to obtain their approval but also to be recruited as an assessor for the native organization. They asked him to carry out tasks that were useful to them, such as a systematic census of the villages, and since then he has regularly collaborated with them, as well as with other groups in the upper Amazonia of Peru, on issues such as the demarcation and legalization of territory and bilingual education.

The trial of return

PC *The ultimate stage of ethnographic work is the return home, to which you alluded earlier as a potentially very difficult experience. Could you describe the experience of returning to the world of the familiar? What are the different stages involved in returning home?*

PD That was, indeed, a difficult period for me, mainly because one rapidly acquires habits that are quite different from those one had prior to leaving. For us—and I believe this to be the case for many anthropologists placed in similar circumstances—it was, first and foremost, a kind of parsimony that had become second nature. When one has spent several years with very little in the way of material comforts and realizes that one does not actually need them, one finds oneself quite out of sync with the condition of overabundance of objects and with the central value placed on material wealth. Eating at least once a day, being sheltered from the rain while sleeping, bathing in clear river water—these become one's highest aspirations, such that one finds oneself bewildered in a world mired in objects. This struck me upon my return home, when I had to buy basic things, such as a pair of socks, and would find myself amid a thousand different pairs of socks. I would sometimes leave the store empty-handed, unable to make up my mind. In such circumstances, one cannot but be struck by the pertinence of Marx's analysis of "commodity fetishism." For Marx, capitalism is characterized by the fact that relationships between people are mediated through commodities, which one ends up considering as more real than the social and moral world. Although almost a century and a half old, this analysis seems strikingly relevant when you are hardly back from fieldwork and each person you come into contact with is shrouded in a jumble of objects and riches that, however modest they may be, get in the way of more direct relations (or at least relations that are mediated in other ways), to which you have become accustomed during fieldwork.

The return home is thus an occasion for intense questioning of one's society of origin. For most, these are questions that were already present before departure, of course, but less starkly formulated, and the contrast with recent experience makes them all the more glaring. In the case of the Achuar, it is the contrast in the relationship with nature that appeared the most striking one, and I have already discussed it quite a bit. But there was also this curious way of experiencing a collective destiny without resorting to a clearly expressed ethnic identity. Even if the Achuar know that they are different from their neighbors, they do not hold up this difference as a mark of superiority, or as the expression of common interests, or even as a heritage of unique cultural traits—perhaps with the exception of a few who nowadays deploy such arguments with the state, for political reasons. Rather, their common existence is based on a sense of sharing the same way of living social connections and relations with neighboring peoples, and this sense is asserted without any real national consciousness.

80   *An Amazonian Sojourn and the Challenges of Ethnography*

Their perception of time is also radically different from our ordinary way of experiencing it. To understand the difference, consider myths. With the Achuar, as elsewhere in Amazonia, the time of myths prevails, not because these people sleepwalk through life as if it were some kind of daydream, but because it is this time that unfolds at each moment the conditions of possibility for humans and nonhumans alike. Indeed, what is an Amerindian myth? It is a narrative, often somewhat quirky, of how an animal or a plant species has acquired the appearance it currently has. In the time of the myth (and this is actually an inappropriate turn of phrase, which I am using here for the sake of convenience), all living beings had the same body and culture, such that the differences between them could be perceived only in their names—Achuar, Toucan, Grasshopper, Cassava—and in their particular habits and inclinations: in their house, the vulture-people ate carcass ceremoniously, as if it were boiled meat, and the jaguar-people lapped up blood as if it were manioc beer in calabashes. The myths recount the events that prompted each of these forms of life, that of humans included, to acquire bodies that fitted the uses to which they were put without actually losing their subjective capabilities. These are stories of speciation, stories that set out the accidental conditions for sudden changes of state.

At first glance, these myths are thus rather close to historical narratives, minus the factual truth of the event. In reality they are thought experiments through which a given fact of the world—that nonhumans have an interiority like ours and bodies all different from ours—can be conceptualized. The solution arrived at is that of a metamorphosis, a switch of perspective that suddenly makes visible in a body a set of dispositions that preexisted—in short, the actualization of a potentiality. It is a very abstract operation, reminiscent of the social contract in European political philosophy— the contract that put an end to the state of nature and legitimized political sovereignty. To paraphrase Rousseau himself, just as the state of nature is a theoretical fiction that does not exist, has never existed, and will never exist, the time of myth is a necessary fiction for an ontological condition to receive the illustrated expression of its actualization. To say, as is always done at the beginning of a myth, that the events about to be described took place a long time ago is not really to assign to these events a place in time; it is more like assigning a time to an axiomatic system. True, there is a time for an axiomatic system and a time for demonstration, but that does not make the axiomatic system a period *sui generis*.

The trial of return 81

And yet—and this is where the beauty and the subtlety of this conception of time lies—axiomatic time is still very near, it is two or three generations ago, perhaps; for the memory of recent time does not exist. Many Achuar have forgotten the names of their grandparents, the place where they lived, their achievements; and there is little attempt to retain events beyond individuals' living memory and what they have themselves seen. In short, time is flattened out, because with each generation it is brought back to the still very recent past, when it was the condition of possibility of the immutable present. Mark the contrast between such a regime of time and that of a world like ours, where the weight of filiation and of what we owe previous generations and past centuries constantly looms over us and where the past is supposed to determine what we are and to herald the shape the future will take. A society in which none of this makes sense, however much it might be governed by custom, gives an impression of unlimited individual freedom: one is free of these multiple legacies, of the weight of ancestral forces and history.

All these differences mark one for life and further reinforce the sense of incompatibility with the ordinary world that I invoked at the beginning of our interview, now combined with a kind of split of one's personality. This experience is common to many anthropologists. We watch ourselves playing our roles on the stage where circumstances have placed us, but we do so through the eyes of the population whose daily existence we shared for a time. We are no longer truly from here, without ever being completely from there either.

PC   *Upon return, anthropologists also find themselves between the two worlds of literary narrative and scientific demonstration. How did you experience the compromise between the "Proustian" recovery of past experience in narrative reconstruction and the need to conform to academic standards of writing?*

PD   Edmund Leach has said that all anthropologists are failed novelists, and there may be some truth to this. But instead of drawing the stuff of narrative inventiveness from the spectacle and experience of a nearby world, like Proust, we draw from ethnographic experience the stuff of plausible reconstructions. I say this because anthropologists, just like historians and sociologists, have to deal with questions of scale, as they try to convey an accurate

82 *An Amazonian Sojourn and the Challenges of Ethnography*

picture through a narrative of the collectivity they have studied. Some elements will have to be eliminated because they cannot be scaled down—namely a large part of what daily life is made of, on which the literary mind feeds. Others will need to be altered because, out of the qualities of the social object the anthropologist has described, only a few will be held to be relevant for analysis. And all this contributes to the production of a kind of miniature, which is the most plausible possible rendition of the small world in which the anthropologist was immersed, even while taking into account the specific constraints of putting it into words. So ethnographic writing will never be an exact copy of lived experience and of the social fabric itself—just as a novel is never only pure description, or a painting is not only the faithful reproduction of an object— but it will deliver a scale model that reveals the salient features of social life and conveys them to the reader.

To deliver it, we resort to literary techniques. First of all, we attempt to strike that precarious balance between composition— through which we select, from the flow of events recorded in our notebooks, the moments or utterances whose meaning appears to be exemplary—and generalization—through which we assign to these behavioral fragments a paradigmatic value. This is how, on the basis of an observed behavior or of an utterance overheard and repeated by several individuals, we move from a singular narrative—"so and so said..."—to a general proposition—"the Achuar think...." Anthropologists are well aware of the audacious character of this kind of conceptual and narrative craft. Our justification is that the generalizations produced in this way are the result of accumulated experience and of the capacity derived from it that I described earlier: the ability to anticipate, in some sense, what the people with whom one has been living for some time will say or do. If, in a given situation, this kind of prediction can be made accurately, then there are indeed predictable behaviors, and therefore also habits and norms that govern them. This technique of composition is similar to that of the novelist but its aim is to reveal the synthetic character of social experience in general.

Another technique very commonly used in anthropological and historical monographs is contextualization. This is the art of making a given practice understandable, and sometimes also morally acceptable, by inserting it within a more general set of practices in which it makes sense. If we take the example of cannibalism, it is clear that, severed from its ritual and symbolic

The trial of return 83

underpinnings, eating fellow human beings appears as a revolting practice. But when cannibalism is contextualized, its apparently outrageous character is dispelled and attention turns to how those who practice it think about what they are doing in relation to their conceptions of identity, the life cycle, eschatology, bodily substances, and so on.

The comparison with novelists is thus justified, if only because we have to use techniques of literary representation. This is paradoxical, since the rule of ethnographic description has long demanded that our observations be conveyed in the most neutral fashion, without rhetorical flourish. There is indeed a contradiction here, since the relevance of a piece of information to the reader of an ethnographic monograph is assessed thanks precisely to the description of the conditions under which a situation was observed or a remark overheard, which means that a reconstruction is required of the subjective dimension of what was witnessed. For a long time, the sudden arrival, center stage, of the knowing subject and the literary techniques that enabled this presence were frowned upon in the profession. I have always found it striking, for example, that an introspective writer as great as Michel Leiris had so little to say about himself in his technical ethnographic texts, for example in his books on possession in Gondar and on the secret language of the Dogon, and confined all discussion of the circumstances of his fieldwork to his travel narrative, *Phantom Africa.*[10]

It may be these inhibitions regarding writerly artifice in scientific writing that have led French anthropologists, myself included, to write what Vincent Debaene has called "a second book"—a more personal, reflexive, and literary account, which highlights the conditions under which fieldwork was conducted.[11] In addition to training in philosophy, this is another characteristic of French anthropology. In other countries, the books produced by anthropologists who depart from the rules of scientific monograph are of a different sort from French "second books." Nigel Barley, for instance, has provided very eloquent and witty accounts of his fieldwork experience, and older books such as *Return to Laughter* and *The Savage and the Innocent* have become classics of the genre.[12] But these are collections of fieldwork anecdotes with little literary ambition—not the kind of reflexive, philosophical essays that characterize a French anthropologist's "second book." They aim to endear anthropology to a broader public and they belong rather in the genre of travel writing, where the British are masters.

84   *An Amazonian Sojourn and the Challenges of Ethnography*

PC   *Some critiques of anthropology have seized precisely on its literary dimension to deny it the scientific status it has claimed for itself and to cast this form of knowledge as a set of subjective projections. Do you think this is an inescapable impasse of fieldwork?*

PD   The line of critique to which you refer began in the United States with the publication of the book by James Clifford and George Marcus on ethnographic writing.[13] Their reflections represented a profound challenge to the discipline worldwide, but I believe that they are closely tied to the specificities of American culture, where this reflexive tradition—which in France took shape in the more personal "second book"—was largely absent. Indeed, until the 1980s, American anthropology was characterized by a positivist ambition and adopted a factual and empiricist approach that presented itself for a long time under the form of monographs in the tradition of Franz Boas. And, of course, that kind of writing was replete with implicit statements and surreptitious literary and rhetorical effects, whose political implications Clifford and Marcus were right to expose. But I believe that the conclusion that has sometimes been drawn from these analyses—that anthropological writing says more about its author than about its subjects—is a vast exaggeration. One thing that is very striking to me is that, even though each situation, each observation, and each ethnographic experience is of course singular, in the end the sum total of these experiences never amounts to the mere accumulation of singularities. Very likely as a result of the homogeneity of transcription techniques, no matter how much anthropologists attempt to distinguish themselves from one another, the information one gleans from these different studies is comparable, even consistent—which only goes to show that the accusations of subjectivism are unwarranted.

    If one looks at ethnographies of any given society over the course of a century, for instance, since we now have examples of this kind, one will find no doubt variations that spring from the temperament of anthropologists, their gender, their national tradition, their theoretical approach, their specific areas of interest, their historical circumstances, and so on. And these variations are rather easy to spot. But the information—the basic data on the society described in these different ethnographies—remains stable. And this is what matters and what shows that ethnography is not just the expression of an individual gaze. These ethnographies engage with a persistent ethos. Beyond the variations, often linked to the passing of time, one

The trial of return 85

finds a continuity of practice that may be perceived or explained in various ways, according to the personal dispositions and theoretical affinities of the particular anthropologist. But we are dealing with constants that, although reinterpreted in slightly different ways over the years, are not the product of the anthropologist's fantasies or imagination.

3

The Diversity of Natures

The four corners of the world

PC   *Let us now turn to your later work, and especially the genesis of* Beyond Nature and Culture, *your wide-ranging comparative study. First I would like to know how the specific circumstances of Amazonia influenced your conception of the relationship between nature and society.*

PD   I have long wondered whether there was a determining relationship, or at least some correlation, between the Amazonian environment—the rainforest—and how the populations who live in it conceive of their relationships with plants and animals. In other words, I wondered whether living in a milieu of such exceptional biodiversity, where high population concentrations of the same animal or plant species are therefore rare, had not prompted Amerindians to look at ecological relationships as interpersonal ones, relationships among singular individuals who are all different, unlike what happens in regions of the world where the relatively uniform environment may prompt you to see it all as a whole, as a natural world outside the human.

But the ethnographic literature on the great North made me see that it would be a mistake to posit such a simple causality between environmental properties and the social imaginary. Indeed, the environmental characteristics to be found throughout the circumboreal region are the exact opposite of those of the rainforest. For, rather than being an ecosystem with a very large number of species and a very low number of individuals per species, the boreal forest contains fewer than half a dozen tree varieties; as for animals, it

The four corners of the world 87

has vast herds of caribous, clouds of migratory birds, schools of salmon, and colonies of seals. The northern part of North America is peopled by two large ethnic groups: the Amerindians, who speak Athapascan languages in the West and Algonquian languages in the East, and the Eskimo groups, which include the Inuit, the Yupiit, and the Iñupiat. Despite their diversity, all these societies have developed the same kind of relationships with nonhumans as in the Amazonian region. This goes to show that the idea of an empirical relation between the environment and the mental representation of nature does not hold, since similar relations have surfaced in very distinct natural contexts.

There is another characteristic of both Amazonia and the great North that is perhaps even more relevant to accounting for this conception of nonhumans. One of the striking characteristics of Amazonia, and especially of the zones of dispersed habitat such as the one I lived in, is that the human inhabitants are few and far between, whereas the nonhumans are very numerous. This means that in these communities the social interactions we all constantly engage in in Europe, be it in a rural or urban context, take place only in the domestic sphere, or on occasional visits to other houses. Hence they concern a small number of human individuals and a rather limited number of possible occasions. Once you leave the house, you can walk in a straight line for an entire week without coming across anything but nonhumans, and mostly plants and insects at that. The Amerindians are de facto immersed in an ocean of disparate beings, whose behavior they watch closely and whose habits and mores they know well, both for practical reasons and out of scientific curiosity. It is therefore not entirely impossible that these life conditions, which have rendered Amerindians very familiar with the ethology of animal species, with their modes of reproduction, and with symbiotic, parasitic, and mimetic behavior, have led them to think of animal and plant populations as forming a social group that is almost dominant, insofar as it is the one with which the forest inhabitants are most in contact. This everyday sociability with nonhumans is also characteristic of the sub-Arctic area, despite its very limited number of species; for there, too, the number of humans is quite low. And there, too, relations with nonhumans, and especially animals, are dominant outside villages and hunting camps. Animals are the ones who become interlocutors, if not the primary ones, the ones who take a very important role in everyday interactions.

88 *The Diversity of Natures*

PC   *What you describe here, this resemblance in forms of interaction with nature despite ecological differences, corresponds in the end to the concept of animism as you have defined it. More broadly, what role did these kinds of comparisons and contrasts play in your turn to systematic comparative work?*

PD   The development of my thinking on these questions was the fruit of a seminar I taught at the École des Hautes Études in the 1980s and 1990s in which I began to explore forms of relations to nonhumans systematically—among Amazonian populations first; then I moved gradually northward and explored the ethnographic literature on the native societies of northern North America. This drive northward was guided by the idea that attitudes to nonhumans very similar to those observed among the Achuar could be found there, attitudes that could therefore not be interpreted, as they generally were, simply as characteristics of hunter-gatherer societies. This was certainly the case in the circumboreal area, but not at all among the Amazonian Indians, who have cultivated plants for millennia. I have tried to continue on that path, across the Bering Straits, to Siberia and Central Asia, pursuing social and cultural continuities along the way. There were of course gaps in this geographical progression, as well as significant discontinuities: the Andes, the entire southern North America, and Central America had to be skipped over, because the forms of interaction with nonhumans observed there were obviously quite different from those observed in Amazonia, Chaco, Patagonia, and in northern North America. Nevertheless, given my need to develop these seminars in a systematic way over the years, I gradually acquired a solid ethnographic knowledge of societies that clearly shared the same relationship with nonhumans, while living in very different environments. This took a long time, during which I had the chance to rediscover work that had been somewhat forgotten and had become inaccessible, such as Sternberg's studies on the societies of the Amur River in Siberia, or the work of Bogoras, a Russian specialist of the Chukchee, and Hallowell on the Ojibwa of the American Great Lakes.[1]

One of the first discoveries I made in this exploration of the ethnographic literature was that my observations on the Achuar largely echoed those made by other ethnographers before me, even if those had never been systematically theorized. This is how, as I was grappling with the nature of this very peculiar relationship with plants and animals, I came to dig up the concept of animism—essentially in an attempt to characterize it by comparison with totemism, as paradigmatically defined by Lévi-Strauss in his book *Totemism*. I have already explained why that definition of animism as inverted totemism, so to speak, seemed to me at the time a good starting point for putting together all the material I had collected, assembling it into a stable category that highlighted the contrasts with other configurations of symbolic and practical systems.

In this early phase I was very much influenced by André-Georges Haudricourt, whom I have already mentioned, and especially by his article "Domestication of Animals, Cultivation of Plants and Human Relations."[2] In this very short text Haudricourt compares and contrasts two ways of dealing with humans and nonhumans or, to use his terminology, two forms of treating nature and others, which he calls respectively "direct positive action" and "indirect negative action." Each one encompasses certain agrarian techniques, forms of animal husbandry, and conceptions of political authority that he considers to be radically opposed. The first form of action is that of cereal growers, essentially European societies, even if it may be expanded to include, for example, cereal growers in Africa. They treat plants as a bloc and with brutality: the soil must be turned before it is planted, the sheaf cut with a scythe, and the grain threshed, which means beating it or, in the old days, having cattle trample it. Thus, at every stage, the cultivation and harvesting process entails direct and, one may say, violent forms of intervention on the plant, all collectively thought up. This is contrasted with the individualized handling of plants that is observed in the Melanesian area Haudricourt was familiar with: there the cultivation of yams required that each seedling be given space in which it would be able to grow by itself. The work is done not so much on the plant itself as on its environment, to provide it with all the conditions necessary to its flourishing. He described this form of action on plants as "careful friendliness," which in his view characterized the relationship of indirect action with domesticated species.

Haudricourt goes on to say that the treatment of domesticated animals obeys a similar division. In the West, and especially around the Mediterranean basin, it is the relationship between shepherds and their flock of sheep that best illustrates this. The shepherd exerts direct and permanent action on the animals, guiding them, choosing their watering holes, carrying the newborn, protecting the flock from predators. This is very different from what can be observed in Asia, for instance in Indochina, where Haudricourt

90 *The Diversity of Natures*

spent time: there boys escort herds of buffaloes that are five times bigger than they are and, if a tiger threatens, the beasts may even encircle their little guardian to protect him. Haudricourt would say that these two very contrasting ways of treating nature can also be found in the political treatment of humans. Indeed, the ideal of the sovereign as a good shepherd has developed in the West, both in ancient Greek philosophy and in the political ideology of Mediterranean empires, and encompasses the Bible. But on the other side of the world, in Asia and Oceania, both in Confucian philosophy and in the political ideology of Melanesian chiefdoms, the idea was to encourage the advent of things, to build consensus through discussion with each element, and not to impose an arbitrary perspective. In Haudricourt's view, this parallel between the agrarian and the political schemas revealed that, in both cases, humans and nonhumans were treated in the same manner.

I found this proposition very interesting, because at no point does Haudricourt say that either technical action or social action governs the other or acts as the general matrix of all attitudes. Thus it is not a technical system that determines a social system, nor is it a social system that has an impact on the relationship to nature; it is a simultaneous movement toward humans and nonhumans, which are simply treated in the same way, through the same shared schemas. This idea struck me as remarkable, at once simple and enlightening. I attempted to use it in a more systematic way in my subsequent work and, in particular, it prompted me to challenge my original idea of a symmetry between totemism at one end—or the use of natural categories to conceptualize social categories—and animism at the other—or the use of the elementary categories of social practice to conceptualize the relationship with natural objects. I could see that this proposition, which I had arrived at in the early 1990s, had a major drawback: it did not in the least conform to the symmetry that Haudricourt had suggested but instead was founded, under the influence of Lévi-Strauss's classificatory theory of totemism, on the idea of a separation between nature and culture and of the alternating superiority of one over the other. In totemism, nature enabled the conceptualization of society; in animism, it was society that enabled the conceptualization of nature. Evidently, such a stark distinction between social and natural systems was hard to accommodate with the ethnographic data I had on societies that I have called animist, where the distinction does not make much sense. So this was clearly a dead end.

The four corners of the world 91

The evolution of my ideas was thus linked to reading Haudricourt, but also to exchanges with various colleagues who worked on the same kinds of issues. I have in mind especially Tim Ingold, one of the great figures of environmental anthropology and a discerning expert in the sub-Arctic world, and Eduardo Viveiros de Castro, a brilliant Brazilian specialist of Amazonia, who both played an important role in the evolution of my thinking. Thanks to conversations with them, I managed to rid myself of the analytical classification grid I had borrowed from Lévi-Strauss and adopt instead behavioral forms and modes of interactions with nonhumans that allowed me to develop a comparative analysis of the structures of practice. Among the critiques that helped me make progress, there was for instance an article by Ingold that challenged the way in which I opposed animism and totemism and argued that in this I relied on an inadequate characterization of totemism that was borrowed from Lévi-Strauss.[3] Ingold put forward various arguments drawn from Australian ethnography, the region of reference as far as totemism was concerned. And that critique reminded me of an earlier article by a Canadian colleague, Luc Racine, who also challenged the relevance of Lévi-Strauss's classificatory definition of totemism when confronted with the facts of Australian cases.[4] Racine was an anthropologist well-read in theory and an expert on ethnographic literature as well as an admirer of Lévi-Strauss, and so his critique was not to be taken lightly. Tim Ingold's objections, together with Racine's article, encouraged me to delve more deeply into the literature on aboriginal Australia, which I did not know well, and this is how I eventually came over to their view. Relationships with nonhumans, as they had been described in Australia, could not be brought under the classificatory rubric of Lévi-Straussian totemism, and I thus had to reconsider both the definition I had given of totemism and the way in which I had opposed it to animism.

The second set of critiques that led me to revise my position came from exchanges I had over a long period of time with Eduardo Viveiros de Castro about the general contrast between animism and the modern western conception of nature. To the animism and totemism pair, I had added a third term, which I labeled "naturalism" and defined by default, simply via a comparison with animism. It designates the belief that there is a realm of reality that lies outside human action and in which nothing happens without a cause, a realm populated with beings who have their own regime of development; this realm was originally captured by the Greek

92   *The Diversity of Natures*

concept of *phusis* [nature]. In my view, the term "naturalism" aptly described a mode of being, characteristic of the West since the Greeks, that modern science has gradually defined as its object; and it represented a third approach, alongside animism and totemism, but one that had no direct logical link with them—in short, a kind of anomaly. Viveiros de Castro objected that by defining naturalism in this way I failed to take it into account that western nature was, rather systematically, the symmetrical opposite of Amazonian animism, in a way that he himself had outlined. Indeed, Amazonian animism is based not only on the generalized attribution of a soul, subjectivity, and moral conscience to nonhumans, who thereby find themselves endowed with a particular perspective on the world; it is founded also on the idea that each species has its own bodily dispositions, which give it access to particular worlds, and whose point of view varies according to whether the animal is hunter or prey and according to its system of perception, its living environment, its mode of locomotion, its means of defense, and so on. This reading of things is the opposite of how moderns construe the relationship between humans and other entities in the world: indeed, in naturalism, it is the exclusive dimension of human interiority that makes the human species radically exceptional among beings that are deprived of subjectivity while being still governed, like humans, by universal physical laws. This reading would entail, then, a total inversion between a system in which only humans have a subjective perspective on a singular nature and one in which the natural world consists of the multiple perspectives of various species—or, to use Viveiros de Castro's term, a "multinaturalism."

Viveiros de Castro's remarks were spot on, based as they were on ethnographic elements that I, too, had observed; and they led me to modify radically the definitions I had proposed earlier. I kept the three terms I had initially adopted—animism, totemism, and naturalism, that is, the three ways of perceiving continuities and discontinuities between humans and nonhumans—but reformulated them according to a more systematic set of contrasts. Animism still served as a starting point, since it was the ethnographic anchor for this reflection, but I now defined it as the extension to nonhumans of the human form of interiority, with an awareness of the physical discontinuities between the various classes of living beings in the world. These various living beings are not merely animal species in the classic sense—since, to use a very telling example provided

The four corners of the world 93

by Bogoras, in the view of the Chukchee, the shadows that their figures cast on walls live in villages where they depend on hunting. In this case, the morphological identity of a class of beings with similar physical properties was deemed sufficient to give them a collective coherence and to differentiate them from other classes of living beings. With this revision of my concepts, naturalism was no longer defined simply by a belief in the existence of an external and objective nature but through the systematic inversion of the terms that characterized animist societies in general. The point was no longer that nature and culture are opposed (since humans have both natural and cultural dimensions), but that interiority is perceived as marking the discontinuity between humans and the rest of nature— which is not the case in other ontologies.

As a result, I also had to revise my conception of totemism, since the Australian data made it impossible for me to continue to hold the definition proposed by Lévi-Strauss. Moreover, totemism had to be placed in a relation of contrast with animism, as I had redefined it. One of the difficulties of this operation was in the very use of the concept of totemism in relation to Australian societies. The term has a long history in anthropology; it was first introduced in the late eighteenth century by a pelt merchant in the American Great Lakes region. It derives from a word in the Ojibwa language whose meaning gradually stabilized to refer to animal emblems adopted by human groups or individuals. It was eventually associated with Australian communities, since that is where this kind of relationship was most often found, even if its exact definition was the object of heated debate in the early twentieth century. In the past thirty years anthropologists working on Australia had grown reluctant to use the term "totem," whose meaning had become confused and which harked back to an earlier state of anthropological debate. However, I decided to revive it, giving it a new meaning. Australia offers a very original conceptualization of the relationship with nature, both ontologically—the kinds of beings that exist in the world—and taxonomically—the way these beings are grouped together. Indeed, the groups we call "totemic" are constituted jointly of humans and a wide range of nonhumans endowed with similar qualities, which are generally subsumed under the name of an inclusive quality. It is that name, which most often corresponds to that of an animal species, that refers to the totemic group and to the ontological mold from which all the members of that category originated, human and nonhuman alike.

94   *The Diversity of Natures*

This idea appeared to me very clearly when I compared classical ethnographic literature, for instance the works of Spencer and Gillen in the early twentieth century, or later studies by A. P. Elkin, with more recent or contemporary research. And here, again, it was accidental circumstances that played a decisive role. I was reading a rather austere work by the linguist Carl Georg von Brandenstein on the names of totems in Australia. It is a semantic study of the formation of these names, and it is based on examples taken from a very large number of Australian languages.[5] Elkin points out that the names of the totems are for the most part names of animals, even if there is considerable inventiveness in this field, as terms are sometimes taken from the contemporary world, from the technical domain imported by westerners. He said, in a footnote, something that struck me and whose significance he probably did not fully measure himself: the names of animal totems are not names of species—taxa, as in the classifications we are familiar with—but qualities that are used, by extension, to refer to animal species. In other words, what comes first is not the relation of a group to an animal—as Lévi-Strauss, and Boas before him, had very rightly pointed out in response to Frazer's theory—but the subsumption of a group under a particular quality, which itself applies both to the human and to the nonhuman members of that group.

Let us take the example of the Noongar tribes, in southwestern Australia, who were organized in exogamous moieties named after two birds: the white cockatoo, whose native name, *maarnetj*, can be translated "the catcher"; and the crow, called *waardar*, which means "the watcher." The names signify attributes, which then serve to designate animal species. And these two totemic prototypes are the source and the physical embodiment of two opposite sets of material and spiritual properties—character traits, bodily structures and abilities, psychological dispositions—which are deemed specific to all human members of each moiety as well as all to the nonhumans affiliated to them. Indeed, this community of humors and temperaments within hybrid collectivities had already been noted by Spencer and Gillen, who in speaking about central Australia remarked, more than a century ago, that humans think of the creatures that serve as their totem as being the same as themselves. In this case, the identification is not with a crow or a cockatoo that might be observed in the environment; rather these species represent exemplary objectivizations of a relationship of physical and moral identity between specific entities of the world, a relationship that

The four corners of the world

transcends apparent morphological and functional differences and underlines a common essence of ontological similitude.

By shifting the problem in this way, we eliminate questions related to the animal considered to be a parent or ancestor—questions that polluted the debate for a very long time—and we change the equation regarding the classificatory dimension of totemism. Contrary to what Lévi-Strauss had surmised, the point was no longer the homology between natural and cultural classes but the common membership of some humans and some nonhumans in a class defined by an original quality, which is hypostatized in an animal-totem. These qualities may be, for instance, being quick or slow, angular or curved, light or dark, depending on the attribute embodied by the totem animal. The latter is thus an illustration of that quality, just like the humans in that category and other species that are affiliated with it. This is what makes me think that we are dealing here with a conceptualization of the continuities and discontinuities between humans and nonhumans that introduces a new formula, distinct from that of animism and naturalism. Indeed, we have sets of physical and moral qualities shared by humans and nonhumans, qualities that make them identical because they come from the same ontological mold, the same prototype. And each of these human and nonhuman assemblages is different from others, which are characterized by other qualities. These mechanisms that distribute both physical and moral properties among the beings of the world are also found in animism and naturalism, but here they lead to mixed classes of beings defined by relatively abstract qualities.

So this third formula is in contrast both with animism, which is defined by continuity between humans' and nonhumans' interiority and discontinuity between their physical attributes, and with naturalism, which is defined by moral discontinuity between humans and nonhumans and physical continuity between all beings. It places emphasis on the fact that there is moral and physical continuity within a certain set of humans and nonhumans and then discontinuity at another scale, between each of these sets of humans and nonhumans, which are called "totemic groups." This definition of totemism is quite far from that of Lévi-Strauss, but it maintains one of his profound intuitions, developed in *The Savage Mind* and *Mythologiques*, which is that human thought always operates through the registers of the continuous and the discrete and draws on observations of the world in order to build symbolic systems characterized by the dialectical dynamic between these two poles. This brilliant

96 *The Diversity of Natures*

intuition found confirmation here in the fact that, in each case, there is an interplay of continuity and discontinuity. For a mode of identification to stabilize, it needs to achieve an ordering of all the realities of the world by having them enter into that play of resemblance and difference that makes it possible to situate them and make them intellectually and practically manipulable. This is what matters.

To arrive at the combinatorial framework of *Beyond Nature and Culture*, a fourth formula had to be identified that could logically follow from the first three. It would be a system in which humans thought that all the elements of the world, both physical and moral, were different and discontinuous, and in consequence formed so many singularities. This hypothesis corresponded to systems that were evidently neither totemic nor naturalist nor animist, some of which I was rather familiar with. In my career as an Americanist, I had been quite interested in the Andean world and in Mesoamerica. Indeed, these were my first areas of study, as I already explained. In these cultural areas, the communities are configured in a way that does not conform to any of the three previous formulas. They rather seem to present a sort of general fragmentation of interiorities and physical characteristics: decomposition, distribution, and recomposition of these multiple entities into meaningful sets organized according to systems of correspondences. For a world that remains a pure aggregate of singularities is both inconceivable and unlivable. Analogies must be drawn between these miscellaneous elements in order for us to structure these singularities by weaving them into series of symbolic correspondences. It is because of the central role of analogy in this process that I have labeled this fourth formula "analogist." Not, of course, because this is the only one in which analogical reasoning is employed—it is universal—but because it is systematized to a degree not found in any of the other formulas.

The animal double in Mexico provides a good illustration of the forms of discontinuity and analogy used in this formula. Most often called *tona*, it is an animal whose life cycle parallels that of each human being, since it is born and dies at the same time, and anything that causes harm to one simultaneously causes harm to the other. But one never knows the identity of one's *tona*, and it may happen, for instance, that a hunter will kill his own animal double, thus condemning himself to a certain death. Anthropologists had originally called this belief, observed throughout Mesoamerica, "nagualism" and treated it as evidence of a lack of differentiation between human and animal that was similar to what had been

The four corners of the world 97

seen in Australian totemism. However, there is a clear difference between the commonality of fate between the human individual and its double and the material and spiritual continuity imagined by the Noongar between the totemic prototypes and the members of each moiety: first, because the animal is here an individual one and not a prototypical species with shared properties; and, second, because humans are not endowed with the idiosyncratic traits of the *tona* with whom they are paired and of whose nature they are often unaware. On the contrary, humans and their animal alter egos must be distinct in essence and in substance for an analogic relationship to exist between them, such that the accidents that happen to one of the terms affect its correlate, through a kind of reverberation.

At this stage, the main challenge was to fill in some of my ethnographic and historical lacunae: even though I was familiar with the literature on Mexican and Andean societies, it stood to reason that this system must exist in other areas as well, and so I had a lot to read on these other lands where analogism held sway. As chance would have it, again, I was rereading Foucault's *The Order of Things* as I was looking into the origins of the expression "the prose of the world," of which I am very fond. In the chapter that bears this title, Foucault describes the means employed in Renaissance thought to bring to light analogies between the various elements of the world, and these means correspond well to the logic that I was trying to draw out. At the same time, I had begun reading Marcel Granet's work on China, notably *Chinese Thought*, which describes the intellectual operations employed in Chinese medicine, arts, and crafts—what we might call Chinese "philosophy"; and they appeared to correspond rather well to what Foucault described about the Renaissance. Granet goes so far as to assert, about ancient China, that "society, man, the world, are the objects of an overarching form of knowledge that is constituted through the use of analogy alone."[6] The discovery of these references played a decisive role, since this was what made me realize that, rather than being seen as the moment of the advent of the modern cosmology that gave rise to naturalism, the Renaissance should perhaps be thought of as the point of culmination and ultimate refinement of that specific form of identification that I have labeled analogism. I was thus led to identify in this system a much broader phenomenon than I had originally imagined. The definition of analogism I had formulated was at first rather impressionistic, given the very large number of collectives it encompassed and of the sociohistorical elements it had to account for. Yet it allowed me to

98   *The Diversity of Natures*

grasp the logic at work in a great many collectives in Asia and Africa that I had not yet explored and that did not fit into the cosmologies I had identified up to that point.

This is how the project evolved from an attempt to define the various forms of continuity and discontinuity between humans and nonhumans, which I have called modes of identification, into a system of contrasts between four distinct schemas of composition of the world.

Methodological questions

PC   *What you have just described is the genesis of the typology in* Beyond Nature and Culture, *whereas the book itself presents the final outcome of this development in structural form, with each ontology on an equal footing with the others. How much did that formal exercise, which consisted in identifying a systematic pattern, impact your thinking?*

PD   There is always a disconnect between the economy of discovery and that of exposition. Indeed, I could have chosen to narrate *Beyond Nature and Culture* as an etiology of the genesis of these four formulas, as a kind of ethnography of the concepts. This is in part what I did with animism, first because it was the starting point of my reflection, but also because the definition of it I provided had changed over the years and I wanted to clarify what had led me to alter my sense of that term and to avoid misunderstandings—at least inasmuch as they can be avoided! I should also say that I am not a fan of neologisms and have followed the classic practice in anthropology, which consists in using the traditionally sanctioned terms while giving them a different definition. For instance, in the history of the discipline, "totemism" has designated very different things, as the concept variously expanded around the central core of the Australian social system. From this perspective, all I did was to add yet another layer of alternative meaning, and the same is true for what I did with the concept of animism. This is probably an old philosophical habit that was passed on to the social sciences and goes back to classical thought, where everyone used the terms "substance," "cause," "attribute," and "soul," even while giving them distinct meanings each time. This is how a common field of intelligibility develops, with internal and historically defined references—by

Methodological questions 99

contrast with neologisms, whose creation often seems to me a way to change the packaging so as to keep the same stock-in-trade. I prefer it to be the other way around.

I was probably also influenced by the great expository modes of French anthropology, especially that of Lévi-Strauss in *The Elementary Structures of Kinship*. I found it useful to provide a kind of philosophical, epistemological, and cognitive basis for what I was proposing, as Lévi-Strauss had done. Granted, there is something paradoxical in this model, because the foundation Lévi-Strauss offers at the beginning of the book—the passage from nature to culture, the incest prohibition as condition for the exchange of women and as index of the emergence of society—all this was an abstract philosophical construction, a thought experiment, and in the end it had little to do with the analyses of matrimonial systems that followed, which in several instances even contradicted the idea of a clear separation between a state of nature and a state of culture for humanity. So I hope that the theoretical basis I offer in *Beyond Nature and Culture* does not simply appear as a preemptive legitimation of my position—as if this position could just as well be severed from it—but truly informs the concrete exposition that follows.

I should perhaps elaborate on the two main aspects of this theoretical foundation: the contrast between interiority and physicality on the one hand, the role of schematism on the other, both of which draw on work in cognitive psychology. The idea that humans, when identifying objects in their environment, detect in these objects physical properties and inner states that are of the same nature as those they themselves experience in their corporeal and psychic lives—this idea has two sources. First, an ethnographic one, since in both animism and naturalism a clear distinction is drawn between what may be described as an individualized deep interiority and a body endowed with certain attributes that enable it to act on the world. For these two formulas at least, a contrast between the order of interiority and that of physicality is operative. In addition, the distinction between these two orders corroborates findings in developmental psychology that suggest that, long before they can speak, humans interpret the world around them through intuitions, which are probably innate, concerning the material behavior and the psychic dispositions of the objects it comprises. These intuitions range from an awareness of the permanence and solidity of objects in space and time to a tendency to treat animate objects as

100   *The Diversity of Natures*

if they were conscious beings and had interior states. It was thus not illegitimate to think that, whatever shape local ontologies may take, they always develop around a series of contrasts between these two dimensions of physicality and interiority, which are universally perceived in the objects of the world.

As for schematism, it is a central piece of the structuralist apparatus, inherited from Kant and Piaget, but recent studies in psychology have given it a more solid experimental foundation. The idea is that an important part of what humans do rests on the activation of abstract structures that organize understanding and practical action without mobilizing mental images or any explicit knowledge that can be organized into propositions. These schemas, which are acquired through socialization, govern most of our capabilities and proceed from "knowing-how," which is effective because not conscious, rather than from "knowing-that." Examples can be found in Mauss's techniques of the body, in Bourdieu's habitus, in image composition through linear perspective, in the recognition of shapes as described in Gestalt psychology, and in Haudricourt's two types of interventions on nature and on others. I used this very early on, in *In the Society of Nature*, to describe what I called "schemas of practice," that is, forms of behavior toward humans and nonhumans that are simultaneously quite distinctive and yet never explicitly discussed as such. Recent research, for example the work on mental models, connectionist models, and schematic induction, has brought empirical support for our understanding of the nature and functioning of these schemas, which ultimately validate a rather old hypothesis on the automatic and repetitive character of some inferences, interpretations, and courses of action. This is what I drew on in order to posit that the four modes of identification are integrative schemas of practice.

My background in philosophy also explains, in part, my keenness to present a synthetic model right from the start; it is not easy to let go of the foundational tradition! When I was younger, I was fascinated by the method adopted by Pierre Bourdieu and Jean-Claude Passeron in *Reproduction in Education, Society and Culture*, which is modelled on the geometric exposition in Spinoza's *Ethics* and on his model of formal rigor. I am also a fan of Georges Pérec and, more generally, of any literature with formal constraints, since, in philosophy as in poetry, the playful side of having to submit to very strict rules of expression comes with a powerful stimulation to inventiveness. Finally, I must confess to having a soft spot for

Methodological questions

the elegant principle of Occam's razor, which says that the most powerful scientific explanations are often also the most parsimonious, those developed from a very small number of simple rules. For all these reasons I have sought to provide a philosophical and epistemological basis for a work that then becomes more properly anthropological.

Yet I would warn against adopting a dogmatic reading of the combinatorial analysis of modes of identification. I have found it convincing from a philosophical and conceptual point of view, but it is above all the power of the analytical criteria it supplied that interests me. It may be that this matrix can be empirically validated at a cognitive level, and I am in touch with a team of developmental psychologists to explore the kinds of experimental protocols that could be devised to provide possible confirmation for my hypotheses. But in the end it does not really matter. For the combinatorial analysis I have proposed is, first and foremost, an anthropological model designed to resolve anthropological issues, in other words to explain correlations and incompatibilities that have long been observed between categories of facts studied by anthropologists. Why is it that a given type of cosmology is most often combined with a certain theory of the individual and a certain form of social organization? Why is shamanic activity prevalent in societies where hunting plays an important role, but it is rarely present where sacrifices are practiced? These kinds of questions cannot be solved by the crudest forms of mental reductionism— evolutionary psychology, for instance—if only because the latter, in projecting the conjectural conditions for the emergence of universal psychic dispositions into a remote past of our species, fail to explain how cognitive mechanisms that are supposedly common to all humans have engendered such a wide diversity of institutions. By contrast, with very simple and perhaps even inaccurate cognitive hypotheses, I am able to propose a highly productive contrastive matrix that accounts for these anthropological logics of compatibility and incompatibility that I just evoked. To be honest, quite independently of the psychological plausibility of this grammar of ontologies, it is the use that can be made of it by anthropologists, historians, sociologists, and geographers that will be the ultimate test of its merits. As I have already mentioned, initial results are promising, especially in the field of history, and I was the first to be surprised by the enthusiasm with which medieval historians, sinologists, and Hellenists have seized on this analytical instrument. I may

102   *The Diversity of Natures*

well have accidently stumbled upon a very powerful tool whose
utility I did not immediately grasp, a kind of experimental machine
that can capture certain properties of the real and then organize
them contrastively into meaningful sets.

PC   *This combinatorial approach is also a way for you to take advantage
of the rigor of the structural method while adapting it to your
own objects of study. To what extent would you say your work is
structuralist?*

PD   To answer your question, it may be a good idea to briefly review
what makes structural anthropology so original. There are in fact
two aspects to it. It is, first of all, a method for understanding
and analyzing certain kinds of social facts—a method inspired by
structural linguistics, which Lévi-Strauss and others after him have
fruitfully drawn upon. But it is also a particular perspective on the
very nature of social facts and on the epistemological conditions of
apprehending the real—a perspective that Lévi-Strauss developed
alongside his method and that came to represent the core of his
doctrine in the eyes of most observers outside the discipline, philosophers above all. One may make use of the structural method while
not sharing all the philosophical and moral convictions that inform
the Lévi-Straussian vision of human experience; and indeed nobody,
except Claude Lévi-Strauss himself, has ever done so.

So what exactly does the method consist of? The first objective
is to isolate the phenomena that can be subjected to analysis. For
the most part, they are those that Lévi-Strauss has called super-
structures—elements of the real that the unconscious activity of
the mind is supposed to organize into meaningful and systematic
sets: rules of kinship and alliance, classifications, myths, dietary
rules, and artistic forms. In these systems we focus on the relationships, realized or not, that bring together elements characterized
not by their intrinsic properties but by their position in relation to
one another. The aim is to highlight in a table of permutations all
possible combinations between these elements. The structural model
that results from this does not seek to faithfully describe any social
reality; it is a heuristic mechanism that supplies the syntax of the
transformations that enable the move from one variant to another
within a category of phenomena. Structural analysis in anthropology is limited to revealing and ordering contrastive traits so as
to point to the necessary relations that govern certain sectors of

Methodological questions 103

social life, for instance culinary techniques, or ways of circulating the women among individuals and groups. In other words, it is a very powerful method for reaching the goal of all anthropological analysis: detecting and ordering regularities in enunciations and practices.

And then there is the Lévi-Straussian perspective proper, on the nature of the social and on the aims of anthropological understanding, certain aspects of which one might share. I can say a few words about the ones I have learned to recognize as my own. First, Lévi-Strauss's perspective is profoundly semiological: social life, in his view, is a network of exchange of objects of various kinds, which circulate the same way signs would. This is right, so long as signs are not limited to symbols, and thus to objects that are conceived of analogically with how language works. If you want to combat the anthropocentrism of the social sciences, as I do, our analysis of the sign system must be expanded beyond the human, to include other kinds of signs that humans share with nonhumans: iconic signs— that is, images—and indexical signs—that is, the traces left by beings and phenomena.

Lévi-Strauss also placed a great deal of emphasis on the role of the unconscious. According to him, the unconscious activity of the mind accounted for the structure and functioning of symbolic systems, the variations between their contents being a contingent effect of the natural and historical environments in which they operate. Hence his famous proposition that anthropology is in the first place a psychology. I confess that I am more skeptical of this project, which consists in extracting, from the black box of the unconscious, bits of objectivized thought in the form of institutions, to deduce from them the laws that govern how the mind works. Even if I am indeed convinced that a considerable part of our cultural dispositions is acquired, employed, and passed on in unconscious ways, rather than deducing these kinds of dispositions from the social expressions they make possible, I find more convincing, as a way of explaining them, what cognitive psychology has begun to establish with regard to the application of non-propositional knowledge. I have already talked about this. Another important piece of the Lévi-Straussian system is a theory of knowledge characterized by the radical rejection of Cartesian cognitive realism and by the concomitant affirmation of a natural continuity between "subjective states and properties of the cosmos."[7] I fully subscribe to this monist gnoseology, even though I find it just as well articulated in Merleau-Ponty, Francisco

104 *The Diversity of Natures*

Varela, James Gibson, and even Spinoza, as Lévi-Strauss himself pointed out.

In the end, what Lévi-Strauss and structural anthropology have contributed to other great models of interpreting social facts, for instance historical causality or functionalism, is the idea that no human phenomenon makes sense in and of itself and that it comes into relief only when contrasted with other phenomena of a similar kind, such that the object of inquiry is not the description of phenomena so much as the logic of contrasts. This method has often proved to be very productive, especially since it relegated to the background the question of causality—environmental, psychic, technical, economic, political, and ideological—which had long contaminated all attempts to explain social facts. It also brought to the fore a dimension that I consider crucial: the conditions under which common worlds are composed, that is, the principles that govern the compatibility and incompatibility of institutions, practices, ideological systems, values, and so on. Anthropology's mission, as I see it, is to highlight these principles, to understand why, in given circumstances, certain elements have come together and given rise to social formations of a specific kind. Its mission is also to explain why these relations of compatibility and incompatibility recur in rather similar forms in very different regions of the world: the same kinds of things work well together and exclude others. Structural anthropology is a very effective tool for explaining the laws of organization that govern these aggregates, precisely because it is attentive to the systematicity of differences and the compositional effects of phenomena that pertain, at first sight, to very different fields of practice. This may be a simplistic way of presenting the virtues of structuralism, but, as far as I am concerned, if there is one fundamental point to be retained, this would be it.

In a more technical sense, structural anthropology achieves the ends I have just described thanks to a very original mechanism: transformation, which I have myself used. By Lévi-Strauss's own admission, this was the cornerstone of the sort of analyses he practiced and, in my opinion, also what seems to have been most productive in his approach. If the notion of structure as a system of contrastive oppositions was borrowed from linguistics, he gave it an analytical dynamic that resulted from his capacity to organize the orderly transformations between models of the same group, that is, those that applied to the same set of phenomena. A structure is not a

Methodological questions 105

system. For there to be a structure, there must be invariant relationships between the elements and between several sets, relationships that enable the passage from one set to another via a transformation. As I have discussed elsewhere,[8] Lévi-Strauss makes use of transformation in two distinct ways, which are related to two different morphogenetic traditions: that of D'Arcy Wentworth Thompson, to which he explicitly refers, and Goethe's, about which he remains far more discreet, and which directly inspired me. It may thus be useful to dwell on this dimension for a bit.

The first type of transformation is the one Lévi-Strauss makes use of in *The Elementary Structures of Kinship*. The invariant relationship is here the exchange of women, which is an expression of the reciprocity principle, itself the positive form of the incest prohibition: to proscribe the women in one's own group is to force oneself to give them away to the men in another group and obtain those men's women in exchange. All the forms of matrimonial union that Lévi-Strauss analyzes are as many transformations of that original principle, whose forms Lévi-Strauss studied on the basis of their increasingly complex departure from the simplest sociological form that the reciprocity principle may take: the dualist organization, in which society is divided into two classes that exchange women according to the rule of exogamy. This is restricted exchange, a minimal organization of reciprocity below which no social life is possible. It is followed by a series of transformations that illustrate the possibilities of that original invariant: the Australian four- or eight-class systems that are based on generalized exchange; the Kachin system in the Burmese highlands in which generalized exchange is combined with marriage by purchase; and, finally, the various combinations of limited and generalized exchange that characterize the kinship systems of India and China. This tree diagram of the forms of marriage closely resembles the methodical variations of an *urform* in the Goethean sense—in this case, the exchange of women governed by the reciprocity principle, of which Lévi-Strauss lays out the whole range of logical consequences in so many morphological types of matrimonial union. Just as Goethe harbored the dream that one day he could discover the primordial plant—the prototype from which all the characteristics of all plant species, current and logically possible, may derive through transformation—Lévi-Strauss identified in the reciprocity principle the original form of all matrimonial alliances, for which he suggested a developmental law.

106 *The Diversity of Natures*

In contrast with this conception of variation as the development of a complex prototype, in his analysis of myths Lévi-Strauss adopted an entirely different approach to variations, one that he said was inspired by D'Arcy Thompson. In his master work *On Growth and Form,* the latter proposed a transformational grid of a geometric kind that made it possible to move from one form of organism to another, through continuous deformation, without ever considering any complex original form from which all other forms were derived. Abstracting from evolutive lines of descent, he could move from the cranium of an extinct species of rhinoceros to the cranium of a contemporary species of tapir, and from the latter to the cranium of a horse. Lévi-Strauss adapted this method to the analysis of myths. A myth's transformation is the set of myths that contains on the one hand all the variants of a myth that have retained the same structure, including those in which the structure was reversed, and on the other hand all the myths, often of neighboring societies, that can be shown to have been mutually transformed through the borrowing of episodes—what Lévi-Strauss calls "mythemes"—whose pattern can be reversed and whose function can be switched around. Thus the transformation of organic forms and of mythemes proceeds in the same manner, through a continuous series of small variations.

Yet there is a major difference between myths and organisms, namely that the transformation group within which myths operate forms a virtual continuum from which the analyst takes ideal cross-sections in an arbitrary fashion. On the basis of her knowledge and imagination, the analyst chooses, from an immense store of myths and variants, the mythemes whose contrastive potential will be highest. From this perspective, the variants of a myth do not in and of themselves hold to a discontinuity principle. But the specific and generic differences between organisms depend on disconti-nuities in their genetic code. In other words, the transformation through continuous variation that D'Arcy Thompson applies to the morphology of organisms requires that stable forms—the rhinoceros and the horse—be provided as starting points and endpoints in order to reveal the physico-mathematical principles that enable the movement from one to another through continuous deformation. There is nothing of the kind in the structural analysis of myths: each analyst is to trace the path of transformations according to his fancy.

In short, depending on whether it concerns organisms, images, social types, or semantic units in certain categories of enunciations, the change from one form into another can be considered from the perspective of either a "Goethean regime" or a "Thompsonian regime." In the former case, the transformation is a development into various forms of an initial plan of sorts, itself constructed through a comparison between empirical objects that belong in the same set. In the latter, the transformation is a deformation through continuous variations, within a space of coordinates that apply to already given forms. It was the first method, developed by Lévi-Strauss in *The Elementary Structures of Kinship*, that inspired my approach when I attempted to organize the various forms of continuity and discontinuity between humans and nonhumans starting from an original relationship between interiority and physicality. This dynamic represents a hypothetical invariant that is neither more nor less plausible, as a foundation, than the imperative to exchange women that Lévi-Strauss identified as the necessary and sufficient condition from which the various kinds of matrimonial systems could be deduced. But, rather than proceeding through an increasing complexification of the logical conditions for the implementation of the invariant, as is the case in *The Elementary Structures of Kinship*, the transformation is here based on the use of the four combinations made possible by the original relationship: humans and nonhumans have the same interiority and distinct physicalities, or they have the same physicality and distinct interiorities, or both their physicality and their interiority are the same, or, finally, both are different. As in kinship systems, the transformation here is the hypothetico-deductive expression of all the possible consequences of a core that is posited as invariant. The arbitrary dimension, for there is one, is in the choice of the original relationship. But, once this relationship has been posited, it must account for all the possible forms, and this is indeed its only justification, a posteriori.

Indeed, once the elementary matrix was established on a universal fact, it became possible for me to show how the initial ontological contrasts could be found in other domains of human experience— from the way communities were formed to relationships with nonhumans, theories of the subject, and the organization of space. This table of the various modes of identification perhaps comes closest to what Lévi-Strauss sometimes called "the order of orders," namely the higher level of structural articulation of the various systems that compose social life. Here this level operates as such, not as a function of its integration of analytically predefined orders but as the effect of a hypothesis about what comes first in how we

108 *The Diversity of Natures*

experience things: the process of discerning qualities in the objects around us; and that of inferring the relations with them that these qualities allow. Yet the matrix of identifications here does not play the role of a philosophical prime mover. Rather it is a kind of experimental machine that allows for the capture (hence the establishment) and the selection (hence the combination) of phenomena in order to bring out the syntax of their differences. Having said that, I also tried to remain faithful to the fundamental principle of structural analysis according to which each variant is a variant of all the others and not only of one of them, which would thus be privileged. For, if I put the matrix of ontological relations center stage, none of the variants it reveals at its own level (animism, naturalism, totemism, and analogism) and none of the variants that can be isolated in other systems that are its transformations (in the sociological, epistemological, cosmological, or spatio-temporal orders) are endowed with any primacy over the others. This was a requirement I had in mind from the start, so as to produce a model of intelligibility of social and cultural facts that had to remain as neutral as possible regarding the assumptions of our own ontology. This is why that ontology, naturalism, is only one of four possible variants of the ways of objectivizing the world.

Conceptual reform

PC *The use you make of the term "ontology" gave rise to some misunderstandings among philosophers as well as among anthropologists. Yet you also use other, similar notions such as "worldview," "cosmology," and "mode of identification." Could you comment on the use of these terms and how they have structured your approach?*

PD It is true that the term "ontology" came to enjoy a certain prominence, in the anglophone world especially, after the translation of *Beyond Nature and Culture*—so much so that, along with Bruno Latour and Eduardo Viveiros de Castro, I have become one of the figures of the "ontological turn," which has been the subject of considerable debate in anthropological and philosophical circles, as well as between them. As far as I am concerned, the most accurate expression for talking about the various forms of composition of the world—that is, about the architecture I was just describing of these continuous and discontinuous relations between beings—is

Conceptual reform 109

"mode of identification." It is in fact an expression I borrowed from Marcel Mauss, who wrote that "man identifies with things and identifies things with himself, having at the same time a sense of the differences and the similarities that he establishes."[9] Varying the modalities of these elementary identifications that structure the relationship to oneself and to others, I have attempted to describe the fundamental economy of interactions with the world. It is through this process that humans identify themselves as humans, as a specific category of beings, emphasizing different forms of similarity and dissimilarity with other beings; the opposition between nature and culture is only one among other possible variants of such forms. In my view, an ontology is just the established result of a mode of identification—the particular form, discernible in language and images, that one of the four regimes of continuity and discontinuity takes on at a given time and in a given region of the world. To give you an example, there are many differences between the ontology of classical China and that of ancient Greece—in the number and nature of beings identified, in the forms of relations between them, in the types of networks they constitute, and in the keys that make them interoperable. Yet the principles that govern the constitution of these ontologies are reducible to the same mode of identification: the one that I have labelled analogism.

By comparison with the mode of identification, cosmologies refer simply to the distribution of the components of an ontology in space and to the relations that tie them together. In *Beyond Nature and Culture* I made sure to specify that the modes of identification are further defined by the dominant relations—exchange, predation, gift, production, transmission, protection—that give these modes a style of their own. If we were to draw a parallel with political systems, the mode of identification would refer to the general form of government—monarchy, democracy, aristocracy; the ontology, to the kind of constitution that, in each of these regimes, delineates the balance of powers, the nature of the assemblies, the forms of representation; while the cosmology would correspond to the legal and regulatory instruments that govern how we live together.

As for "worldview," this is a term I try to avoid, even if it is not always easy to do so, since for the general public it comes closest to what I call ontology. But there is a major difference between the two, which accounts for my reticence: indeed "worldview" supposes that there is a world, a nature, a single system of objects, which each culture then perceives in its own way. I am convinced, on the

110 *The Diversity of Natures*

contrary, that there is no such thing as a world that is a self-sufficient and preexisting totality awaiting representation from various points of view, but that there are, rather, diverse ways of worlding, of actualizing the countless qualities, phenomena, and relations that may be objectivized or not by humans on the basis of how the various kinds of ontological filters with which they are endowed allow them to discriminate between what their near and distant environment offers to their direct and indirect perception. These ontological filters are systems of inferences about the nature of beings and their properties, and they are enabled by modes of identification. A naturalist ontological filter will not generate an animal spirit, while an animist ontological filter will not generate a quark. So, once the movement of worlding is underway in an ontological regime, it does not produce a "worldview," understood as one version among others of some transcendental reality that only science or God could fully access. It produces a world in the true sense, saturated with meaning and teeming with multiple causalities, a world that, at the margins, overlaps other worlds of the same kind, themselves actualized in other ways by other agents. It is this overlap that makes anthropology possible.

That said, I understand that speaking about ontology, and especially about ontologies, in the plural, may seem rather presumptuous on the part of an anthropologist; but I am not at all using this term to signal the conquest of a domain that was previously the reserve of philosophy. If I have used it, in a somewhat militant way, I admit, it has been mostly to make clear that I believe that anthropological analysis should position itself at a more elementary level than the one at which it has hitherto operated. I am now convinced that we cannot account for the system of differences at play in the properly human ways of inhabiting the world if we consider these differences to be the outcome of some institution, economic organization, technical infrastructure, value system, worldview—in short, of all the dimensions of collectives that have been hypostasized by the social sciences as determinants, in order to bring to light determinations. All these dimensions are, however, the stabilized result of more fundamental intuitions about what the world contains and about the relations maintained by its human and nonhuman components. The word "ontology" seemed to me fitting to designate this analytical level, which in the language of phenomenology we might call prepredicative. This is why I began to use it, sparingly, in the 1990s. In the end, insofar as I did contribute to an "ontological

Conceptual reform 111

turn"—an expression I have never used myself—it was out of a need for conceptual hygiene: the roots of human diversity must be sought at a deeper level, that of the differences between the basic inferences humans draw about the kinds of beings that populate the world and the way these beings are linked to one another. From these differences come the kinds of collectives within which common life unfolds, as well as the nature of their composition—forms of subjectivization and objectivization, regimes of temporality and forms of figuration, indeed, all the richness of social and cultural life.

PC   *For some time now, anthropology has tried to rid itself of the somewhat cumbersome term "culture," which encompasses collective habits that are perhaps somewhat superficial. Is the notion of ontology a way of moving beyond culturalism, of offering a different formulation of the nature of collective existence?*

PD   As we have just seen, "ontology" is in no way synonymous with "culture"—contrary to what may have been thought in anglophone anthropology along the path once taken by Irving Hallowell, a precursor of the phenomenological approach among anthropologists in the United States.[10] The confusion probably comes from a persistent misunderstanding about what anthropology should take its object of study to be. In North America and, by extension, in a growing number of countries, the stuff of anthropology is culture, understood in the tradition established by Franz Boas and the German heritage that inspired him. But, since it is impossible to study culture in general in the sense of a mechanism that mediates all natural human determinations, North American anthropology has focused on particular cultures—human groups that share the same values and the same ways of life and modes of interaction—or on the interfaces between them. And the theorization of culture operates through progressive generalization from these individual ethnographies, that is, through inductions that draw regularities from behavior and habits on the basis of these empirical amalgams. By contrast, the object of French anthropology has never been culture in general, even though many French anthropologists have provided very thorough ethnographic descriptions of human communities that one may call cultures. But, as I have already said, in France the object of anthropology is not these aggregates of cultures from which generalizable lessons are to be drawn; it is the models that are built to account for a totality that comprises all observable variants

112   *The Diversity of Natures*

of the same type of phenomenon and to elucidate the principles of their transformations.

I therefore find myself in complete agreement with the movement that seeks to distance itself from the notion of culture; and one of the most powerful inspirations for that movement came, paradoxically, from the United States, in the form of Roy Wagner's masterwork *The Invention of Culture*.[11] Wagner was well placed to diagnose the dead end to which culturalism led, but for a long time he went relatively unheeded in his own country. For my part, one of the primary motivations of my theoretical work has been to pursue the critical relativization of the concepts in use in the social sciences. The key notions in these disciplines—"culture," "nature," "society," "history," "economy," "politics," "religion," "art"—have revealed dimensions of our collective condition as Europeans and have put names on realities that were in the process of becoming perceptibly autonomous from the early eighteenth to the end of the nineteenth centuries. These were two crucial centuries during which were forged the main concepts that enabled Europe to define itself reflexively, as a collectivity anchored in a historical process. These concepts are thus anything but ahistorical; they are the product of a very singular social and cultural history—that of this peninsula, located at the westernmost tip of the Asian continent and commonly called "the West." Intrinsically connected to the sociopolitical destiny of modern Europe, they were then reemployed in the social sciences to describe and explain non-European societies, as if their descriptive value were universal. This quiet conviction that our societies could serve as the standard in describing any form of society is in fact linked to the then dominant evolutionary ideology that considered all human groups to be destined to go through the same stages and one day perhaps become, with a little help from colonization, "societies" comparable to those of Europe, with the same kinds of institutions, the same kind of division between economic, political, and cultural domains. In the meantime they were just clumsy rough drafts, from which anthropology could nonetheless discern the still embryonic shape of their future accomplishments.

It thus appeared to me that the principle of relativism that had been developed by anthropology in the early twentieth century had not been taken to its logical conclusion. Relativism—as a method, and not as a moral precept—consists quite simply in not taking the observer's values and institutions as a standard by which one should assess the values and institutions of the observed. Anthropology

Conceptual reform 113

has very effectively employed that principle, especially to describe the various kinship systems and forms of family organization. For instance, the European monogamous heterosexual family, organized as an economic and procreative unit, is anything but an anthropological invariant. It is but one possible variant within a vast array of formulas, in which the number and the sex of the partners, their mode of residence, their way of obtaining children, and the status granted to the latter may vary. Anthropologists do not consider these other formulas as deviations from a norm, but as so many instituted forms that enable humans to partner with one another in order to meet their needs and produce offspring. However, this principle of methodological relativism has not been given its full measure, which is to challenge the general framework in which our own values and institutions have taken shape. And this general framework is the ontology we are so familiar with that I have labelled naturalism, an ontology in which, unlike in others, there are societies, nature, historical destiny, cultural habits, a clear separation between the social and the economic, and so on. In the end, contrary to what some have accused me of, I have sought to develop analytical tools that are as free as possible of the historical particularisms of the concepts currently used in the social sciences. Terms such as "gravitation" and "photosynthesis" hold universal value; this is not the case with notions such as "society," "culture," and "nature."

It therefore seemed necessary to push the reflection further, to not be content with the critique of this or that notion from the sociological repertoire but move to a deeper level, that of the elaboration of the common world—more specifically, to the level of detecting regularities in the world that, when they are systematized, have the effect of producing forms of collectives, conceptions of the subject, and theories of action specific to large social universes. Proceeding in this way, I no longer considered "societies" to be preexisting realities, as was customary in the social sciences. I tried to understand rather how different collectives developed, some of which indeed thought of themselves as "societies." This is what the ontological turn consists in: it is not a thesis on what the world is about, but an investigation of how humans detect the various characteristics of objects so as to make worlds out of them. It is because these initial modalities of identification of the world are slightly different that the forms of the collectives that humans will come to imagine also differ. Humans will be immersed in political configurations, types of exchange, and the kinds of relations between themselves and with

114 *The Diversity of Natures*

nonhumans that vary widely and change radically through history. But my ambition was to bring the critical aim of social science down to the most elementary level, to make social science capable of grasping the general form of interaction between beings. From this perspective, we should really no longer speak of "social" science, since the social here is more an effect than a cause; we should speak instead of a science of beings and relations, a science still to come, to which anthropology and philosophy could contribute along with ethology, sociology, psychology, ecology, cybernetics, and history.

PC *What you are suggesting here is that the history of your discipline, and of the social sciences more broadly, plays a fundamental part in your thinking. Could you say more about your relationship with the anthropological tradition and with the history of science in general?*

PD One thing that is patently clear about the social sciences—and many social scientists have already pointed this out—is that the genesis and conditions of possibility of a science form part of its object of study. This means that the science in question can be practiced only by those who are aware at all times of the history of its emergence and its metamorphoses. This is not true of the natural sciences or of practical sciences like medicine. One can very well be interested in the history of medicine, out of curiosity—as a mandarin in her field may be, in retirement, when she has the time to delve into the writings of early pioneers. But this is absolutely not essential to being a good doctor, and it is even less relevant to being a good biologist. In some domains such as physics, it can be important to learn about the evolution of ideas in the field in order to better understand recent developments, but this is still far from constituting the systematic reflexivity that is required in the social sciences. The work of generating new concepts in these forms of knowledge indeed entails the constant reworking of the theoretical heritage at one's disposal, and even requires that that be the starting point. Gradually, while becoming aware of the specific historical experience linked to that heritage, we come to realize that the concepts are not quite adequate to describe unprecedented situations, that they are less general and less operational than was previously thought.

This attention to a "presentist" form of history—one envisaged not in and of itself, but from the perspective of contemporary intellectual issues—is of course connected to the critical ambition of the social sciences, to the fact that they are not external to what

Conceptual reform   115

they are talking about. But neither I nor other anthropologists who have engaged in similar pursuits have ever had the intention of systematically tearing down everything out of vanity, for the sake of having one's name attached to a moment of conceptual reconstruction. In France, the fact that anthropologists and sociologists are often trained in philosophy might have whetted their appetite for the constant reworking of the concepts through which thought develops, since this is a highly philosophical practice. As far as I am concerned, and I believe this to be the case for most anthropologists, my sense of the need to reflect on method and history came from an initial ethnographic shock. It was my encounter with a radical alterity that made me aware of the fact that the conceptual toolbox I had brought with me into my fieldwork was not going to be of much help in making me understand what was happening around me. That state of shock, that initial jolt coming from the gap between ways of using the world, amplifies one's natural curiosity and inclination to question things, because the critical distance that philosophy cultivates becomes a fact of daily life.

With philosophers, the inclination not to take anything for granted comes from within, so to speak. Kant is a perfect illustration of that intellectual heroism, combining as he does an incredibly orderly petty bourgeois daily life and an incredibly original form of thought for his time. I find this kind of adventurous imagination absolutely extraordinary, but I am myself incapable of it. It took the experience of sharing the life of people whose behavior is often enigmatic and whose remarks are very strange, a life that runs counter to ways of being that are considered normal, for me to realize that I had to question the intellectual tools with which I was seeking to grasp this strangeness.

Indeed, the ethnographic experience resonates in a very curious way with one's prior knowledge of anthropological theory. In my case, you may think that it was somewhat naïve of me to be surprised by the fact that the Achuar treated plants and animals as persons and engaged with them in social relations. Indeed, a large part of the anthropological literature since the second half of the nineteenth century deals with this kind of phenomenon. There are good reasons to believe that the discipline itself was born out of the need to resolve the apparent logical discrepancy, when the early ethnographers, missionaries, merchants, and soldiers began to bring back to Europe the strange news that peoples in the farthest fringes of the world considered animals to be their ancestors and conversed with plants. Their apparent ignorance of the distinction between

116 *The Diversity of Natures*

nature and society, which seemed to go without saying, was thus one of the constitutive issues of anthropology, and all the founding fathers of the discipline devote attention to it. This is true of Edward Burnett Tylor's *Primitive Culture*, of James George Frazer's *Golden Bough*, of Émile Durkheim's *Elementary Forms of the Religious Life*, and, somewhat later, of Lucien Lévy-Bruhl and many others. When I started off on my fieldwork, I had of course read all of them, but a bit like one may have read treatises in theology or medieval philosophy—that is, as works that speak of abstract realities that function as pretexts for undertaking exercises in intellectual virtuosity. This is due to the fact that these classic works generally dealt with remarks taken out of context, as was the famous proposition "the Bororo are Araras," which Karl von den Steinen reported and which has since been the cause of so much spilled ink.[2] These mysterious fragments of discourse are recomposed into very complex theoretical elaborations, which are also very distant from their original realities. Reading Durkheim, one is not immersed in the world of the Australian aborigines, just as reading Plato one is not immersed in the Athenian symposium.

This is what makes the practice of ethnography so different from the reading of anthropology. When you are doing fieldwork, what had been only relatively abstract propositions—ideological constructions, systems of thought, visions of the world—becomes incredibly concrete. It thus becomes increasingly urgent to find ways not so much of putting an end, in scholarly fashion, to the logical discrepancy, as of understanding why I, a random individual who was brought up tens of thousands of kilometers away, find it so difficult to share in these ways of seeing and doing. Since the beginning of anthropology, this experience of incongruity has been a powerful spur to the kind of conceptual reform I was talking about, and to considerations of its philosophical implications.

PC *One of the main consequences of this synthetic work is that it reshuffled the cards between a certain universalism and the relativist imperative of anthropology. In your view, how are we to find a new compromise between these principles, which are often opposed to each other?*

---

[2] Translators' note. This ethnographic fragment—which suggests the possibility of humans identifying with animals, in this case birds—was taken out of its original context by Lucien Lévy-Bruhl, as part of his discussion of the "primitive mentality." It subsequently became the subject of much abstract philosophical and anthropological debate.

Conceptual reform 117

PD   The main question raised by the critical exercise of refocusing that I engaged in is the following: how are we to develop analytical tools that are neither founded on a form of universalism that comes out of the development of western thought nor entirely segmented according to the type of ontology that we are dealing with? This is a complicated challenge, requiring that we take seriously on the one hand the diversity of modes of actualization of the world and the fact that each of them has specificities that make any comparison difficult and, on the other, the need to put all these differences into relation in a way that meets our ambition for comprehensive knowledge. And, despite the difficulties that this latter dimension of my work entails, I have no desire to give up on it, for it seems to me that, among naturalism's legacies to thought in the world, this is an important one. I am well aware that, for many researchers today, the very idea of articulating various ways of composing worlds into an overall synthesis has something of an imperialist, or even neocolonial air about it. Indeed, some think that a western naturalist point of view necessarily contaminates the demand for universality and that, by implicitly granting scientific priority to naturalism, we would confirm and legitimize the politically dominant status that the West has long assumed. However, I think that we ought to dissociate the scientific objective of universalism from the history of European domination over the world, even if this is a difficult task, given that the two have for so long been in league with each other in the project of colonial expansion: an understanding of the other served to subjugate that other, and this subjugation was all the more successful as a solid knowledge of the other had been acquired. Universalism demands that we seek to articulate all the modes of being in the world through concepts that are interoperable, which means that they allow us to see ourselves as we see other societies, so that the particularity of our point of view no longer acts as a bias in the analysis but as an object of that analysis among others.

Rather than a militant universalism, what I aspire to is thus a form of symmetrization that would place the anthropologist on an equal conceptual footing with the people they study. The point to such a symmetry is neither to generalize the scope of a local principle, as was done in earlier days with *mana*, nor to provide a philosophical counter-model inspired by native thought, as Viveiros de Castro has done with perspectivism. The purpose is to build a combinatorics that accounts for all the states of a set of phenomena by revealing the systematic differences between the elements of the set. This is of course a basic

118 *The Diversity of Natures*

principle of structural analysis, but how is it a symmetrization? It is such, very simply, because the totality is never given a priori, as the privileged vantage point from which anthropology can structure the world under its imperial gaze, but results rather from the always unfinished operation through which cultural traits, norms, institutions, and qualities are identified as variants of one another, within a group that not only can be reconfigured in another way if other elements are added but has indeed no other purpose than to subsume the variations for which it provides a stage. This kind of symmetrization is entirely dependent on the numerous properties that can be variously detected in phenomena, and all it requires, in terms of an overarching perspective, is a bit of erudition about the diversity of objects one is dealing with, which is in the end the only concession I am prepared to make to universalism as it is traditionally conceived.

In addition, it seems to me that it is only through its capacity to analyze actual situations that this project will prove itself capable of making conceptually interesting findings. You can tell whether you are making progress at the conceptual level only by looking at whether or not it works in specific empirical situations. I began to do this with images, for instance (and we may talk about it later), because it seems to me that they work well as a way of trying to understand this interoperability of concepts. Later on I would like to do the same with political systems, that is, with forms of collective organization and their ways of exercising sovereignty, a classic domain of anthropological analysis. I am not at all sure that I will manage. But one thing is certain: it is through structuralism that I have come to believe this to be a legitimate and achievable goal. Indeed, if ever there was a remarkable example of this kind of analysis, it was in Lévi-Strauss's work on the study of myths. His analysis was based on revealing the properties of things—plants, animals, meteors, diseases, artefacts—that mythic narratives put into relation. This required a very solid botanical, zoological, gastronomic, astronomic, and cultural understanding of the specificities of these properties. Yet this analysis did not in any way involve an imperial perspective, since the elucidation of the distinctive oppositions between the properties of the objects that the myths deal with could follow any path. So long as the analysis is done in a rigorous manner, any possible pairings in the body of myths will be able to give it a meaning. And that is what matters most, more than access to any definitive truth about the selected objects: an analysis that tends toward synthesis, but never exhausts its object.

Conceptual reform 119

PC *The concrete articulation between the various ontologies you have identified has also raised questions. And, indeed, we can think of different models to describe how cosmologies have interacted historically, how they were brought into contact and and how they combined. How do you see this issue?*

PD Traditionally, until the early twentieth century, anthropology accounted for the transitions between major social and cultural formations principally through the schema of evolution. Today we have abandoned this simplistic model, but that does not mean that we have abandoned the idea of chronological sequencing between the various cosmologies. We have a few well-documented cases of shift from one mode of identification to another, and especially of the transition that concerns us, the one from analogism to naturalism, between the fifteenth and the seventeenth century in Europe. It is rather difficult to identify clear historical markers for that long birthing process. On the basis of the history of science and philosophy, I had initially located the pivotal moment in the seventeenth century, since that is usually the period identified with the "scientific revolution," which is the most visible expression of the hold of naturalism on cultivated European elites. The year 1632—that of the publication of Galileo's *Dialogue Concerning the Two Chief World Systems*—may be taken as a watershed moment for this shift. But, in light of the pictorial documents and the history of modes of representation that I subsequently studied, I have come to think that the dawn of this shift can be traced back in images at least two centuries earlier. Indeed, if you agree that the two cornerstones of the naturalist mode of identification are the distinctive inner life of the individual human being and the physical continuity between beings and things within a homogeneous space, then there is no doubt that these two conditions were beginning to be realized in Northern European art in the fifteenth century. In Burgundy and in Flanders a new style of painting was emerging at that time, a style that brought the representation of individuals to the fore, first in manuscript illuminations, then in paintings characterized by the continuity of the spaces they represented, the incredibly precise rendition of every detail of the material world, and the individuation of human subjects, endowed, each, with their own individual physiognomy. Naturalism thus appears in images, through the emergence of two novel genres: the painting of the soul—in other words the representation of inner life as evidence of the singularity of the

120 *The Diversity of Natures*

human person—and the imitation of nature—in other words the representation of material contiguities within a physical world that merits observation and description for itself.[12]

While abstract evolutionary schemas are surely unreliable, specific transitions such as this one can be analyzed. The difficulty with such an approach lies in the fact that, for most of the other historical situations, we lack material. The global expansion of what I have called analogism in systems that were previously most likely of the animist kind is very difficult to trace in empirical documents other than archeological remains, which are difficult to interpret from this point of view. When considering societies that have developed writing systems and thus kept traces of events, such tracing is possible, but in other cases, which are more numerous, it is out of reach. I am not ruling out the evolutionary dimension, but one must be very careful not to fall back into the errors of nineteenth-century conjectural evolutionary anthropology, as practiced by Morgan and Tylor, by merely substituting ontologies for the stages of "savagery" and "barbarism."

Other articulations between cosmological models present themselves less as a gradual succession than as a sustained combination that may take either the shape of a gradual hybridization of modes of identification where one will gradually establish its hold over the other or the shape of a coexistence along a border between two ontological fields that may remain stable over a long period. The former appears for example in situations of domination, conquest, and colonization. One system gradually contaminates the other and subordinates the reproduction of the latter to its own ends—while it is not necessarily always the politically or militarily dominant system that gets the upper hand. With all due precautions, it is likely that, when the Aztecs proceeded to migrate from Northern Mexico to the valley of Mexico City, they fell under an animist regime and gradually "analogized" through contact with civilizations of the central plateau. This kind of situation opens up a vast field of research that has the potential to enrich the evolutionary model, and raises questions of a Marxist type regarding relations of domination between cultural formations. When evolutionary models were abandoned, anthropologists made the mistake of giving up on the study of phenomena of large-scale change—with a few exceptions, including Alain Testart and the archaeologists. This disaffection is due to an understandable mistrust of the coarse technical and environmental determinism

Conceptual reform

of earlier days and of the growing importance, especially in the United States, of the hermeneutic approach to anthropology, an approach that led more and more of its practitioners to cease to see it as a science.

One of the most important mechanisms for grasping these phenomena of transformation and hybridization, it seems to me, is what is called "exaptation." This term, which originates in biology, refers to processes through which, over the course of history and as a result of the mutations imposed on the social system, a given institution that emerged to fulfill a certain function comes to take on a different function, which may be very far from the original. In these kinds of processes, an institution that is characteristic of one system may continue to exist in another and yet serve other functions. To give you a simple example, slavery strictly speaking did not exist in Amazonia, but it was customary to capture men, women, and children among the enemy and to integrate them into the victor's domestic unit, where they were generally treated as any other member of the group, although some of them could sometimes be ritually put to death after a number of years. Consequently these captives were not really captives and did not try to escape when they had a chance; more often than not, their almost invisible status was manifest only in the names they were given, in a distinctive sign they wore, and sometimes in their ultimate fate. This practice, which is typical of animist predation, was subverted when colonial powers created the conditions for a servile labor market for plantations. Then some of the tribes came to specialize in slave raids, transforming the animist incorporation of enemies into a commodification of captives that enabled them to acquire manufactured goods in exchange.

For my part, I have pursued a different approach to the transformation of the modes of identification, following a structural logic. In this approach, the emphasis is no longer on historical evolution but on the formal conditions for the shift from one mode to another, through a continuous series of intermediate variations, which can sometimes be found in human collectives spread out along a kind of transect across continents. In *Beyond Nature and Culture*, for instance, I studied the transitions between what I called donor animism and a form of analogism that is characterized by hierarchical relations of transmission. The former is specific to the animist and egalitarian ontologies of subarctic Amerindians: these are marked particularly by the idea that the gift—from animals to humans—and sharing—among humans—are cardinal

122 *The Diversity of Natures*

values. The latter is typical of the cattle-raising people of southern Mongolia and represents a reorientation of some of the traits of animism toward the more hierarchical analogist communities, where protection, both of humans by divinities and of cattle by humans, plays a central role. In the space in between, that is, from Chukotka to northern Mongolia, we find gradual variations that lead from one form to the other, not unlike in the D'Arcy Thompson model of organism transformation that I have already described.

It appeared to me that, moving in this way through space against the grain of the historical settlement of the American continent, we could see how the different adjoining forms represented stages in the transition from one form to the next. We do not really have proof of any historical evolution from one to another, or of a relation of dependence of one on the other, or of loss suffered by one to the other's advantage, but this approach nonetheless helped identify how the transformation of sometimes minor components of a collective could enable a shift from one intermediary state to another, how the simple accumulation of small differences could eventually lead to a new and unrecognizable system, which differed radically from the previous one. I am aware that I am indulging here in a kind of history-fiction, since I do not have all the elements to trace these minor differences, but this is no conjectural anthropology, since it is possible to identify the elements that have undergone simple transformations, especially relationships to animals. This method is similar to that of Marx in the chapter titled "Forms Which Precede Capitalist Production," in the *Grundrisse* manuscripts of 1857–1858. Its interest lies mostly in the regressive approach he adopted: he proceeded from a structural definition of the capitalist mode of production and reconstructed its emergence from the decomposition and recomposition of elements of feudalism.

PC *Could we imagine a social situation in which elements characteristic of different ontologies would be represented at the same time, and thus in which several possible ways of structuring the social world would be present?*

PD Examples of this kind do exist, and I have begun to work on a few, especially through the use of images. The northwest coast of America, for example, presents elements that are manifestly animist and others that are just as clearly totemic. With regard to animism,

Conceptual reform 123

it is quite simple: throughout that region nonhumans, and especially animals, are said to see themselves as human and to be endowed with a subjectivity, institutions, and a culture that are analogous to those of humans, with whom they maintain person-to-person relationships. Yet, when one turns to the representations produced by these societies, the animist dimension seems partly erased. Specialists of this cultural area all insist on the fact that, on the contrary, the most common representations, especially the heraldic poles, are for the most part crests. One of the northernmost groups, the Tsimshian, offers a good illustration of this combination: one finds, side by side, a system of crests of several hundred named coats of arms with heraldic animal figures and another iconographic system, in which animal spirits are represented along with their transformational ability and the powers they can pass on to humans. From these a typology can be drawn that clearly distinguishes two kinds of representation: the first represents a group of contrastive qualities that are embodied in a totem endowed with an animal or human form, whereas the second is of an animist type and is intended to make spirits, generally animal spirits, visible and present. These representations reveal a hybrid regime—also manifest in ceremonies and ritual enunciations—that combines all the characteristics of an animist ontology and a few salient traits of a totemic ontology of the Australian variety.[13]

New Guinea provides yet another example that I find utterly fascinating. For this region of the world, I have indeed had a lot of trouble isolating truly pure forms of one or another of the cosmologies I have defined, historically embodied forms of the ideal types that the modes of identification represent. Indeed, we find forms that would seem rather animist, for example among the Kasua and the Kaluli of the "Great Plateau" region, where, to judge from all the descriptions, one could almost believe we are in Amazonia. But if we go up toward the valley of the Sepik River, for example among the Manambu, we find a configuration that resembles more closely that of Australian totemism. And elsewhere still, one sees clearly analogist elements. I sometimes have the sense that the whole of New Guinea is a vast group of transformations, in which a large range of elements are combined in very diverse ways, within a rather limited area. Therefore more comparative work would need to be done on all these variations, work such as Pierre Lemonnier began in *Guerres et Festins*. This is a remarkable book on the various forms of political power, war, and matrimonial exchange in the highlands of

124 *The Diversity of Natures*

New Guinea, but it does not take into account all the elements that contribute to the constitution of ontologies.[14]

For example, one striking feature of New Guinea is that both the circulation of women and the circulation of the dead involve two forms of exchange, which I have labeled "homosubstitution" and "heterosubstitution."[15] In the former, only humans can be traded in exchange for other humans. For example, in the marriage system, a group acquires a woman and gives away another woman in exchange, even if this might not happen at the same moment in time. In the same way, in cases of homicide, someone in the group that is held responsible for the homicide is killed. In heterosubstitution systems, by contrast, it is possible to trade material goods in exchange for a woman—most often pigs, or cowries—and the same goes for the dead. In this case, then, wealth may play a role in social exchanges, whereas in the other it cannot. In Amazonia, by contrast, homosubstitution is the only possible mechanism; there is no avenue for equivalence or compensation for humans in the form of material wealth. From that perspective, New Guinea is a remarkable conceptual laboratory for trying to understand how combinations of this kind can be articulated with one another and accompanied by different modes of identification.

This type of situation highlights one of the main functions of the model I am proposing: to understand the conditions of compatibility and incompatibility between various elements of the social world, that is, to understand why certain things are generally present together and others never. To return to the contrast between homosubstitution and heterosubstitution, we can surmise that the former is characteristic of animist systems in which the person, human or animal, forms a compact totality and is not diffracted and decomposable, as it is in analogist systems, where heterosubstitution is very commonly found. In the latter, then, pieces of a person can have a wealth equivalent and can symbolically circulate in different exchange networks, since each human is a composite in perpetual disequilibrium that is shared between groups. In this way, on the basis of our general knowledge about the kinds of institutions that are found in different contexts, the emergence of something new that was hitherto held to be incompatible with this context will help further our understanding. The overall logic that governs the coexistence and compatibility of institutions, ways of behaving, and representations will indeed be enriched when we can observe major and unexpected transformations. Lévi-Strauss had drawn a parallel

Forms of figuration 125

with the periodic table of chemical elements that does indeed give a sense of what, in my view, anthropology is all about: bringing to light the elementary components of the syntax of worlds and the rules that govern their combination.

Forms of figuration

PC   *You have recently put this combinatorial approach to the test on a particular type of cultural object, namely images—pictorial figurations of the world. How did this interest emerge, and how did it affect your initial model?*

PD   Previously I had mostly focused on discursive systems, and it seemed to me that I had to turn my attention to other types of socially shared phenomena. Images appeared to be an excellent resource, because they are to be found in nearly all human societies and generally are closely connected to the way the composition of the world operates. In addition, as I suggested in *Beyond Nature and Culture*, the modes of identification come first and then draw along behind them other registers of collective activity, such as the ones I have called "modes of relation," as well as particular relations to time, to the organization of space, and to figuration. To look briefly at the example of time—that is, to the objectivization of certain properties of duration that are based on different systems of computation, spatial analogies, cycles, cumulative sequences, and remembrance and deliberate forgetting—I have already discussed how, for the Achuar, the time of myth was singular and entailed a kind of amnesia around the immediate past and a flattening out of duration. And this conception is probably generalizable to other Amazonian animist communities. In addition (and I have not had a chance to discuss this point yet), it seems quite clear to me that each of the great modes of identification has a corresponding dominant model of the experience of time. Cyclical time, for instance, which Mircea Eliade called "the myth of the eternal return," is characteristic of many analogist communities throughout the world—in the Andes, in Mexico, in East Asia—and consists in an alternation between universal destruction and rebirth. In this temporal regime characterized by a succession of catastrophes and returns to precarious balance, the directional orientation of time typical of naturalism is of course inconceivable, such that there

126 *The Diversity of Natures*

cannot be cumulative improvement, progress, or historical destiny, since all the cards are reshuffled at regular intervals, each time a world collapses and then rebuilds itself.

But let us return to figuration, understood as the act through which real or imaginary objects are represented in two or three dimensions using some sort of material medium. It seemed to me a good way to test the validity of my hypotheses, and so I undertook to verify if the same kinds of contrasts I had brought to light in relation to modes of identification could be found in images. I initially proceeded rather naïvely, taking images as illustrations of modes of identification, and I sought to identify the figurative systems that may be typical of animism, totemism, analogism, and naturalism. I have since come to see that, even if there was perhaps no other way to proceed at first, this approach was far from ideal, as it tended to turn images into simple servants of a preexisting model that had to be confirmed, instead of taking them for what they are, namely configurations of signs and agents of social life endowed with considerable autonomy.

The first lead I followed to enrich this initial approach was to delineate several forms of pictorial representation within each of the cosmologies I had identified. By delving into the production of images in societies that seemed to typify one mode of identification or another and by immersing myself in their universe, I gradually became aware of the wide variety of forms that the mode in question could take within a single ontology. With regard to animism, for example, I chose to begin by looking at Amazonian images, since this was always my empirical starting point. And in that region of the world images are generally not iconic—they do not resemble the outside world as we perceive it. Indeed, rather than producing images of human and animal bodies that resemble their models, Amazonian Indians have sought to turn human bodies themselves into images, borrowing for that purpose patterns and attributes of animal bodies. In so doing, they appropriate for their own benefit the biological aptitudes of animals, and thus the effectiveness with which the latter make use of their environment. This appropriation takes two complementary forms. First, body ornaments made of animal parts—feathers, down, fangs, skins, bones, claws, beaks, elytrons, scales—characteristic of the form and aptitude specific to each species are added to, and thus enhance, the capabilities of human bodies. Following sound animist logic, the point is for humans to capture for their own benefit a fragment of the experience of the

Forms of figuration 127

world that other species have thanks to their particular physicality. But, second, humans borrow not only appendages from animals, they also borrow images from them, that is, patterns that adorn the bodies of the various species and that the Amerindians use to adorn their own bodies. For these patterns, which they see on the bodies of animals—spots, eyespots, stripes, scales—are thought to be perceived by fellow animals as body paint on humans, since the animals perceive themselves as human. And the humans, who want to be perceived by the animals as members of their community, do not paint the patterns as they perceive them, but as they think the animals themselves perceive them, that is, as distinctive signs adorning human bodies.

I then worked on the contrast between these forms of representation and those we encounter in northern North America, where there is the same attempt to combine human and animal qualities, which is one of the distinctive features of animism, albeit distinctive in a very different way. For there the effect is achieved through masks, in particular transformation masks, spectacular examples of which are found among the Kwakwaka'wakw (formerly known as the Kwakiutl) of British Columbia. Such masks are also widespread further north, among the Yupiit, who speak an Eskimo language. These are masks with movable flaps that can be pulled up or down, to reveal a human face behind the representation of an animal head. For the Amerindians, this representation of human traits does not designate humans as a specific species. It reflects instead the interiority of the soul, the fact that the animal is endowed with a subjectivity analogous to that of humans; and it is human traits that serve to figure that animal interiority. This kind of pictorial mechanism makes visible the double nature of the animal, who is endowed with both the body of its corresponding species— represented by the distinctive head of a bear, eagle, or crow, for example—and an interiority analogous to that of humans.

This type of material enabled me to provide experimental validation for my hypotheses, which I had the opportunity to present in an exhibition I organized in 2010 and 2011 at the Musée du Quai Branly in Paris under the title *La Fabrique des images* (*The Making of Images*). The exhibition was based on the conviction that the contrasts that I had brought to light between the various kinds of images and that appeared to me to correspond to differences between the various modes of identification should be put before the general public. If ways of figuring the world follow truly different models,

128   *The Diversity of Natures*

then this had to be perceptible to everyone, including those who are not art historians or specialists in ethnographic art. From this perspective, an exhibition highlighting these contrasts constituted a valuable test of whether I was being followed by the uninitiated. And the reactions I received, both through discussions with guides who conducted tours of the exhibition and by reading comments left in the visitors' books, gave me the impression that the general point had been understood.

Another form of experimental verification was supplied by images from vastly different regions of the world that I unexpectedly came across and that established the same correspondence between visual mechanisms and a common mode of identification. Let me take the example of the transformation masks of northern North America I just mentioned. Among the Yupiit, we find both the masks with moving flaps described a little earlier and masks with a lateral asymmetry that feature an animal half face on one side and a human half face on the other. By oscillating from one side to the other, one moves from the perspective of the animal's body, the visible "vestment" that bears the specific traits of its species, to the perspective of the animal's interiority, which is figured as a human face. This is the most economical way of representing metamorphosis, a process that characterizes animist ontologies. It turns out that I had identified, simply from ethnographic descriptions, typically animist traits among some of the native populations of Malaysia. But I had no idea what kind of images they produced, until I stumbled across a shaman mask of the Ma'Betisek of Malaysia at the house of my friend Maurice Bloch. He had received it from Wazir-Jahan Karim, a Malaysian anthropologist whose doctoral work he had supervised in London. This remarkable mask came as a pleasant surprise, since it featured a lateral asymmetry that was very similar to that of the Yupiit: a human face on one side, a tiger face on the other. It was displayed as part of the Quai Branly exhibition. One could thus find, at a distance of several thousand kilometers, animist figurations that used the same codes to represent metamorphosis.

Discoveries of this kind are a source of tremendous satisfaction, because they show that the fundamental characteristics of a mode of identification can be activated and made visible by two groups in a similar way, in the absence of any direct contact. This is also a method of fleshing out structuralist principles, since the continuities and discontinuities that appear in images are completely linked to rather simple logical possibilities, which are bound to

Forms of figuration 129

appear independently in different places. This came as something of a surprise to the art historians with whom I have discussed this phenomenon, since their discipline has long been essentially focused on artists' direct influence on one another and, more generally, on the study of the economic, political, philosophical, and, of course, aesthetic contexts in which images are produced. This approach, which is based on relations of historical and spatial proximity, makes it quite impossible to bring out relevant similarities and differences between, say, a Flemish painter and an Amerindian mask from the Northwest Coast. To do so, one must return to a more fundamental order of formal possibilities, which are both iconological and cosmological. Such an order has generally received little attention from art historians, with the possible exception of a few eccentric figures such as Aby Warburg and Aloïs Riegl.

Another dimension of images that is important from the anthropological perspective is their power to anticipate phenomena that may appear in discursive form only later. As I have already said, naturalism is a good case in point: its emergence is clearly manifest in images from the fifteenth century onward, whereas in discourse it surfaces only in the seventeenth. Indeed, these images openly express a desire to render the interiority of humans visible; they work especially on the gaze, on resemblance to the model, on the plausibility of the situation—and all this to underline the fact that what is being depicted is a singularity. The representation of people in medieval imagery is, by contrast, much more typological: those are generic human figures, while in a later period they become individualized. Art also expresses the desire to make tangible the organization of the objects of the world in a coherent space, structured according to geometric laws, which no longer has anything to do with the symbolic space of most medieval imagery. In the latter, for instance, the elements of the image would be placed according to their theological importance in a sacred scene, whereas in later forms of representation the laws of geometry gave each element its place and dimension within a purely mathematical frame of reference. In this precise case, images made visible an inflection in the composition of the world that was not yet visible elsewhere. I think naturalism was thus born in images before it propagated to other registers of thought and action. This transformation of visual culture that spread like wildfire through the illuminated manuscript and through painting workshops made apparent continuities and

130 *The Diversity of Natures*

discontinuities between beings that were subsequently picked up in philosophy, theology, and so on.

I believe that the unsettled quality of late naturalism in our contemporary world emerged with a similar abandonment of the visual codes through which it had expressed itself in art until the early twentieth century. A good example of this process is how radically the privileged status of man as a subject and of his relationship to universal material laws changed in visual culture. Philosophical thought has devoted a lot of attention to this issue, and one of the ways in which it has tested the validity of this frame of thought was to suggest, following biology, that the mind was but a property that emerges from matter. The soul, or subjectivity, or interiority would thus be not a thing in itself, endowed with a specific reality, but something reducible to a specific conformation of the physical body, which develops certain receptive capacities. This position has found many expressions, from the classical materialism of the eighteenth century to the contemporary philosophy of mind. And it has resulted in shaking one of the founding pillars of naturalism—the distinctive character of human interiority—even while consolidating the other: now everything is physical, everything is nature, the human mind included. I believe that images bear witness to a still earlier evolution in this direction and, in a sense, offer us a first experience of what the subordination of the subjective dimension of humans to their physical dimension may be like. What small groups of scholars imagined in philosophy, psychology, and biology was made conceivable through images—and, in my opinion, especially through seventeenth-century Dutch painting.

In genre painting of the Dutch golden age (as we call it), a form of genre art that represents the profane and sometimes even prosaic dimensions of daily life, the interiority of the persons represented has become largely undecipherable, in contrast with the efforts that were made earlier to convey it faithfully. This tradition is much studied by art historians, who have commented on the edifying virtues that these paintings were held to possess, but have not accounted for the often undecidable character of facial expressions on the figures and of the relationships between them. For the Quai Branly exhibition I used, as an example, a famous painting from the Louvre painted around 1652 by Gerard ter Borch and entitled *The Reading Lesson*. In it a young woman has a little boy—believed to be the artist's half-brother—read a book, probably the Bible. What is interesting is that they are together in the same scene and in a common endeavor,

Forms of figuration 131

yet seem very far from each other: the young woman appears to be thinking about something entirely different, and the little boy is looking at the book but he, too, seems to be elsewhere. This is a situation in which the individual singularity of the persons is erased in favor of a network of relations between them. In the paintings of Ter Borch, Dou, de Hooch, or Van Hoogstraten interiority plays only a secondary role and, rather than being the attribute of individuals that it used to be, it now emerges from their conjunctural interaction.

Gradually we see the emergence of images that are entirely focused on the depiction of movement and life. In the eighteenth century, Honoré Fragonard, a cousin of the famous artist, produced arresting anatomic reconstructions of the human body that highlight our physical dimension. Later still, thanks to the chronophotographic process, the physiologist Étienne-Jules Marey gave visual expression to the decomposition of movement—the clearest expression of life. Nearer to us, neuroimaging has brought this logic to its conclusion: by unveiling the physical structure of thought, it makes this setting aside of interiority its very objective. Of course, the value of these images does not lie in what is classically understood as their aesthetic or artistic dimension. But, for me, this is not an important criterion. This is precisely why I speak of images and figuration techniques, and not of "art." In my view, images make visible a reality that is not present, either because it does not appear immediately before our eyes or because it is difficult to represent it, to figure it. In the present case, these pictorial representations provide evidence of a gradual transformation of the relationships between the physical and mental dimensions of humans, a transformation that was also being expressed in other domains of our collective experience.

PC *With this shift from cosmologies to images, it is quite clear that your combinatorial approach, focusing as it does on the search for relations of continuity and discontinuity between beings, applies to a wide range of phenomena. Are there limits to the versatility of this method, and, if so, in what domains or in relation to what questions does the method come up against its limits?*

PD I am a confirmed empiricist, as opposed to what the sometimes slightly philosophical tone of my work might lead one to believe. This is therefore a question that can be answered only through inves-tigation, and only if we are wary of adopting an overly systematic mindset and are prepared to recognize, in every case we examine, evidence that confirms my hypotheses as well as evidence that invalidates them. Mercifully I am not alone in this endeavor. As I have already mentioned, young researchers have taken up these ideas in order to put them to the test, in a wide variety of domains. I pay attention to their work, whether it confirms or refutes my own. All I can say at this stage is that we need to be very careful with what could be called "conjectural" ontology, that is to say, with attributing an ontological regime to a community or to a type of practice on purely formal grounds. This is why, for instance, I have never taken as material for iconological analysis images on which I did not have reliable information as to the reasons why they were made, the meanings and effects they were endowed with, the way they were received, and the uses they were intended for. I have thus carefully avoided the minefield of prehistoric cave art. However, I do not exclude the possibility that the interpretations I have put forward regarding well-documented images can perhaps be extrapolated by others in a more speculative way, to interpret images we know nothing about.

4

The Contemporary World in the Light of Anthropology

We moderns

PC   *I would like to turn now to a dimension of your work that has implications for all the social sciences as well as for philosophy: the status that you have granted modernity and that you call naturalism. What is striking in your work is that, from the point of view of animism, we appear as a strange people, which has put in place a division of the world that has nothing intuitive about it.*

PD   As I have already said, the reflexive gaze onto our own social and cosmological specificities is, first and foremost, a function of an epistemological process. Insofar as anthropological reflexivity is accompanied by a reform of the concepts of the discipline, it also entails challenging the means by which Europe has thought about its own historical development, and then about that of the rest of the world. This can be achieved only by looking at the West as the particular expression of a system of objectivization of the world, and not as the model on the basis of which a scientific analysis of what is foreign to it can be carried out. From this point of view, achieving reflexivity is a movement within the discipline that is linked to the experience of fieldwork, but also to a desire to break out of the deadlock of political action, at least as I had envisaged it for a time in my youth. Yearning for the state to disappear thanks to the rise of a single party that would represent the common interest—which was the common horizon of all hues of communism—indeed proved a utopia, and a dangerous one at that. Against these kinds of considerations, the interconnected fates of the various peoples of the world and of the nonhumans with whom they are

134   *The Contemporary World in the Light of Anthropology*

assembled gradually appeared as a political emergency—and one that profoundly called into question our historical trajectory, which could be borne by anthropology.

I believe that the forms of emancipation that come from Enlightenment philosophy have played an important role by generating, in Europe, forms of living together that are increasingly acceptable to a large number of people on the surface of the earth. But these forms still seem to me to disqualify other ways of being present to the world and of creating community. They also seem to make it difficult, if not impossible, to better take into account the nonhumans in our political assemblages. From this point of view, making Europe and the western world into one particular case, one anthropological variation among others, is an invitation to refuse the idea that the aspirations and institutions that have developed in European democracies over the past two centuries and have subsequently spread to a good part of the planet represent the end of history. Indeed, one of the main characteristics of this political and institutional heritage is that it does not leave enough room for nonhumans in the processes of political representation and has inhibited other forms of political community, which are more open to those beings. I use the term "nonhuman" only for lack of a better one, and above all in order to avoid resorting to the concept of nature, but I believe that it is important to take the measure of the critical dimension of these nonhumans. And when I say "critical nonhumans" I am referring not only to farm animals, tigers, and whales but to the multitude of entities we are in constant interaction with, from CO_2 to glaciers, to viruses, and to bacteria. In the end, this is a way of talking about the common fate of things and people in a world where their separation no longer makes sense and where it behooves us to rethink their collective existence.

PC   *In discussing naturalism, you often make use of philosophy, that is to say, of a form of reflexivity applied to our spontaneous ontology, whereas for the other combinations you draw on forms of ordinary experience. Why did this shift seem necessary?*

PD   There is indeed a big gap between ritual systems, hunting practices, and kinship relations on the one hand and, on the other, scholarly expressions of thought such as in philosophy, theology, and law. But in fact I chose to proceed the way I do in order to make up for the gap in the relationship we have with traditions of thought, both our own and those of others. Indeed, the reflexivity we have long enjoyed using on Amazonian and Australian societies and on most African ones comes from the work of understanding and objectification carried out by outside observers, often anthropologists. This introduces a mediation through which things that, if presented in raw form, would not have been otherwise understandable become legible and make sense to us. There are linguistic reasons for this, of course, as well as formal ones, such as the fact that these forms of thought are often incorporated into acts, especially ritual acts, and do not abide by the canons of presentation of reflexive thought, which we are familiar with. If I were to talk about Achuar animism in a way that reproduces a purely Achuar perspective, I would have to confine myself to chants, magical incantations, dream narratives, and all kinds of things that, without interpretative mediation, do not make much sense for people who are not used to these discursive registers. But this is in fact the material from which I have constructed a reflexive perspective on Achuar animism, and one could say the same of the other civilizations I was referring to earlier.

Since in talking about Africa, Australia, Amazonia, North America, and Melanesia I used texts that were formulated in the idiom of western thought, I had to adopt the same perspective to render our own ontology. In other words I had to grasp it through the prism of the reflexivity produced by philosophy, the history of ideas, the history of science, and literary works. These are also attempts to give shape to a collective experience. To this must be added that, while for the Achuar I have at my disposal raw materials from which a reflexive vision can be extracted, as a simple subject whose own experience is configured by this way of composing the world I am immersed in naturalism. I did not conduct the sociological and anthropological fieldwork on the modern world that would have allowed me to maintain a scientific distance from it. What is more, the immense diversity of this world, as well as the enormous mass of information that circulates about it, makes it necessary for anyone who attempts to synthesize it to draw on reflexive operations that have already been done by others.

Some specialists in modernity, for example Bruno Latour, have reproached me for being elliptical in my presentation of naturalism— for either calling on the intuitive and implicit experience that we all have of this cosmology, and hence failing to develop its specific issues any further, or relying too much on the official version of it—as one may describe it—provided by philosophy, epistemology,

136   *The Contemporary World in the Light of Anthropology*

and the social sciences. There are two reasons for my proceeding in this way. First, I am addressing readers who are themselves from the naturalist world and who in consequence understand what I am referring to, however allusively, when I speak of naturalism. With regard to animism and totemism, on the other hand, only a handful of specialists know already what I am talking about, and I must therefore clarify in a much more thoroughgoing way the premises of the systems to which I refer. And then there is the fact that modernity is not my area of expertise and, as a result, I tend to see it through the lens of the cannons of my education. I believe that this constitutes a good illustration of the average understanding that a competent participant in the world of modernity may have of the way it operates. This average understanding is analogous to that which Achuar use in the world they interact with, and hence it is comparable to it. A path must be sought between the intuitive experience of competent participants and the scholarly formulations that interpret it; so this was a choice I made—to give equal treatment to all modes of identification.

PC   *Yet not all philosophers embody a perfect form of naturalism: while Descartes conceives of a typically modern dualism, others, for example Montaigne and Spinoza, seem to go against this trend. Does this mean that naturalism has a singular capacity to become aware of its own specificities, to examine and critique them?*

PD   Undoubtedly. I would even say that this is one of the essential characteristics of naturalism. I have tried to describe this kind of difference within each ontological regime, through the notion of "mode of relation." If each cosmology defines a general arrangement of existing beings, then the space of continuities and discontinuities between them and the relations that they knit with each other can take different forms. This means that within each ontology relations can be instituted in various ways, notably according to the relationships, hierarchical or not, that are established between beings beforehand. In most ontologies there is thus a unity in the way humans and nonhumans are treated; this unity gives a very distinct aspect to the ethos of a collective, yet it can take various forms. In the naturalist world various forms of relation coexist that give it its multicolored, reflexive, conflictual, and dialectical dimension. The coordinates of naturalism seem to enable a wide variety of perspectives, which generally clash with one another, since they rely on

We moderns 137

ascribing different values to beings. When I was working on these questions, I was inspired by the work of Luc Boltanski and Laurent Thévenot on the economies of worth. I see in this diversity an equivalent of what they called "polities," which represent different universes of reference characteristic of late naturalism.[1] Indeed, the constitutive division between what comes under nature and what comes under society introduces a kind of apartheid in the way the moderns deal with the beings of the world and prevents the implementation of a scheme of interaction that would have the same synthetic power and simplicity of expression as the relations that structure nonmodern collectives. If transmission does play a role, for instance in the worship of history and in the cult of commemorations and memorials, it does not have the same integrative power that characterizes it in analogist collectives, where the living owe nearly everything to their ancestors. The gift has almost entirely disappeared, except in intimate rituals or as atonement, through charity, for acquisitive greed. There is still exchange, of course, the basis of mercantile and then industrial capitalism; but, as Marx has taught us, it is completely rigged, and hence quite different from what it activates in many an animist collective, where, with its fussy concern for strict equivalence, it functions as the main motor of interactions between humans and nonhumans. In short, it is impossible for moderns to schematize their relationships with the diversity of existents through an all-encompassing relation.

In the other ontologies, the range of possibilities seems narrower. In animist collectives such as the Achuar, what is most striking is the unity of perspective. It has sometimes been suggested that in traditional societies there is an opposition between masculine and feminine universes on which a dissociation of representations of the world might be based. But I do not think that these oppositions acquire the same importance as they have here; nor do class differences and the associated forms of domination. In the analogist ontologies, perspectives may differ according to the specializations of distinct castes or crafts, as happens in India. But here, again, such differences have not reached the same proportions as in naturalism, where the diversity of conflictual conceptualizations is quite unique. Michel Serres wrote a very entertaining little book,[2] which offers a variation on the categories I have defined in *Beyond Nature and Culture*. He interprets the works of European writers, scholars, and philosophers as representative of such and such a particular mode of identification. As he demonstrates, this undertaking is entirely

138   *The Contemporary World in the Light of Anthropology*

feasible: in Leibniz, the proliferation of monads harmonized by a calculating God represents a reformulation of analogism into the categories of modern metaphysics; Spinoza's one substance corresponds to a radical monism, or to the version of naturalism that is achieved when the distinctive dimension of interiority in relation to physicality has been eliminated. The tradition of free debate, in which the fundamental terms that structure thought are subject to questioning, goes back to ancient Greece. Once scientific and political concepts were caught in a logical vice, as was the case in that context, philosophical systems emerged, all comparable to as many different mini-ontologies within larger cognitive schemes. This kind of intellectual and political configuration is rather exceptional in the history of humanity, even if similar situations did arise elsewhere.

I suspect that the roots of naturalism are to be found in the fertile ground of analogism, where indeed it sprouted on several occasions and in different places, but failed to ever reach maturity—that is, the age at which reproduction and dissemination become possible. Such is the case with the atomists of antiquity. For instance Democritus, whose radicality was unrivalled, eliminated all teleology, granting humans total autonomy amid a soulless and aimless nature reduced to being an arrangement of atoms governed by the principle of necessity. But this objective nature is a metaphysical construction, the condition of a demanding morality that leaves humans to their own devices in a disenchanted world. Classical atomism did not give rise to a physics; the rigor and fortitude of the soul that this uncompromising materialism required limited its implementation to a few sages, who were focused on self-mastery rather than on the propagation of a new cosmology. The same may also be said of certain Chinese thinkers, especially Wang Chong, who lived in the first century CE and has sometimes been compared to Lucian and Voltaire. He was a skeptic of fierce independence and consequently remained entirely marginal, a powerful mind that exposed the superstitions of his contemporaries. This caustic critic was more interested in mocking illusions and pretenses than in engaging in cosmological reform, which would have required founding a school and hence seeking the protection of the powers that be. Finally, even though this is a domain in which I am rather ignorant, it is likely that, between the ninth and fourteenth centuries, Arab philosophy and science paved the way for a shift to naturalism that was ultimately never completed. In other words, even if naturalism remained a mere potentiality in classical antiquity, in ancient China, and in medieval

We moderns 139

Islam, its realization would not have been completely incongruous in these three analogist configurations, whereas it is quite impossible to find even the slightest trace of it in animist and totemic collectives that are known to us thanks to ethnography.

PC *What role can be attributed to writing in bringing about these reflexive developments?*

PD Writing probably played a decisive role, but it should not be dissociated from other techniques of recording mnemonic traces. There are great analogist collectives, such as the Incas, who were nonliterate but developed very sophisticated systems of calculation and memorization, for example the famous *quipu*, in which strings of different colors attached to a rope and knotted in various ways were used to record numerical data. Writing is thus but one graphic technique for the expansion and maintenance of mental capacities, alongside pictographs, counting strings, notched tally sticks, and other such memory aids. And the link between these apparatuses and analogism is self-evident: in this ontology in which beings are diffracted into multiple singularities, one needed to connect them and forge interpretive paths. We know for instance that predicting the future played an important role in these collectives and was closely connected with the ability to associate material signs that were visible and manipulable with various elements of the world. From this point of view, graphic techniques not only fulfilled practical functions (the management of cattle, population, crops, trade, etc.) but also made possible the stabilization of singularities and the repeatability of the connections between them, as required for purposes of divination. And it took specialists—physicians, surveyors, soothsayers, accountants, geomancers, astrologists, fortune tellers, priests—to use these computation systems and to master these processes of memorization, recording, and information storage. These specialists, often organized in highly selective colleges, were motivated by a robust *esprit de corps* and openly competed for the patronage of laymen and the favor of the powerful. They were trained to observe and detect regularities and recurrences in the movements of planets and the appearance of meteors, in the symptoms of ailing bodies, in the behaviors of animals, and in the events of daily life. They could expand the network of connections through complex mechanisms such as equivalence and conversion tables, algorithms, and scale models. In short, it was in analogist

140   *The Contemporary World in the Light of Anthropology*

collectives and only in them that we could find the aptitudes, techniques, and institutional frameworks necessary for integrating and stabilizing the singularities that inhabited them—means that are quite clearly and directly echoed in the combination of aptitudes, techniques, and institutional frameworks necessary for the practice of science, as it flourished in Europe with the advent of naturalism.

Writing is surely one of the most effective means of achieving this kind of objective, especially as it allows for the perfecting and relaying of argumentative techniques that would perhaps not have evolved as rapidly, had they not been stabilized in this form. The major difficulty we have in assessing with any greater accuracy how much writing contributed to the development of these domains is that we do not know exactly how stable orally transmitted discourses remain over the long term, over several centuries. And the reasons are obvious; for we do not have old enough recordings of these discourses. Even if the hypothesis that writing constituted a rupture is reasonable, we know that, in the absence of written support, there are other mnemonic techniques, which are quite rich. For instance, the work of Frances Yates and Mary Carruthers on the "art of memory" has highlighted the central role, in educated circles in antiquity and the Renaissance, of mnemonic techniques based on establishing a correspondence between an imagined itinerary through space and bits of spoken language mentally placed along the way. The work of my colleague Carlo Severi on primitive pictographs has also revealed how these series of images, which are rough sketches of places and situations, in fact refer to key moments of an oral narrative and serve as an effective tool for marking mnemonic traces, being quite reminiscent of the art of memory. Far from constituting an unfinished form of writing, primitive pictographs are rather an alternative to it, a particular way of consolidating through images the relationship between memorized and spoken words. In short, the various computational and mnemonic techniques, including writing, together with the institution of colleges of specialists who pass on esoteric knowledge and compete with one another, probably contributed to the rise, in a few analogist collectives, of the reflexive dispositions you were referring to.

PC   *The founders of the social sciences have all sought ways to characterize the modern experience: Durkheim described the passage from mechanical to organic societies; for Weber, it was the disenchantment of the world—and so on. Where does your proposition fit within this panorama? And what is your relationship with these classic references?*

We moderns   141

PD   The great authors you cited broached the question of modernity straight away. In their view, modernity had to do with relatively recent and poorly described social innovations such as the emergence of capitalism, the role of the individual in society, the transformation of the state, and the like. And, under these conditions, they had to invent new approaches that could grasp the historical present. Even though both Weber and Durkheim also defined modernity from a comparative perspective, respectively via China and via Australia, it was in the first place what they had before their eyes that preoccupied them most. For me, it was the reverse, in that the definition of naturalism I propose is the result of a process of elimination. Naturalism emerged negatively, in contrast with other formulas: it was not problems within modernity that guided my thinking, but first of all the forms of existence of societies very different from ours. In a way, a blank square appeared in the combinatorics I had developed, and it became that of naturalism. This is also why I do not accord it the exact same treatment as the others, as I explained earlier—the notion I have of it is also informed by the experience I have had of this thought process.

But, if this formulation was initially peripheral to my work and almost unintended, I have nonetheless tried to develop certain aspects of it and to consider its possible implications by reading the history of science and philosophy as well as the history of images, political institutions, and law. This amounts to a potentially endless task, and it is therefore difficult to make it the central axis of one's work. But, for me, the main objective has been to understand the echoes that giving by default such a characterization of naturalism may have on the work of other authors. For instance, I recently read Carl Schmitt's *Nomos of the Earth*, after a long period of time during which I harbored strong reservations about this author, for obvious political reasons. It is a book on the relationship between modern legal conceptions and space, and on the impact of the great discoveries of the sixteenth century on the legal framework for the exercise of sovereignty in the territories of the great European empires. What struck me there was how much the law, and jurists as knowledgeable as Carl Schmitt, are saturated by a specifically western sense of the relationship with the land, even though the book was written at a time when an abundant ethnographic literature had become available. From that literature I became aware of the fact that our relationship with the land and with territory is quite exotic, even if most of us, like Carl Schmitt, think of it as more or less universal.

142   *The Contemporary World in the Light of Anthropology*

Lacking a conception of sovereignty that would bring the land under a clearly defined political authority, and in the absence of mappable frontiers, for instance with the enemy, the political space of Amazonian societies does not look anything like that of Europe. Readings of this sort thus elicit very interesting shifts and surprises, leading me to consider what I already know from a new angle and to marvel at things that used to be familiar. Yet, in spite of all this, I remain aware that work on the specificities of western modernity must be carried out by specialists and through empirical study.

PC   *In presenting naturalism within a combinatorial logical, there is a risk of freezing it in an eternal present. This intellectual and social configuration has, however, experienced numerous transformations and imposed itself over other elements, often in conflictual ways. How much importance do you give to the historical dimension of modernity?*

PD   The first thing to say is that it is difficult to define the kind of historical existence that is specific to naturalism. Indeed, this would require a comparative approach that placed it side by side with other similar forms of transitions, for instance by examining how an analogist collective has emerged from an animist base. Unfortunately, sources are lacking if we wish to document and track this process, as we have been able to do for the shift from analogism to naturalism. The other difficulty would be to avoid the pitfall of reducing the history of naturalism to a linear and intentional path from darkness to reason—which is in a sense a return to the thesis of a heroic modernity guided by science and definitively conquering the foundations of our common life, treating them as the laws of matter and life.

As for me, I have developed an interpretation according to which the elementary intuitions that characterize naturalism—humans' inner life makes humans exceptional in the world, but they relate to other beings in their physical dimension—are part of the basic equipment of humanity but, for historical reasons that remain to be specified, they were instituted and stabilized only once. We have good reason to think that this systematization began to take shape several times, in Greek, Chinese, and Indian philosophy, as well as in the Arab–Islamic world. The big question is why this embryonic systematization did not reach fruition. Why did the mechanism of its establishment, which would have made these ideas into the essential bearings of a society, become blocked at a certain point?

We moderns 143

We do know that, in a given historical context, several competing conceptualizations may coexist, but the logic that accounts for their relationship is more difficult to clarify.

Through my work on images I was led to look into the Arab–Islamic case, where a form of proto-naturalism began to surface in philosophy and is visible from the eleventh century to the thirteenth. It seems to me that one of the reasons that may explain why naturalism remained thwarted has to do with visual culture. In Europe, techniques for representing the world took off, in a way, from intellectual developments and, as Alain de Libera's work has shown, over the very long course of the Middle Ages they gradually led to the emergence of the thinking subject and individual human identity. Through the force of their immediacy, images have thus contributed to the spread of naturalist intuitions into the common culture. This was of course not the case in the Muslim world. Verifying this hypothesis is no easy task, of course, but it shows in any case that a study of the abortive germs of naturalism would be very instructive about how we have came to be modern and about the kinds of obstacles that had to be overcome. And one can say this without assuming any superiority in kind for this intellectual style over others.

The debate on the history of naturalism also recalls the amicable, engaging, and engaged exchanges I have had with Bruno Latour, for several years now. The discussion began around the importance of the idea of symmetry for us both, that is (even though the term has other meanings in his work) the necessity of introducing nonhumans onto the scene of social life other than as resources or external surroundings. From this perspective, doing symmetrical anthropology is not to explain the life of humans through the influence of nonhumans, but to appreciate the composition of a world in which both humans and nonhumans take part as actors—actants, Bruno Latour would say—with their own properties and modes of action, and therefore are, both, objects of equal interest to the social sciences. But we have our differences, too, as when Latour declared, in *We Have Never Been Modern*, that what I call "naturalism" has never actually existed because, despite what the moderns themselves have proclaimed, they never severed nature from culture. In his view, our world is peopled by hybrid beings, halfway between natural and social, and this is the reason why he denies any relevance to the division between science (which establishes indisputable facts) and politics (which regulates deliberation on uncertainty). I would

144   *The Contemporary World in the Light of Anthropology*

not define naturalism as a pure and simple separation of nature and culture; but I set great store by the intellectual and social consequences of the idea of a unification of phenomena under the concept of nature, an idea specific to the modern world. It seems to me that this transformation in intellectual orientation has had observable consequences in practical life, on the forms of access to nature that have characterized the industrial world. It is thus not just a figure of speech, as Latour claims, a justification that science has found in bad faith, in order to impose itself, and that epistemologists subsequently took at face value.

Our disagreement has not yet been settled, even though we have tried on several occasions at conferences; but I did notice that Bruno Latour now borrows the term "analogism" to define the earlier period, and thus implicitly admits that there is a demarcation between modernity and another historical stage that preceded it. The question then becomes: if we were analogists but never have been modern, then what are we now? Are we still naturalists, are we analogists who have become coherent, or do we live in a historical period where no single structuration of experience prevails? Even if I do not consider myself to be a specialist in naturalization, that is, in the "becoming naturalist" of the West, I continue to raise the question of the "becoming modern," of what is different between our experience and analogism. Naturally, these questions can find only empirical answers. Verification necessarily arises from the study of particular objects, which will determine whether the hypotheses I have put forward hold up in light of new material.

PC   *Beyond this disagreement, you and Bruno Latour are the main witnesses to, and thinkers of, a kind of exhaustion of naturalism. You suggest this yourself in* Beyond Nature and Culture, *where you discuss the present as an experience of the intellectual and political limits of the modern constitution. Would you say that we are facing a historic impasse?*

PD   We may indeed be facing an impasse, or at least a semi-impasse, if I may put it this way. The problem here is that we need to make a clear distinction between the normative judgment that this kind of expression implies and a simple statement of what can be observed. On the one hand, we could give credit to Latour and recognize in the division between nature and society a vestige of our intellectual

We moderns   145

history that is of use only in philosophical dissertations. From this point of view, the foundation of our modern constitution, to use Latour's terminology, has collapsed and given way to an increasing interpenetration of natural and social phenomena, conventions and physical processes, especially through science and technology. We have thus been led to use combined expressions such as "socio-technical," to account for the networking of things that used to be opposed and to escape the trap of the ready-made categories of modern thought. The compromise that led to a division between specialists in the social and specialists in the natural has thus exhausted itself, and this is precisely what makes possible work such as ours.

I do believe that we must take the full measure of the historical transition that such a dissolution of the classic duality implies. The notion of nature gave us a remarkably powerful tool, which encompassed a large number of cardinal conceptual oppositions. This is what Heidegger meant when he wrote that the notion of nature was the foundation of the modern world. It was in his view the central reference, the standard that defined all the fields of knowledge and human practice—history, art, society, religion were in fact, all of them, thought in contradistinction with nature.[3] I agree with him when he said that it was on this notion that the cogency of modern concepts was based and that, if we were to make it disappear, many of the elements of that modernity would dissolve. This is actually what we are witnessing, insofar as that notion does not account in a relevant way for the arrangement of beings that surround us and for the relationships between the major fields of knowledge and collective life. For instance, the autonomy of the moral and social spheres comes under pressure from increasingly physicalist positions, but I doubt that our mode of identification could be entirely reconfigured through such processes, for the intuition of a persistently autonomous interiority is enduring among most moderns. One could be the most confirmed materialist and yet find it difficult not to experience our reflexive consciousness and our imagination as manifestations of a "mind" that is both specific to each of us and specifically human. What seems more likely to me is that we will experience an increasingly radical divorce between the naturalist mode of identification and its constitution, or the ontology that results from it—between the spontaneous inferences we make about beings and their relations, on the one hand, and, on the other, the way these very beings are composed in the public

146   *The Contemporary World in the Light of Anthropology*

sphere, the way they are taken charge of by objective institutions and political processes. Insofar as the ontology in which we are evolving is no longer in keeping with our common experience, the productive apparatus of this ontology, which is its mode of identification, will necessarily be affected.

We are then left to wonder whether a new constitution can really appear and stabilize around a mode of identification whose development is necessarily slower and more uncertain. I believe that this is not impossible and may take the form of a shift toward the extreme possibilities of naturalism. We can thus imagine a system in which interiority is no longer conceived of as one single block, as the distinctive property of a being that is radically different from others. On the contrary, an evanescent and pluralized interiority would be distributed across all things, while physicality would remain universal, in a way that is reminiscent of what can be observed in analogism. That new analogism would thus be characterized by the diffraction of the value that used to be placed on human interiority and its dispersal over a broader and more open range of beings, one that includes nonhumans but where the scientific method based on universal laws of matter remains valid.

Such a transformation opens up a horizon of hope, as it allows us not to feel locked into a self-enclosed naturalism, limited to possibilities that have already been realized in history. And, since it seems highly improbable that we return to animism or totemism, which are now profoundly incompatible with irreversible elements in our society (if only at a material level), the development of a new analogism looks to me both more probable and more desirable: it is the most capable mode of including nonhumans into our sociopolitical constitution. It will probably be necessary to invent novel forms of coupling between beings, since the most common and effective form found in large analogist collectives—be it the Indian caste system or the system of orders of the *ancien régime*—is hierarchy, which is no longer tolerable in a world that has known the emancipation of the Enlightenment.

PC   *You have very much insisted on the importance of paying attention to compatibilities and incompatibilities between social worlds. From this point of view, a question arises concerning naturalism. Does its specificity not lie in being compatible with all the other ontological formulas, which makes it able to absorb them, to accommodate them even as it exerts its own logic?*

PD   I do not think in any way that collectives are imprisoned each in its own mode of identification and that they exist as closed worlds. Quite the opposite: they are permeable—but permeability is possible only up to a point. Nowadays shamanism holds a fascination for a part of the western population and it is easy to take online courses in shamanism and participate in New Age rituals in the forest of Saint-Germain in a Parisian suburb. But this does not mean that naturalism has fully assimilated animism or analogism. For, in the examples I cite, we are dealing with forms emptied of content, where only the most superficial elements of these cosmological systems are being retained. From this point of view, I am not sure that there is a profound effect on the current reorganization of naturalism: in the end, only what is most compatible with the preexisting system is being absorbed.

But in some cases the tension between two ontologies reaches a level beyond which only two possibilities remain: either the process of absorption stops or the system topples. In *Beyond Nature and Culture* I gave a few very interesting examples of absorption provided by the process of evangelization. What is quite striking, when you look further into this phenomenon in the Americas, is that it took quite different forms—in the analogist worlds of Mexico and the Andes on the one hand and in the animist worlds of the Amerindians of Amazonia, the Gran Chaco, and North America on the other. In the Andes and Mexico, at the time of the conquest, the Spaniards encountered worlds endowed with technical systems that were quite different from their own but not totally remote from an ideological point of view. Contrary to what is often said, there were noticeable continuities between the world of Europeans at that time and the great empires of Central and Andean America; and the Spanish chroniclers did not fail to pick up on them. If they were shocked by human sacrifice and polytheism, they were also quite ready to recognize certain dimensions of social life that they were familiar with, such as the presence of astrologers, calendars, and priests, or systems of thought such as humoral medicine and the doctrine of signatures. At the same time, nothing made sense anymore in the lowlands of the animist worlds where the conquistadors and missionaries ventured; there Christianization proceeded in fits and starts, much to the chagrin of the clergy, whose members could not figure out what earned them sudden conversions and what prompted just as sudden rejections of the Christian faith. The Indians could conform for a while

148   *The Contemporary World in the Light of Anthropology*

to the model the missionaries expected of them, then gave up on it when it was no longer compatible with the pursuit of their normal activities—a pattern of behavior that continues to the present day and that I myself witnessed with the Achuar in the 1990s regarding evangelical Protestantism. The problem was not the sincerity of their faith, but an incompatibility between different registers of action. One can point to many similar examples, such as that of Jesuits at the Chinese imperial court. As in the Andes and Mexico, there were quite a few common points between European Jesuits and Chinese scholars, steeped as they all were in analogist cosmologies, and this enabled a lasting acclimation to western thought in China—and vice versa. But, upon arrival in South America, these very Jesuits were completely at a loss when it came to converting the Tupinamba or the Jivaro. In other words, naturalism's mechanisms of absorption of systems of thought that are very different from it must be taken with caution. We often imagine naturalism, lazily, as a linear and uniform process of globalization under the guidance of the western world and its representations, but this is often overly superficial.

PC   *Do these reflections lead to a nuancing of the idea of a global hegemony of naturalism, and to a conception of cultural innovation made possible by compatibilities and incompatibilities?*

PD   As an anthropologist, I have a mental repository that makes available to me a very broad diversity of cultures and systems of thought, and I am naturally inclined to deplore any erosion of this diversity. This problem is very real: most of the systems studied by anthropologists in the twentieth century have now disappeared or no longer exist in the same form, and this includes the Achuar. Indeed, with each of the four generations of anthropologists that have succeeded one another since ethnographic fieldwork became the norm, the concern has been voiced that in future years nobody would be able to see what they had observed. This is both true— the pace of change, especially in the material conditions of life, has considerably accelerated in the past sixty years—and untrue, because significant elements remain that anthropologists of subsequent generations have had no trouble identifying. But, generally speaking, a background in anthropology makes one particularly sensitive to the loss of these philosophical treasures, which represent so many utopias for those of us who do not experience them directly.

One must nonetheless abstract from this knowledge, at least provisionally, and examine what is actually happening in situations of cultural hybridization. It then becomes clear that entirely new phenomena of coupling and assembling take place between elements that did not seem compatible at first glance. The expansion of certain western cultural and ideological traits—such as Christianity, as I just mentioned, or individualist morality, or the profit incentive—have provoked all kinds of reactions at the local level that are, all, relevant phenomena from the anthropological perspective, as they enable us to broaden the way we think about the conditions of agreement between worlds.

In some cases we find a re-creation of elements borrowed from the modern world that are made partially compatible with preexisting conceptions and practices. This can lead afterwards to quite bizarre syncretisms. Melanesian "cargo cults" is one of the classic cases in point: a set of ritual practices developed by local prophets to capture the material wealth of the Whites. The sudden influx of manufactured goods, and especially of military supplies and equipment unloaded from the planes and boats of the warring parties during World War II, had caught in particular the attention of the Melanesians, who saw in it an attempt by Whites to appropriate the gifts that local gods had originally intended for the native inhabitants. The cargo cult was an attempt to highjack these flows, mostly by replicating the infrastructure through which the goods were transported—landing strips, wharfs, warehouses, radios. The objective was not so much to accumulate coveted merchandise as to reestablish relations of equality with Whites. For the ostentatious gift of riches is a central element of political prestige in Melanesia, where such prestige often rests on the incapacity of those who receive the gift to give equivalent gifts in return. The Melanesians as a whole had been placed in a subordinate position, and the cargo cult was an attempt to escape the humiliation of a one-way flow of riches. In other examples elsewhere, we encounter a form of cultural misunderstanding presiding over the adoption of foreign traits. Certain external signs of a foreign tradition are adopted, while the domestic framework in which they are reformulated remains intact—as in the cases of western shamanism and the evangelization of Andean societies that I just mentioned.

What we should retain from these moments of hybridization and their complex character is that the model of globalization that we have is completely inadequate. There is no simple spreading

150   *The Contemporary World in the Light of Anthropology*

outward from the hubs that London, Paris, and Berlin once were, or that New York, San Francisco, and Singapore are now. This process is polycentric, and the diffusion does not proceed from a "center" to a global periphery, in a state of cultural passivity. This is due to the fact that such disseminations take place through all sorts of local mechanisms, and even the extreme case of the disappearance of a culture does not leave behind an unchanged global situation, where the cultural universe remains essentially the same, minus one element. For example, in Latin America we perceive, at a very general level, a certain cultural homogeneity. However, this obscures the emergence of local and regional cultures, which are less visible on account of their smaller scale. These regional cultures are the product of a complex history, which combines various reactions to the experience of colonialism and various contributions from rather different traditions, depending on whether one is in the Brazilian Nordeste, in the Argentinian Chaco, or in Quito. Thus the institutions, music, values, attitudes, and types of interpersonal relations of any one of these cultures can take over and spread beyond their initial locations—generally towns, both small and large—to the surrounding hinterland. In this dynamic, the more peripheral populations, such as the Achuar, are not immediately transformed into Los Angeles suburbanites but turn rather gradually into inhabitants of the rural Ecuadorian world, a population that is as opaque to a Parisian as the Achuar. Thus, between the global and the tribal levels, which are the two extremes of classic anthropological thinking, multiple and distinct regional identities gradually develop.[4]

PC   *In* Beyond Nature and Culture *naturalism seems to be uniformly embodied in each individual, as a representation that is equally shared by all. But do you think that we could posit that, on the basis of class or position in the social world, naturalist beliefs may be unevenly distributed? Or that we do not all adhere in the same way to these beliefs?*

PD   It is likely that this kind of logic is at work in the construction of ontologies, but it goes largely undetected in the social sciences, which are sciences of relatively standardized individuals, amalgamated into a multitude. And this is true even of anthropology and history, even though, among all these sciences, these are the ones most attuned to individual particularities. Among the Achuar I found a certain

We moderns 151

variation in the degree of adhesion to typically animist conceptions. When I ask people about the spirits of game animals, I would generally receive rather clear answers regarding the existence of such entities. The characters mentioned in the *anent* were described in detail, the circumstances of the encounter were recounted, and thus these accounts seemed to have a considerable degree of cognitive consistency. But I also met someone whom we might call agnostic, who refused to say whether they actually existed. And, in any case, he did not seem very much interested in the question. He was a sort of proto naturalist, an iconoclast.

However, the homogeneity of belief is of course very strong in these kinds of contexts. In the West, social and intellectual competition between different classes and the unequal distribution of symbolic and cultural capital have given rise to a wide variety of positions. I have indeed constructed an average person that is emblematic of the typical inferences of this ontology, but this is a function of the level of generality that we are dealing with in anthropology. This figure would likely become less and less credible as our attention to detail increased. But I remain convinced that, if we were to carry out a statistical inquiry, most of the answers provided to a questionnaire on the basic elements of naturalism would reflect the premises I have described. The basic intuitions of the modes of identification are universal, but their systematization is not. Speaking to your cat qualifies as an animist intuition but does not make you an animist; reading your horoscope is a typically analogist impulse but does not make you an analogist.

PC   *But this variety within naturalism does raise questions about the process through which it has been systematized. And one of the questions it raises would be, quite simply, who were the first bearers of naturalism and how did they manage to impose these views on others?*

PD   I concede that I have not given much thought to these important questions in my work. Perhaps they have as much to do with historical sociology in the style of Norbert Elias as with anthropology, but either way they raise the issue of the mechanisms of circulation and stabilization of a mode of identification, and also the issue of the first bearers of these views. I think I see rather clearly how it works in collectives of the kind I have studied, such as the Achuar. In these situations, individuals are steeped in a world whose cosmological bearings are never inculcated in any formal or explicit

152   *The Contemporary World in the Light of Anthropology*

way. There is no schooling, but a vast amount of information is gleaned daily, and rites, major and minor, do the work of teaching schemas of thought and action. Rites, and especially initiation rites, bring forth intense emotions, often fear, and almost always pain and deprivation to sear into the flesh behavioral schemas that often present in condensed form the prototypical attitudes prescribed by the collective. This is a form of stabilization and diffusion that is quite characteristic of traditional societies. The other model that is also found in collectives where there is no formal education is one of recurrent narrative schemes, which are heard over and over from a young age. These narratives create expectations from children—so that, when they are confronted for the first time with situations that adults have talked about, they already have at their disposal a normative model of behavior and interpretation, even without necessarily being aware that they follow some established rule. This is what happens with spirits in Amazonia. Rarely spotted during waking moments, they tend to be detected only through discreet signs of an unexpected presence in the forest: a surprising sound, a gust of wind, a vague shape glimpsed in the vegetation, a strange eddy in the river. There are plenty of stories of these encounters, and they generally follow the same narrative code as the hunting stories that men tell upon returning in the evening. And when a child who has regularly been exposed to such stories is then confronted with occurrences of the same kind, that child is of course likely to interpret the latter in the same way.

Our naturalist collectives are more complex and feature many more mediations between ordinary individuals and the prescribers of normality. For several centuries, the main producers and intermediaries of dominant paradigms have been scholars and teachers, as well as the clergy. There is thus a category of the population whose speech is exalted and whose role is to transmit models of thought and behavior through repetition. This model is now in crisis as a result of the dispersal of information and public speech on the Internet, but I am not sure the proliferation of sources will lead to a plurality of interpretive models as long as the quasi-viral process of imitation leads to confirming rather than questioning ontological normativity. Conspiracy theories, rumors, and rage against the technostructure have no trouble accommodating naturalism. If you look at ancient Greece, where the initial ferment of our naturalism first emerged, you will see that scholarly conceptions of nature developed in the very enclosed world of philosophers—'physicists',

We moderns 153

as they called themselves—and doctors. As Geoffrey Lloyd has shown, the Eleatic school of thought—which was the first, around the fourth century, to try to identify regularities specific to the physical world—only involved a very small minority of people.[5] And indeed, the assertion that phenomena could be explained other than in terms of the whims of gods was a provocative claim that could not be held as true by the majority.

That period, during which the most resolutely naturalist conceptions were minority positions limited to highly specialized social circles, lasted for a very long time. Similarly, when I speak of the advent of naturalism through images in the fifteenth century and its stabilization in scientific discourse in the seventeenth, as well as of the emergence, in the nineteenth, of an explicit opposition between nature and culture that would come to organize the division of knowledge, I am necessarily referring to the practices of a small minority. At the other end of the spectrum, studies have also been conducted on the mass of the population, the world of peasants, and then of industrial workers. When you read, for instance, the work of Le Roy Ladurie on the peasants of the Languedoc region before the French Revolution, or that of Daniel Roche on the population of Paris under the *ancien régime*, you quickly understand that in many ways they were not terribly naturalist.[6] But what is still lacking is more fine-grained studies of the interchanges between populations, between the social categories that bear highly naturalist representations and uses and others. How was it that the peasant of the Languedoc was naturalist in certain circumstances? Under whose influence? And to what end? This would be a social history of the circulation of naturalism and of the political logic that governs it.

One possible approach to this kind of research might be the epidemiological model of representations developed by Dan Sperber.[7] It is part of a broader materialist conception of culture that he has developed in his work, which consists in tracking, at a granular scale, the mechanisms through which elementary ideas are replicated and passed on from one consciousness to another. He adopts a Darwinian conception of selection that he applies to ideas, to show that they reproduce and spread by respecting a number of constraints linked to the social milieu that makes them more or less germane. Of course, this model has elicited many objections, the main one being the identification of elementary units of information, but I believe it can contribute to shedding light on the phenomenon of diffusion of

154   *The Contemporary World in the Light of Anthropology*

representations and on the way they are stabilized as shared norms of thought.

From anthropology to ecology

PC   *Another specificity of naturalism is its capacity to transform the material environment in incomparably deeper ways than any of the other ontologies. Indeed, the impact that the modern world has had on the environment since the Industrial Revolution appears irreversible, as well as defining of our historical condition. How much importance do you give to this?*

PD   The material history of societies is of the utmost importance, and I think there are two possible ways of thinking about it. On the one hand, one can look at the modes of ecological transformation induced by nonmodern societies and their unintended, sometimes catastrophic, consequences. In *Collapse*, the geographer and ecologist Jared Diamond gives considerable importance to cases of environmental degradation that are in fact rather exceptional in the history of humanity, at least until now, such as the Easter Island example.[8] He has shown that key resources in highly circumscribed and fragile ecosystems can become completely exhausted, which poses a real threat to the simple material reproduction of human life. But such examples do not help us think about the environmental dynamic of traditional societies in general. On the other hand, we can consider how traditional societies have sometimes shaped their environments in ways that are less visible. As I have already mentioned, my work on the Achuar, alongside the work of other researchers, has revealed how the Amazonian rainforest is in part the product of several millennia of plant management by Amerindian populations. Their practices have shaped the forest as we know it today, and one could say that they have had a beneficial effect, even if, once again, that was unintended. Indeed, the Amerindians have managed to preserve, over time, a high degree of biodiversity, even while increasing the number and distribution of forest species that are useful for human subsistence. There are numerous examples of this kind, as traditional agricultural practices, including those much closer to us, often demonstrate forms of environmental caution that have withstood the test of time. In other words, in these circumstances the use of nature does not conflict with its

From anthropology to ecology   155

conservation—and it is not true that humanity, in itself, is toxic for the planet.

The difference, when it comes to the modern world, is essentially that the unintended effects of our use of nature are such that they imperil the equilibria of ecosystems of which we are a part. The concept of equilibrium should be used carefully, however, because ecological science now deems natural milieux to be not stable and homeostatic but rather characterized by dynamics of instability. Yet the fact remains that its opposite—the idea of ecosystemic disequilibrium—aptly describes the processes of irreversible environmental damage at work. What is threatened, in the end, is the ability of the environment to reproduce itself and to preserve its own dynamic—what experts call resilience. And this is tragic for humanity. It is quite striking, when you look at these phenomena, that, despite the increasingly strident warnings of scientists and the rare politician, we seem incapable of grasping the risk until after the fact. Only once the effects of this damage have become tangible, only once they are impacting our interests directly, do we come to realize their irreversible character; we begin to take their causes into account only once this threshold has been crossed. This lag may well be a feature of human nature, but it is nonetheless a cause for concern.

I remember that, when I was in the Ecuadorian Amazon in the 1970s, the indigenous organization of the Shuar, the Achuar's neighbors who are also part of the Aénts Chicham language group, had decided to endorse extensive cattle raising. There were short-term advantages to doing this: at the time, Ecuadorian law granted concessions of forest land to families and villages, on the condition that two thirds of the area be put to productive use. To all appearances, this provision was in the Shuar's interest: they could thus become owners of the land they had been occupying for several centuries and that had hitherto been considered *terra nullius*—land without any recognized legal title. But to develop these lands, to satisfy the legal obligations attached to these lands, and thus to obtain the financial resources that would enable the community to participate in the market economy and to finance the activities of the indigenous organization, the Shuar proceeded to clear the forest over most of the tract and to plant it with hardy grasses for grazing cattle. Soon enough, the fragile soil of that region of the Amazonian basin was severely damaged by trampling cattle, strong sun, and intense leaching from the rain and the ecological error of this conversion of forest into pastureland became apparent. The local climate began

156   *The Contemporary World in the Light of Anthropology*

to change, endangering the life of all those concerned. Forests do play an important role in stabilizing the level of moisture in the atmosphere, and thus in regulating rainfall. As in all the places where this kind of transformation was undertaken, periods of drought followed, average temperatures rose, game animals disappeared, and traditional hunting and horticulture practices became impossible to maintain. In short, an equatorial piedmont rainforest with a high degree of biodiversity was turned into a biologically impoverished dry savannah. In the face of these upheavals, which resulted from the disappearance of the climate-regulating forest, the local populations eventually reacted. But they did so only thirty years later, once their very survival had been profoundly and irreversibly threatened. Yet, in the 1970s, I held conferences with the leaders of the Shuar indigenous organization in which I warned them about the social and ecological consequences of this decision to clear extensive pasturelands—consequences with which I was familiar because similar situations had already arisen elsewhere. The Shuar listened politely to my arguments but seemed to have no other option but to follow the route of deforestation, since their priority was to gain ownership of their land. This story goes to show that, so long as we have not directly experienced the negative impact of the environmental transformations we induce, it is very difficult for us to project ourselves into the future, which we always perceive as uncertain and whose tragic character we unconsciously try to deny.

We are in a very similar situation today with the Intergovernmental Panel on Climate Change (IPCC) projections, but on a global scale now. Even if we can imagine some of the effects of an increase of three, four, or five degrees in average temperatures on earth by the end of this century, nobody has really grasped the actual consequences of these transformations at a local and empirical level—except in the most extreme examples, such as the submersion of islands and coastal lands. Add to this the naïve and Promethean belief, which the moderns have ceaselessly nourished, that the negative impact of massive environmental transformations can be effectively managed through technological innovations that will correct the perverse effects of previous technological innovations. I am thinking here of geoengineering projects, most of them completely mad, whose unforeseeable effects on the delicate climate machinery could prove more harmful than global warming itself. This is the default mode in which we respond to crises in the modern context, intoxicated as we are with the idea of linear progress and salvation through science;

From anthropology to ecology   157

but today, in the age of the Anthropocene, there are good reasons to doubt the soundness of this reflex.

PC *More radically, are we not forced to admit that naturalism is, in and of itself, incompatible with ecological exigencies because it is incapable of making nature a political issue?*

PD We could say that the conceptual split between nature and culture has led us to conceive of our surrounding environment as nothing but a repository of resources to allocate, appropriate, and exploit, and hence as not a matter of real social concern. But we must also admit that, within naturalist categories, nature has often been conceptualized as a political issue. Indeed, it is enough to think how things external to us—plants, animals, rocks, the climate— determine in part our conditions of existence and, as such, must be factored into the management of human affairs. This is how political ecology has for the most part developed: as a form of management of the environmental externalities of social life that has perpetuated, to a considerable extent, the split between humans and nonhumans. On the contrary, the shift we must now make is toward conceiving of the fates of humans and nonhumans as intrinsically intertwined. The idea of nature has for some time enabled the expression of all kinds of confused aspirations and unspoken projects, and this is the reason why ecology was first conceived of as a project designed to save nature, or to conserve it—a project that consisted simply in ascribing value to something that previously had none. But, notwithstanding the tactical utility of the idea of nature, I believe that it is necessary to insist that this notion has had its day and that we must now try to think without it and imagine institutions that would facilitate the coupling of humans and nonhumans—in order to govern the life of all beings in the same terms.

This may sound a little abstract, but the main point is to stop conceiving of societies as *sui generis* entities, situated in an environment to which they must adapt and that they must shape and transform in order to acquire an identity and a historical destiny. Yet this model is still predominant in our representation of political action. We must therefore insist on the idea that humans are not ingenious demiurges who find fulfilment in work and in transforming nature into resources; what must come first instead is the fragile environments in which humans and nonhumans coexist and in which the realization of the good life for the former

158   *The Contemporary World in the Light of Anthropology*

very largely depends on their interactions with the latter. In other words, the unit through which we should apprehend political life, in my view, can no longer be the society or the nation—no longer a territory circumscribed by state or tribal borders. This model, based on classical theories of sovereignty, must be replaced by a fabric of ecosystems and contexts of life, both urban and rural, interdependent and partly autonomous. And within these spaces complex interactions occur involving exchanges of energy and information that must be conducted as deftly as possible, such that the perpetuation of human life also entails a better consideration of humans' contacts with nonhumans. For the most part, this requires a displacement of the objects that have been traditionally defined as "political"; it also asks us to put our legal, political, economic, and administrative categories to the test of that transformation, since, having been passed on to us through tradition, these categories are inadequate to the task of thinking and organizing the new interactions. There is therefore a considerable amount of work to be done to imagine new governance instruments for all the component parts of worlds, so that citizens who are drawn to public action can make these new instruments acceptable by debating them within communities.

This undertaking is all the more colossal as there is no way one can carry it out in an abstract and universal manner, as Rousseau, Montesquieu, or Adam Smith attempted to do in their day. Let me take an example that gives you an idea of the possible shape of this task of transforming the instruments with which we think of our political interaction with nonhumans—and it is an example that brings us back to South America. We witness today, in the Andean region, an intensification of protests made by native movements against mining projects. These protests are, of course, motivated in part by people's desire to preserve their conditions of daily life and to protect themselves from the risk of pollution and territorial dispossession—in other words, the protests have classic practical reasons. But, more importantly, they are also driven by a reaction to the endangering of some nonhuman entity or other—a lake, a mountain, a river, a cave, a catchment area—which is considered a member of the collective. In the native Andean world, according to the analogist logic that still informs it, these components of the landscape play an essential role in people's conception of social membership. They are full-fledged members of a collective that is much larger than the human community and whose well-being will

From anthropology to ecology 159

impact that of others. It is very difficult to understand this kind of concern and to translate it into our conception of politics, since it breaks from the legal frameworks that we are familiar with and that have also characterized the Bolivarian constitutions of South American nations. The latter are inheritors of liberalism, possessive individualism, and the values of the French Revolution and the Enlightenment, none of which of course takes into account that Andean collectives are made up of a very large number of human and nonhuman elements that must cohabitate and collaborate with one another.

How are we to respond to this kind of political claim? How is the legal and political system to be reconceived in order to satisfy this kind of demand? Ecuador has demonstrated a certain capacity for political innovation when it stipulated, in the preamble to the new constitution adopted in 2008, that nature as such had rights. But there is reason to suspect that this will unfortunately remain a mere declaration of intent. Even though it is very interesting from a legal point of view, the constitution does not really guarantee this promise, for lack of a way to define the rights of nature other than by the standard procedure of having its interests represented by human groups. While these political claims I was referring to do not demand that nature be represented, they emanate from a collective that makes the case that one of its members has been maltreated, which affects the balance between components and, ultimately, the well-being of all. This is a far cry from environmental protection organizations fighting for the protection of a rare species or an endangered site in the name of the abstract principle of the preservation of biodiversity.

Another example would be what we inappropriately call the "sacred sites" in Australia. These are places where, according to totemist cosmology, a long time ago the totemic prototypes sowed the seeds that promoted the existence and individuation of the human and nonhuman members of the totemic group associated with that site. The destruction of such a site is obviously a disaster for Aborigines, not because it is "sacred" in the sense that the religions of the book have given this word, but rather because it is, quite literally, vital. Not long ago, for instance, an Australian mining company was condemned for causing the collapse of a rock formation at Booty Creek, in the Northern Territory. The courts recognized that this pile of rocks was a "sacred site" that belonged to the Kunapa clan and was known by the name of Two Women Sitting Down—a reference to two totemic female prototypes that

160   *The Contemporary World in the Light of Anthropology*

are said to have fought over food in this place. The Aborigines nonetheless protested against the low amount of the fine imposed on the company; they did so on the grounds that, since the site had been destroyed, the people of the Kunapa clan had fallen ill and died. This shows that the disappearance of Two Women Sitting Down has little to do with what might result from the destruction of sacred sites such as the Cathedral of Notre-Dame in Paris or of the cave of Our Lady of Lourdes—which would be traumatic enough, to be sure, but would not cause the immediate death of the faithful. For what is destroyed along with a totemic site is not merely a place for occasional ceremonies but what could be called an "ontological incubator," a place where the identities of the members of a collective, the common roots of a group of humans and nonhumans, are concretely formed. These are not only locations that symbolize the presence of meta-persons but the principle of their very existence and of their vital relationship with an actual community. Yet when the Aboriginal populations defend these sites they make the argument that they are "sacred sites," because this is a meaningful category in our system, which can be received in court.

Giving voice to these complex assemblages of humans and nonhumans in institutions that are deeply anchored in western religious and legal traditions is, indeed, a very difficult task, which will require considerable conceptual effort on our part. This is probably comparable to the efforts of nineteenth-century socialist thinkers when they sought to redefine radically the traditional political categories they inherited. In both cases, the objective is to move beyond categories that initially enabled a form of emancipation, linked to the Enlightenment and the French Revolution, in order to achieve another form of emancipation, commensurate with the assemblages of humans and nonhumans that constitute different worlds.

PC   *At the beginning of our interview, you explained that the Achuar do not exhaustively exploit the natural capacities of their environment, that they keep themselves in a kind of state of deliberate underdevelopment. One of the main reasons for this, in your view, is that, for them, there are symbolic barriers to the exploitation of nature. Do you believe we moderns should also erect such symbolic barriers?*

PD   This would mean, to use our traditional terms, that we need to develop a new religion. When we speak of "symbolic barriers,"

From anthropology to ecology   161

we have in mind taboos, the constitution of a sacred domain in contrast with a profane one. Of course, such oppositions are not at all operative in the societies I have studied, but this is the easiest way for us to understand it.

The main difficulty with this proposition is that the reasons for the deliberate underdevelopment of the Achuar are manifold. It is true that treating hunted animals as social partners is not conducive to carrying out unnecessary massacres, especially since the spirit masters of the game animals are always quick to punish these excesses by sending disease, for instance, or by provoking "accidents." But, more importantly, the Achuar have maintained a state of environmental balance for largely demographic reasons. For a very long time they had a high infant mortality rate, which, together with the toll of war, maintained a very low population density over a rather extensive territory. This comfortable "carrying capacity" also explains why they could "afford" the considerable potential for excess production. In addition, as I have already mentioned, the time they devote to subsistence production is very limited and inelastic. More precisely, they are not prepared to sacrifice the many things they do when they are not working, which is most of the time. We thus cannot simply invoke taboos of a religious or symbolic nature regarding the exploitation of resources, since these other factors also play a role—and in both directions. The Achuar's neighbors, the Shuar, have recently experienced a relative demographic expansion as a result of their proximity to the colonization frontier, a circumstance that allowed them to benefit from infant mortality reduction policies. Demographic growth, deforestation, and competition with poor settlers coming down from the Andes have led them to expand into Achuar territory, which has not been without its share of problems. The combination of material factors of a biological and technical nature with others, which we would consider symbolic, makes it difficult to identify the real conceptual safeguards against environmental depredation. What is more, in a naturalist context these barriers would also have to be erected without our returning to a hypostasized conception of nature.

PC   *Could we say more simply, then, that we need to relearn how to engage in a symmetrical and reciprocal relationship with nature—in other words, we need to force ourselves to take from nature only what we can return to it?*

162   *The Contemporary World in the Light of Anthropology*

PD   This may indeed be a more realistic proposition, and we could develop it by fostering, among a broad public, a better sense of how ecosystems function and of our interactions with other entities that are present within a given environment. The subtle equilibria that govern these relations—at the level of the soil, the water cycle, the relationships between predator and prey, symbiosis, parasitism, and the like—could indeed be respected as having value and given a symbolic significance, if they were better understood. They would no longer be seen in terms of quantitative factors established in scientific laboratories, as they tend to be perceived today, but as intellectual and moral reference points whose significance is public and shared. This is probably a promising lead but, once again, we cannot count on any individual or group of individuals to give it a real social mooring. This will require a much more robust education in ecology as a science, whereas now this field of study is almost entirely absent from school curricula—as is anthropology, for that matter. More generally, it seems to me that there is a tremendous gulf between the importance of ecological issues in the current destiny of humanity and the weak development of ecology as a science, especially in France. The fault lies not with the ecologists themselves, who do their best and would surely be very happy to have more resources for the diffusion of their knowledge, as I have the feeling that they do not receive much support from public authorities. The tremendous importance accorded today to the cellular and biochemical level in biology seems to me detrimental to a more systematic study of organic communities, which is fundamental. A basic knowledge of these organic communities could be acquired in primary and secondary education.

PC   *You have alluded several times to the diversity of environmentalist movements outside the western world and suggested that they sometimes help renew our conceptions of ecology. Have you ever been faced with this diversity yourself? If so, how do you think about it?*

PD   The difficulty comes from the fact that, paradoxically, native environmentalist movements are native only to a very limited extent. The political language that their organizers adopt in addressing the states in which they live and the major mining, forestry, and agribusiness companies as well as the NGOs that operate on their territories is not the language in which they traditionally define their relationship to the environment. They quickly came to understand

From anthropology to ecology 163

that it was necessary for them to formulate their claims against territorial dispossession and in favor of preserving their conditions of life in a language that was comprehensible to non-natives. Hence the proliferation of a standardized ecological discourse, which can be heard from South America to the circumboreal area of Siberia, in some regions of Africa, and in Oceania and South-East Asia—in short, in all the great marginal spaces populated mainly by tribal minorities where resources can be found that whet the appetite of companies, which are most indifferent to the environment and human rights. Local communities in these spaces thus put on an act, presenting themselves as custodians of nature, bearers of an ancestral ecological wisdom that has enabled them, since time immemorial, to live in harmony with their surroundings. This is perfectly understandable, even if they do it only for reasons of effectiveness and to secure, among urban elites in rich countries, allies who are sensitive to environmental questions. And, in a way, it is also true—the fact that the Amazonian forest is, in part, the product of planting techniques developed by Amerindian populations serves to make the case that they are indeed its guardians. Having said that, these communities are forced into a kind of double discourse, which is very striking for anthropologists who work among them. On the one hand, they address the outside world in a rather conventional manner, sometimes through folkloric demonstrations in which fusion with nature is expressed in ceremonies that are largely cobbled together, if not wholly invented. And, on the other, when the members of these communities speak of their relations to natural beings, among themselves, in their daily exchanges, or with an anthropologist, they do not seem to care at all about these demonstrations, which are intended for external consumption.

Ecuador is a good case in point. About twenty years ago, in the southern part of the Achuar territory, they opened a tourist complex, Kapawi Lodge, which has since become rather well known. It is an ecotourism center developed by Ecuadorians with investment from the United States, but in agreement with the Achuar Federation, which at that point had only just been created and since then has been receiving royalties from the center. Located on a pleasant site by a lake, this village, made up of luxurious versions of traditional Achuar houses, hosts wealthy tourists over brief stays, usually of not more than a week. From the village there are excursions into the surrounding forest, with Achuar guides, to introduce the tourists to some of its inhabitants—mostly birds, the others being less visible.

164   *The Contemporary World in the Light of Anthropology*

From conversations with Achuar people who had worked at that center and with a student who had studied this kind of tourist facility in the Ecuadorian Amazon, I realized that they had drawn quite a bit on my dissertation, *In the Society of Nature*, which had been rather quickly translated into Spanish. A few years after its publication in translation, the book circulated among the young Achuar who had learned to read Spanish, providing them with a transcription, into an objectivized form intelligible for tourists, of the knowledge and know-how they had developed around the environment. This was a somewhat paradoxical reversal of roles, which reflected a very common process of knowledge circulation between anthropologists and the populations they describe. And it makes quite a bit of sense, too: if Achuar guides had to explain to tourists what an *anent* was—and many young Achuar nowadays no longer know any—or had to offer commentary on their dreams or take their guests hunting, in short, if they were to deliver in raw form the kind of relationship that they or their parents maintained with nonhumans, that would be utterly incomprehensible to the visitors. And, of course, these environmentally minded tourists are shocked to discover that the Amerindians, whom they hold to be the protectors of the forest, should also be hunters. There is thus an initial filtering process that passes through the gaze of the anthropologist and is then reappropriated, if only to present this knowledge to tourists.

I believe that this back-and-forth between native discourses and their western translations—whether or not they come from anthropologists—is rather widespread. The tours of Europe and the United States that indigenous leaders make in order to protest the havoc wreaked upon their territories by mass colonization, large dams, and oil rigs follow the same logic. These leaders employ concepts such as "nature," "mother forest," and "cosmic harmony," which do not exist in their own language but speak to their western audiences. Recently there has been much discussion of the Quichua expression *sumak kawsay*, "good living." It is a term that circulated in progressive circles in Andean South America and plays an important role in the critique of consumer society and in the demand for a form of development consistent with ecological concerns. This notion was presented as the synthesis of a kind of ancestral philosophy rooted in Quichua and Aymara cosmologies, when actually it emerged from an intellectual complicity between exceptionally far-sighted indigenous leaders, who understood how

From anthropology to ecology 165

the western world works, and Latin American activists, later joined by others in Europe and North America. Today this construction is the bearer of numerous political aspirations—it has inspired constitutional reforms in Bolivia and Ecuador—even if it is sometimes employed to preach a rather superficial ecumenism, which relegates to the background the conflictual dimension of all social life. The idea of *sumak kawsay*—with its goals of harmony, integration, and totalization—is typical of analogist cosmologies and less successful among Amazonian populations, many of which place more emphasis on predation in the relationships between humans and nonhumans.

PC   *There is much debate today about whether it would be a good idea to establish property rights for the ecological knowledge of indigenous populations. Some communities are calling for the recognition of their exclusive rights to benefit from traditional ecological knowledge in order to be able to protect themselves against the resources exploration carried out by major corporations, as well as against biopiracy. What is your position on this issue?*

PD   I should say first that there are extremely lively debates about this among indigenous populations themselves. Indeed, some call for part of their traditional knowledge about plants and their use to be recognized as heritage and protected as such. This entails making an inventory of this knowledge and of the biological matter on which it is based and granting populations exclusive rights over it in the form of patents. This position is quite understandable, given that for a long period of time the labor, territories, and resources of indigenous peoples were appropriated and exploited by others without their consent. Local populations now see these legal instruments as a means for reclaiming what is theirs. We know that Amazonia is a zone of extraordinary biodiversity, and hence a source of potential wealth for pharmaceutical and biotechnology companies, in stark contrast to the extreme vulnerability of the societies that inhabit it. The predatory behavior of North American bioprospecting companies such as Shaman Pharmaceuticals and the International Plant Medicine Corporation, especially in the Ecuadorian Amazon, has been such that the kind of ethnobotany and ethnoecology work I did in the 1970s would now no longer be possible. These small outfits, alongside the major pharmaceutical and cosmetic companies, fund students in ethnobotany to carry out doctoral research and compile inventories of the plant—and sometimes also animal—species used

166   *The Contemporary World in the Light of Anthropology*

by local populations, their healers, and their shamans. After this initial sorting process, which enables them to determine which species are locally believed to have therapeutic powers, specimens are analyzed in laboratories to identify their chemical and biological properties and to verify their effectiveness, and hence their potential economic value. The Indians have thus developed a well-founded mistrust of Whites who come asking questions about the forest and about their biological knowledge.

The situation was made worse by the repeated blunders of the registration agencies, especially in the United States. About thirty years ago, for instance, a US Patent and Trademark Office center in California granted an exclusive patent to the director of a small bioprospecting company for a very common variety of *ayahuasca*, which is a liana used in the preparation of a hallucinogenic concoction. This brew is commonly consumed throughout western Amazonia by a variety of ethnic groups and is a central element in many shamanic practices. It is as if some random guy came and collected a sample of a traditional grape variety from a vineyard in France or California and then obtained exclusive rights to it with a patent. The absurdity of the situation was such that the patent was eventually invalidated, under pressure from indigenous organizations, but attempts of this kind happen regularly and the appropriation of knowledge for commercial ends is not rare.

That there should be resistance to this kind of pillage is thus perfectly understandable, but other native movements have responded differently, refusing to play the game of western property law by patenting local knowledge so as to protect it against external appropriation. In their view, resistance to commodification cannot happen from within the capitalist system, using its own categories. The fight against foreign economic interests requires, in this view, a more fundamental rejection of the very logic on which they rest. I had a chance to express my own position on these issues a few years ago, in debate with my colleague and friend Manuela Carneiro da Cunha.[9] I am very averse to the commodification of knowledge—of knowledge in general, and not just of living beings. I think that knowledge must be accessible to all and usable by all. Even if this sounds utopian, it seems to me that recognizing certain populations as bearers of rights to knowledge is to open the door to a generalized commodification. There would no longer be any difference between a population and a capitalist enterprise—both would be legal persons in the eyes of the law. This is a very great risk against which we must fight, even if

I recognize that the rights of the inventors of technical and industrial processes should be protected. Nothing good can come of the commodification of living things that is currently underway, as we have seen recently with the attempt of biotechnology companies to register patents on the human genetic sequences linked to the development of breast cancer. The line I support probably does involve certain risks for indigenous populations, who are thus deprived of the legal means to defend themselves against biopiracy, but opening up that front seems to me even more dangerous.

Furthermore, it is very difficult to identify the owner of knowledge. Let us take the hypothetical case of a manioc or sweet potato cultivar, that is, a variety that has been selected over time and that may feature specific advantages in resistance to drought or certain diseases. This selection of the plant's properties over time results from an empirical process informed by botanical know-how and knowledge and is not fundamentally different from what big agrobusiness companies do when they select seeds and create genetically modified organisms. But in the case of a cultivar whose breeder cannot be identified, to whom shall we grant property rights? If an ethnobotanist comes upon it in a garden in Amazonia, does it belong to the village, or even to the household where it was found? Does it belong to the entire tribal group in which it has circulated, or, more broadly, to a regional group in which exchanges of cuttings are commonplace, or even to the state on whose territory it was discovered? All this raises insoluble problems, which relate to the fact that, to assign property rights, one must be able to clearly identify the owner. And this is generally impossible in situations of this kind. Identifying the indigenous communities themselves is difficult enough, and in fact most attempts by international organizations to do so have faltered on the complex cultural exchanges and hybridizations that make up the human diversity of a region like Amazonia. Indeed, the technical skills and know-how involved are so complex, spread out as they are across very large communities of practice, that it is dangerous to think that this knowledge can be appropriated by individuals or groups.

The politics of anthropology

PC *Are you inclined to think that the subversion of capitalism and its logic of environmental destruction must take more or less direct inspiration from nonmodern forms of thought?*

168   *The Contemporary World in the Light of Anthropology*

PD   I do not believe that we can take direct inspiration from nonmodern forms of thought, animist or otherwise, for no historical experience is transferable wholesale into circumstances that are different from the ones in which it emerged. Whatever admiration one may have for what one considers, somewhat confusedly, to be the wisdom of ancestral ways of life—and even if the Achuar, the Australian Aborigines, and the Inuit have much to teach us about how to use nature—our present situation is very different from the ones they faced. The fascination for these peoples has given rise to a rather lucrative industry, especially in publishing, but we should be wary of the search for models. And the main reason is that all these societies have resolved issues at a local scale, whereas the issues of modern urban societies are global. More precisely, they involve a constant articulation between local, regional, national, and transnational scales, and all the way up to the terrestrial biosphere. At each of these levels, the responses are different. One of the major challenges we are confronting, for instance, is the re-constitution of the links between urban hubs—where a majority of the world's population is now concentrated—and the vast spaces of production that surround them. The provisioning of cities, the transformation of exchanges between these zones, and the redistribution of wealth, along with attention to the quality of life within these spaces, are the major challenges of modern societies. At stake here is a renewed appreciation of productive activity and the search for a better economic and spatial balance. These are characteristic challenges of the industrialized world, and also of the industrializing world of developing countries. And, of course, the solutions that tribal populations have to offer are of little help in this respect. The same goes for questions of energy moderation. Tribal populations have long practiced it, but at a scale that has little to do with the needs of postindustrial societies. These are all reasons why we should remain cautious about possible analogies between the ways of life of tribal populations and the problems that we, citizens of a world that is rather out of kilter, are confronting.

One can nonetheless sketch some connections between anthropological knowledge and the transformations of the contemporary world. Anthropologists have access to a multiplicity of life experiences—through their direct experience of traditional societies as well as through books, ethnographies, and articles written by scores of scholars for more than a century. This precious body of knowledge contains a host of singular ways of building worlds and inhabiting

The politics of anthropology   169

them, and sometimes also failures, from which we have much to learn, too. Each of these singular ways of world making offers not so much a model to imitate, a cosmology to reproduce, as a proof that the composition of the world as we know it is not the only one possible. The historian François Hartog has called this "presentism": the short-sightedness with which we are so often afflicted, the fact of being immersed in a present that seems inevitable and necessary and that leads us to accept the historical conditions in which we find ourselves with a degree of fatalism.[10] In his view, history must fight this inclination and bring the present back to its historical construction, and I believe anthropology can contribute to that task. Not by investigating the past, which is the job of historians, but by cultivating a familiarity with cultural alterity and a sense of the contingency of our social forms. The multitude of ways the human condition is experienced represents living proof that our present experience is not the only conceivable one. Anthropology supplies alternative ideals; it offers the possibility of other paths. And, indeed, however improbable they may seem, they have been explored, in other places and at earlier times. Anthropology shows us that the future is not a simple linear continuation of the present, that it is rife with unprecedented potentialities whose realization we must imagine if we are to achieve, in the not too distant future, if not a truly common home, at least compatible worlds, more hospitable and more fraternal.

PC   *How do you see the erosion of cultural diversity, past and present? Have you been personally faced with these questions? In your opinion, should we give in to pessimism, or are there reasons to hope for a conservation of this diversity?*

PD   As I have already suggested, I am not as pessimistic as some on this question. Of course, cultural diversity, in the classic form that we have known, is diminishing. We still have in mind a conception of this diversity that was shaped by ethnographic atlases, which take stock of societies that are distinct, each one being endowed with a territory, a language, and characteristic cultural traits. And, even though this conception has always had its limits, for it is in fact very difficult to clearly distinguish discontinuous entities in the cultural fabric of humanity, it did correspond to a certain reality, which is now threatened with extinction. That phenomenon can be measured through the erosion of languages—and the indicators are fairly clear

170   *The Contemporary World in the Light of Anthropology*

in this respect. While I would not defend at all costs the debatable idea that each language represents a culture, or that each culture is linked to a language, it is unquestionable that the disappearance of linguistic competence signals the disappearance of a form of collective singularity.

But it seems to me nonetheless that, all over the world, the reactions to these processes of uniformization, both commercial and ideological, reconstitute a variety that, as I have already pointed out, is no longer at the level of tribal groups but at that of regional ensembles of various sizes. Each of these regional ensembles forms a collective, with its own form of relations between humans and nonhumans that is quite singular. Each one presents us, again, with a social reality that is sui generis and that, when you look at it, appears clearly to be distinct from the reality of the neighboring ensemble. This may no longer really have much to do with cultures, even in a renewed sense of the term. I would rather call it ways of relating to nature and to others, ways of doing and behaving that become characteristic within regional ensembles that may be larger or smaller than nations. I believe that in Latin America this phenomenon is rather obvious to the curious observer, despite the apparent uniformity brought by the Spanish and the Portuguese. Just as one can identify various countries within France, each with its own differentiated way of occupying space, its own form of rural architecture and organization of the landscape, one can distinguish a variety of regional styles when traveling from the north of Mexico to Patagonia, each of which offers a marked contrast with the other regions—not only in the style of buildings, in ways of speaking, dressing, and eating, and in musical forms, but also in ways of being and interacting.

It is indeed regrettable that anthropologists have not taken greater interest in the development of these new regional identities, even if this can be easily explained as a result of their lack of familiarity with this analytical scale. If a more systematic study of these micro-ensembles were conducted, I believe it would reveal a new scene of diversity. As a matter of fact, when I speak of regional ensembles, I mean it both geographically, because they unfold across space, and within each of these ensembles, on the basis of occupational specialization, for instance. Diversity today is thus located at a level that is still poorly understood and remains to be studied in depth.

The politics of anthropology   171

PC   *You invoked the idea of return to a more political anthropology. Is it linked to these kinds of considerations, and could you give us a sense of what this project would look like?*

PD   This project is still in embryo, but it would be for me another way of tapping into my ethnographic experience. The starting point is that tribal societies—in Amazonia, New Guinea, and some of the regions of Africa and Asia—all have very specific ways of responding to the forms of subjection, invasion, and dispossession that are perpetrated on them by the central state or by other entities that appear within their universe. These responses are of course shaped by the social categories that are used locally to think about community and otherness, but they are also in part adapted to the institutions they are intended to fight, circumvent, or hijack. I believe each of these forms of political response offers interesting clues as to how to conceive of the political in a somewhat different way from that of traditional political anthropology.

Political anthropology was, of course, born in a colonial context; it was primarily interested in the political institutions that could be identified in societies subjected to colonial domination. In these situations of confrontation, it sought to identify, in dominated societies, the equivalents of current or past European political forms, as in African kingship, Melanesian chiefdom, clan organization, and aristocratic systems. Indeed, unlike the colonial machine, which, initially at least, refused to credit these societies with any degree of political complexity, anthropologists sought to push back against this implicit discourse of domination. But at the same time (and this is a constitutive paradox of anthropology) it relied on local administrative channels, and hence was de facto complicit with the colonial system. It would have been impossible to do otherwise. Later, however, with decolonization, there was a tendency to place greater emphasis on the capacity these societies had demonstrated to subvert the dominant order and to contest it through effective countermodels.

It seems to me that most of these studies share a common conception of sociopolitical institutions as governing the relationships between humans, on the model of western civil society. The considerable difference between nonmodern politics and our institutions lies in the fact that the former is able to integrate nonhumans into its collectives and to recognize nonhumans as political subjects that act within their own collectives. In other words, the common

172   *The Contemporary World in the Light of Anthropology*

kinds of beings that result from this are not those we are accustomed to, made of human individuals; they are aggregates of humans and nonhumans that may take widely different forms and can also, in that sense, provide food for thought on how to transform our own political institutions. For example, when one looks at what anthropologists call a "clan" or at any descent group of a similar kind, one realizes that it is not merely a group of humans who share the same ancestors, as the classic definition would have it. In fact the clan, the lineage, the Mexican *calpulli*, the totemic group, or even the Roman *gens* comprises much more than men, women, and children; it also encompasses animals, plants, territories, deities, spirits, sanctuaries, pathogenic agents, forms of knowledge and know-how, and many other things that are necessary for life. And these things are included from the outset and in their own right, not as a simple backdrop to the theater of human action. The idea that the analytical unit of anthropology is provided by human beings has thus acted as a blockage, I believe, and has obscured our analysis of the properly political dimensions of collective life—even though this intellectual configuration has its origins in the struggle against the *ancien régime* and in the redefinition of institutions that are necessary for emancipation from prerevolutionary social forms. This redefinition has essentially consisted in a purge: nonhumans were ousted from society, leaving only humans as the sole subjects of rights. For a long time, the representation that the moderns gave of their own form of political aggregation was thus transposed onto the analysis of nonmodern societies, together with a whole series of categories such as the division between nature and culture and our own regime of historicity; and this is what I would like to break away from.

I have already mentioned the protests against mining projects in the Andes. These protests give voice to a nonhuman held to be a full-fledged member of the collective and whose destruction or alteration would thus be of concern to the collective as a whole. This kind of action acquires a political dimension that is difficult to translate into our western categories—which is a good illustration of the inadequacy of both our political categories and our analytical tools. Now, if we consider Amazonian Indians and other animist collectives of the same kind, which are conceived of on the species model, the consequences are different still: each human tribe, as well as most plant and animal species, forms a specific collective that engages with the world on the basis of its members' own dispositions. It is the interactions, both peaceful and conflictual, between these tribe

The politics of anthropology 173

species that make possible a form of living together that, once again, is not reducible to the interactions between humans in the modern public sphere. Such a system is of course highly counterintuitive to our habits of thought, but this does not mean that it cannot be systematized in terms of a decentered political anthropology. This new approach may be able to account for the misunderstandings and superficial alliances that bring together or oppose indigenous organizations and western movements for the protection of nature. Indeed, the idea that a given species should be protected seems absurd in Amazonian categories, because that species is most of the time endowed with a degree of political autonomy that would make it resist any protective treatment exercised from the outside. Humans have no business exercising jurisdiction over it—implicit domination for protection is a form of domination—since it is already endowed with its own political capacity in the collective in which it exists. What truly matters, then, is to maintain the general conditions of life under which the relationships between various tribes and species can go on.

Our traditional sense of what is political and our intellectual grasp of this kind of phenomena seem to me outdated. In Amazonia, the political consists in maintaining the conditions of interactions—which may take the shape of exchanges, but also of predation or of sharing—with neighbors, humans and nonhumans, conceived of as autonomous. The consequences that this definition may have for our conceptualization of the political are indeed significant: we are now invited to adapt political anthropology, not so much to a typology of forms of organization marked, like before, by latent evolutionism—horde, tribe, chiefdom, state—as to the actual modalities by which beings live together in collectives whose forms are no longer predetermined by those we are accustomed to. This is a new domain, upon which the imperative of the decolonization of thought operates and which allows us to rid ourselves of the models through which we have been accustomed to think, under the influence of a rich tradition that goes back to Greek philosophy via medieval reflections on the city-state, *ius gentium*, contract theory, and so on. At stake, in the end, is our ability to take seriously that which native political models impose on us in terms of analytical categories and offer us in terms of political imagination.

PC *Are these ideas a way for you to break with the dominant conception of politics—a conception that tends to conflate politics with the management of current affairs—and to restore some depth to the term?*

174   *The Contemporary World in the Light of Anthropology*

PD   Politics is increasingly conceived of as a professional affair. This is both an advantage and a disadvantage of democratic representation: delegating a part of one's free will in order to form a sovereign political community, to use the classic contract formulation, means giving up a part of one's autonomy. Many will be quite content with this delegation or will take it for granted. However, living together is in fact profoundly political, as it involves constantly forming a community with the world of humans and nonhumans. Our entire existence is political through and through, including when it comes to our dealings with machines, genetically modified organisms, the climate, and viruses—and perhaps especially then. In other words, our conception of the political is too narrow: the space of collective deliberation on the common good, the institutions that enable the exercise of authority, collective decision-making, and the delegation of power by the people do not exhaust the situations and actions that can legitimately be considered political. In collectives that are not endowed with institutions invested with sovereign or representative power and that are found outside the naturalist context, the exercise of political power takes forms that we are not used to considering as such, as I have described earlier. And I believe that this gap bears within it a redefinition of the political, for it is linked to another way of thinking about the collective dimension of human existence, as well as about the latitude we may have to include a larger number of nonhumans in this collective life.

PC   *That brings us to the political vocation of intellectual work. Under what circumstances have you taken on a public role? And, in your view, what function can intellectuals serve nowadays?*

PD   I already mentioned the discussions I have engaged in, from the time of my fieldwork, with populations, local institutions, and political authorities in Ecuador. The objective at the time was to talk to that country's leaders, who had just discovered the advantages of windfall oil revenues without fully measuring the drawbacks, and to explain those drawbacks to them—namely the double problem of the degradation of Amazonian ecosystems through oil extraction and indiscriminate colonization, on the one hand, and of the destruction of a very rich cultural heritage, with threat to the conditions of life of native populations, on the other. Neither Amazonia nor the population then known as the Jivaros were seen in a very good light at the time. Object of a longstanding dispute with Peru, the region

The politics of anthropology 175

called El Oriente in Ecuador was seen as a fetid jungle peopled by insolent and cruel savages. The jungle had to be to cleared and the savages civilized through colonization. This was an excellent way to absorb the surplus rural workforce in the Andes without undertaking any reform of the land tenure system, which had remained terribly unequal—the local form of serfdom, *huasipungo*, had been abolished only ten years before we arrived. The idea we tried to promote was that the dense selva, the putrid swamps, the fierce warriors were not just obstacles to oil extraction; they could even be considered assets for the country in terms of reserves of biodiversity and cultural diversity. Interventions of this sort are hardly original, and many anthropologists have had occasion to make them. At the time, unfortunately, it fell on deaf ears. It was too early and these themes were not yet in fashion. But the solutions I recommended—especially the creation of zones for the joint protection of the environment and native populations—were eventually adopted, thanks to the efforts of others, especially our former students at the University of Quito, who knew how to find the right channels for the dissemination of these ideas.

Defending these systems, which were designed for the protection of people and nature, led me to oppose a form of ecological fundamentalism supported by many international organizations. For many, the human populations, namely the tribal ones, are by definition environmental disruptors, and protecting an ecosystem means evicting such populations from it. The fundamental idea behind this conception of ecology is that natural environments and landscapes must be as disconnected as possible from human influence and maintained in a hermetically sealed manner. I have been very vocal against this idea, since the example of Amazonia clearly shows how absurd it is to evict, from forest areas that one is seeking to preserve, the very populations that have contributed to its current physiognomy! This would be like displacing the farmers from Normandy in order to preserve the bocage. We had to fight against this attitude, which I believe has receded since the early days of ecologism in the 1970s. In an attempt to set things straight on this question, I gave a presentation in 1998 at the fiftieth anniversary conference of the International Union for Conservation of Nature and Natural Resources, one of the biggest organizations for environmental protection in the world, which acts as a kind of unofficial United Nations agency in this field. The World Wildlife Fund has also wavered quite a bit on this question, sometimes finding it useful

176   *The Contemporary World in the Light of Anthropology*

to enlist native populations in biodiversity conservation projects and sometimes deeming them to be a disruptive factor. These organizations are often headed by biologists, who are not sensitive enough to the human dimension of ecology and sometimes dream of scientists' exercising technocratic government over natural parks—scientists who generally hail from developed countries. Here again, I have not been alone in the fight, and I believe that the critique of ecological fundamentalism has gained ground.

The museum

PC   *A major dimension of the public vocation of anthropology has been its contribution to ethnographic museums. In France, the recent creation of the Musée du Quai Branly represented a sea change in the field. What is your view of these transformations, which have provoked the spilling of so much ink over the past few years?*

PD   I am among those, probably the majority of anthropologists in France, who saw the creation of the Musée du Quai Branly as an opportunity to open a new chapter in our ways of working on and thinking about ethnographic objects. This field, at the crossroads of material culture, technology, and aesthetics, was once the cradle of the first generation of French anthropologists, but has gradually fallen out of favor. The Musée de l'Homme had clearly become but a shadow of the great project launched by Paul Rivet before World War II. The absence of a prominent figure at the head, together with lack of adequate funding and lack of autonomy in management, meant that there had not been much research in anthropology at the Musée de l'Homme for decades. The museography was not particularly innovative, to say the least, and the conservation of collections was substandard by comparison with other great museums. The "scientific" approach to ethnographic objects had indeed lost its capacity for renewal in this institution, and the public's loss of interest only made this pathetically clear. When Maurice Godelier—who, in his capacity as anthropologist, was charged by Prime Minister Lionel Jospin with supervising the creation of a new museum—proposed in 1999 that I be directly involved in the project and that I preside over the preparatory committee on the Americas, I happily and enthusiastically accepted the offer. In essence, Jacques Chirac's presidential ambition to leave a legacy, like his predecessors, in the form of a museum provided an opportunity that many of us seized to revitalize a necrotic field of research. It was mostly for this reason that I supported and participated in the creation of the museum.

There has been much criticism of the museum, which developed a reputation for taking an aesthetic, in other words superficial and emotional, approach to ethnographic objects, unlike the Musée de l'Homme, whose approach was scientific, in other words serious and rational. This opposition is absurd and unfair—first, because it is applied only to non-European civilizations. Nobody takes exception with fine art museums; most of them, and the Louvre first, are quite parsimonious with the explanations they provide about the works they exhibit and quite indifferent to the historical contexts in which they were produced. The average visitor does not learn any more about a Poussin painting or an early Italian annunciation than about a Sulka mask or an Olmec statue. But it is the so-called scientific mode of exhibiting ethnographic objects—roughly speaking, the diorama and the organization by distinct culture—that is itself debatable. It appeared rather late, at the beginning of the twentieth century, following on other modes of anthropological museography that are now forgotten. The only museum of this kind that remains is the one in Oxford named after General Pitt Rivers, who inspired its organization. It makes ample use of the model of arms panoply and tries to capture, through its radial presentation of the artifacts, the evolutionary law that governs the forms and mental operations that presided over their production—how the shape of a club evolved into an oar, which then evolved into a spatula, and so on. It is indeed the only ethnographic museum whose presentation is strictly speaking "scientific," or at least demonstrative, seeking as it does to render visible, in the organization of objects, an elaborate theory of the causal links that connect them.

Anthropology was born in museums, and this early connection has had profound effects on anthropological thought, which has in turn supported and legitimized the current organization of museums. The gradual rise, over the course of the twentieth century, of the practice of classifying objects by geographical area began with the first extended ethnographic fieldwork on a single site— in contrast with the "expeditions" typical of nineteenth-century naturalist exploration. This convergence was not fortuitous and has greatly contributed to our habitual conception of cultures as finite collections of characteristic traits that form a systematic whole. Ethnographic information and collections of artifacts echo each

178   *The Contemporary World in the Light of Anthropology*

other and invite us to imagine collective entities as defined by stable boundaries with their own internal logics. They encourage a bloc-by-bloc form of exhibition that projects onto the material organization of museums the contiguities and geographic boundaries of ethnological maps. We thus move from the Central America room to the South America room; and, within the latter, the Amazonian populations are clearly apart from the Andean ones. Such an organization is supposed to convey a sense of continuities and ruptures in the distribution of techniques, artifacts, languages, and social institutions. Thus the exhibition of objects with the same provenance has now become a self-evident mode, replacing the genealogical demonstrations and formal assemblages of the kind that we still see at the Pitt Rivers Museum and that used to be the norm in the second half of the nineteenth century. Indeed, Philipp Frantz von Siebold, pioneer of the modern contextualization approach, himself illustrates the connection between extended ethnographic immersion and museography by cultural area. He lived in Japan in the 1830s, when the country was not very welcoming of foreigners, and returned with a considerable trove of objects and ethnographic information on traditional Japan. He became a staunch advocate of the culture-by-culture exhibition style in Europe, though he himself never managed to implement that approach at any museum.

It was thus not until the first decades of the twentieth century that the precepts of the ethnographic monograph came to inform exhibition styles as well. The notion of context became widely adopted, and even a leitmotif in approaches to museography with "scientific" pretensions. Objects had to be presented in situ and their significance revealed in relation to one another. The contexts in which they were used had to be homogenized and these uses grouped into larger ensembles, deemed to be characteristic of a cultural area. In other words, while ethnographic museums of the nineteenth century mainly sought to demonstrate the validity of one or the other of the two major anthropological theories then in fashion—evolutionism or diffusionism—in the twentieth century they sought to illustrate the functional coherence of cultures, which the new technique of ethnographic description established as self-evident.

The most common way of realizing this objective that is still practised today in most major museums is through what is known as "nylon thread" museography—a reference to the invisible lines with the help of which figures were "staged" in museum display cases as engaged in some characteristic activity and outfitted with

The museum   179

the typical attributes of their ethnic or cultural group. Dioramas were only the most accomplished form of this mode of presentation: they cursorily re-created a typical environment, in which mannequins in typical dress were shown as using typical artifacts to accomplish typical tasks. Yet, despite its noble pedagogical intention, the scientific contextualization approach has many drawbacks. In addition to reinforcing the idea that cultures are closed ensembles separated by intangible borders, it turns them into stereotypes by reducing them to the few traits, customs, and emblematic objects that represent them in the display cases. Such simplification no doubt contributed to the global spread of the "heritage" conception of the singularity of each culture, a conception based on a finite list of material and immaterial characteristics. In addition, the juxtaposition, within a single space, of objects that often reflect different situations, times, and statuses results in an unreal and atemporal construction. The practice of dressing mannequins in their most ornate clothing is a good case in point: while engaged in rather mundane tasks, they are clothed in ceremonial dress and adorned in ritual attire. Until the 1990s, all the great museums of civilization—the Smithsonian Institution in Washington, the Museum of Mankind in London, the Musée de l'Homme in France—had adopted this form of contextualizing museography. And, as a result of its generalization in the second half of the twentieth century, it still stands as the model for many of the "scientific" approaches to ethnographic objects, and hence as the antithesis of the "aesthetic" approach.

Whatever its faults or merits may be, it would be absurd to pronounce on whether or not the Musée du Quai Branly corresponds to what a museum of civilization in the early twenty-first century should be; for such a model simply does not exist. Each museum promotes certain forms of exhibiting that are based on the museographic tradition of its directors, the nature of its collections, local and national patterns of cultural consumption, the assumed competence of its visitors, and the educational or propaganda objectives it sets itself. The role of the architect is also very important. At the Musée du Quai Branly, Jean Nouvel imposed, through the layout of the building, a scenography that corresponds to his imaginary: the long access route up the "river," leading to the darkened atmosphere of the exhibition area, which is filled with giant sculpted masts and cubicles, conjures up a Conradian universe, halfway between an unsettling voyage up the Congo River and a stroll through a

180   *The Contemporary World in the Light of Anthropology*

nineteenth-century colonial trading post. As a result, it is very difficult to imagine any exhibition there that would not be marked by the surrounding space, in contrast with, say, the large rectangular box of the Centre Pompidou.

The most visible diversification in the field of museography is one that has taken place over the past fifteen years between various modes of exhibition within each civilization museum. From the very start, the Musée du Quai Branly followed this route, complementing the permanent collections, which are still organized by cultural area, with thematic exhibitions that present a civilization, a dimension of the human condition, a major anthropologist, or a historical perspective on the western approach to a particular phenomenon. Each type of exhibit offers an opportunity for commentary, sometimes iconoclastic, on a particular aspect of the great anthropological sweep that the permanent collections represent; and it is on this dynamic that I have drawn for my exhibition *The Making of Images*. It is a way of giving voice to divergent perspectives, especially those of the populations whose objects are displayed, of exploring the colonial context in which the collections were acquired, of highlighting the role played by a particular school or scholar in the formation of our anthropological judgments, and even of reflecting on the institution itself and its exhibition practices. It is a compromise that I find to be fair, and many of the museum's temporary exhibits have been able to give welcome expression to original anthropological (and historical) perspectives.

PC   *But then, on the basis of what principles should a truly scientific anthropological exhibition be mounted?*

PD   This would probably be an impossible challenge to meet, but I think it would have to involve following the social life of an object through its multiple metamorphoses. The object would have to be shown in the context of its initial production, which is what anthropologists generally focus on. A ritual mask, for instance, was made in a particular place, under particular circumstances, to serve a particular function, and its form and ornamentation reflect all of this. At that point, the public should be directly informed about the context in which that object is used. However, the circumstances of this use may be terribly complicated. To give you an example, exhibitions of South American ornaments often include a feather diadem of the Brazilian Bororo called *pariko*. A few years ago, a Brazilian

The museum 181

anthropologist devoted to this adornment a scholarly monograph of 270 pages, in which she declared that the feather art of the Bororo was so rich that she had to limit her study to this particular category of ornament alone if she was to provide a rigorous account of its complex meanings! But the life of an object does not end with its original use. The path of the ritual mask would have to be retraced: it may have been destroyed, abandoned, or picked up by a collector or by a missionary. Throughout these stages it became something else, a curio, an art object or a scientific object, depending on the gaze of its acquirer and on the interests associated with that gaze. And under each of these guises the object takes on a different existence, which is based on the context that gives it life. All these stages are legitimate in their own way, even though one might say that some do not do justice to its initial qualities. Ignorance of these properties is of course an issue, but that an object may be appreciated because its physical perfection, the symmetry of its form, or the juxtaposition of its colors strike the imagination of people of an aesthetic sensibility, this is by no means a problem. Objects have complex lives that are subject to all manner of metamorphoses, and a true museum of anthropology would have to account for the complex biography of each object, transposed as it is, throughout its existence, into a host of different circumstances where its significance, its use, its value, both symbolic and commercial, and the effect it exerts on those who gaze upon it or use it will vary widely. Unfortunately there is not one museum in the world that does this for any object.

One of the ideas I sought to convey in the exhibition I organized at the Musée du Quai Branly is that there is no evolution in art. I think this idea did get across, and I am very pleased about it! It is for this reason that I opened the exhibition with animism and then tried to show the overlap between various modes of figuration, so that one would not get the impression that these are completely closed worlds. The visitor would then move straight from animism to naturalism, without transition, being exposed to objects from vastly different regions of the world, but their articulation and their coexistence I hope were clearly apparent. The third room was devoted to totemism, and I selected bark paintings and acrylic paintings by Aboriginal artists of Australia that, from a stylistic point of view, were reminiscent of impressionism. From an evolutionary perspective, which is very hard to shed given our education, jumping in this way from modern art to Aboriginal paintings may seem absurd, but it is precisely this kind of response that I wanted

182   *The Contemporary World in the Light of Anthropology*

the visitor to get over. I had in mind to reshuffle the deck and to highlight new continuities and discontinuities. And even if the complex argument has not always been grasped, I hope to have at least made it clear that all the images are on an equal footing, regardless of our personal tastes. From the point of view of the figurative operation that these images deploy, no difference in kind can be established between them.

PC   *While working on this exhibition, did you have to deal with issues related to the conditions of conservation of these indigenous works, or with the question of the restitution of some of these works acquired under dubious circumstances?*

PD   Not directly within the framework of the exhibition I personally curated, but I am aware of the recent cases that rekindled the debate on restitution. It is legitimate that works that were stolen in the course of large-scale pillaging by colonial armies be returned to their rightful owners, even if these might not always be easy to identify. However, it is also desirable that they be kept in a context that allows for their value to be understood, not just within the social and historical context of their production but also by comparison with other works of the same kind, produced in very different contexts. In other words we must strike a balance between the identity claim and the comparative claim, one that provides a measure of the diverse ways in which the world is inhabited, and one to which we should all have access. The latter—the comparative claim—is rarely taken into account by heritage museums, which often confine themselves to collecting objects from the same region or culture. It is a common impulse of native communities, especially in North America, to create museums that are basically storerooms of objects and images, and thus of the techniques embodied in these objects, which the younger generations can go and see if they wish to restore their sense of pride in a past that was discredited by colonizers. This habit has created a situation where each collective—local, ethnic, or religious—provides its own version of what it truly is, the only authentic version, in its view, and one that serves to discredit competing versions that outsiders or dissidents from the collective may have produced. In British Columbia, collections are generally made of objects that were returned by the federal government from the 1970s onward, after the confiscations of the first half of the century—as the great rituals such as potlatch had long been prohibited. And, depending on who benefits from these restitutions and on the beneficiaries' social status in these highly aristocratic societies, the way the objects are exhibited will vary considerably.

But such initiatives, albeit linked to the concern of indigenous communities to maintain a collective memory by reappropriating objects and know-how, do not make universalist museums of civilization illegitimate. These museums exhibit a wide range of objects from all over the world, all of which have the same function. In this way they can give a sense of the range of human imagination when confronted with the need to represent the world in images or to transform it with techniques. Anthony Appiah offered a vivid illustration of this a few years ago, in an article for the *New York Review of Books*[11] in which he described how the Ashanti king Kofi Karikari had assembled, in his Ghanaian capital, a kind of cabinet of curiosities that contained an eclectic assortment of objects from West Africa as well as from further afield, notably Europe. This was, of course, a court museum, but one that sought to present the diversity of human invention, and such an ambition could not be reduced to a manifestation of European universalist imperialism. That museum was plundered in 1874 by British colonial troops. But, as the Ashanti king reminds us, the project of creating a museum that opens the mind, reveals new things, and knocks down the walls between cultures remains a legitimate one. The demand for historical justice, also perfectly legitimate, must not lock us into a rigid conception of cultural heritage by forbidding its circulation.

Thus claims for restitution must always be weighed against the need for places to exist where a wide range of objects can be seen by the greatest number of people—even though it must be admitted that, for the time being, these places are located in former colonial metropoles. I have an anecdote to illustrate this point: for the centennial anniversary of Claude Lévi-Strauss, the Musée du Quai Branly organized a day-long event with free admission during which certain people were asked to read some of his texts. I was waiting for my turn to read an excerpt from *Mythologiques*, not far from a small video monitor on which a short film of an African ritual was playing. It so happened that two visitors of African descent, clearly of modest socioeconomic status, who had perhaps never set foot in a museum before, were commenting on the film. They were absolutely fascinated, seeming to recognize in the film things that their parents or grandparents had told them and that now seemed rather remote. I spent ten minutes listening to them as they

184   *The Contemporary World in the Light of Anthropology*

commented on the ritual and discussed what they understood or failed to understand, asking each other questions and listening to the commentary in the voice-over. This educational function is in my view absolutely central, and it is one of the things of which the Musée du Quai Branly can be proud. Indeed, it has managed to attract a new audience, especially people of sub-Saharan African descent, which was entirely unexpected, because they never visited the Musée de l'Homme before. This is also a way for France to give meaning to its own multiculturalism. Hence another difficulty with the restitution issue: independently of the inalienability rule for the collections of French museums and of the mistaken interpretations that can be given to objects, the value of exchanging cultural works must be taken into consideration.

There was a rather lively debate recently about the restitution of the tattooed Maori heads, generically called Momokai, that were found in 2006 in the collections of the Rouen Museum. The Te Papa Museum in New Zealand had requested the return of all heads from France, as well as from any other country that had any; but it ran up against the legal principle of the inalienability of museum collections. A new law had to be passed to authorize this restitution, which finally happened in 2011. The resulting discussions were quite interesting and led to a conference organized at the Musée du Quai Branly. One of the questions raised was how these heads should be defined: were they to be considered human remains, works of art, anthropological specimens, or images? And how were they to be handled in each of these cases? Traditionally only people of high status were tattooed, and their heads were preserved in the family after death, to be exhibited at important rituals, a bit like the mummies of royal lineage among the Incas. To these were added the enemy chiefs killed in battle whose heads were also preserved, but in this case as a kind of spoils, which could occasionally serve as an object of mockery. Finally, with the beginning of trade with foreign sailors, the Maoris adopted the habit of tattooing slaves and prisoners of war, who would then be executed in order for their heads to be sold. In short, we are dealing with three very different categories for these heads. First, a sort of ancestor portrait: just as noble and bourgeois families kept paintings of their ancestors, the Maoris kept heads, which were in fact a kind of image. Next, the heads of enemy chiefs were trophies somewhat similar to hunting ones. And, finally, the heads of slaves were trading goods, of a grisly kind to be sure, but without much significance for the Maoris

The museum 185

beyond the revenue they could provide. If the diversity of these processes is not taken into account, we will misidentify these objects, as well as their radically different functions and uses.

This recalls another classic example that I happen to know well: that of the Shuar shrunken heads, *tsantsa*. A shrunken head is a kind of identity document, captured from another group and made up so as to sever the token from its identity and to transfer it to another individual. It is not an ancestor, for *tsantsa* were taken from enemies in the same linguistic area but who spoke another dialect and were thus distant enough to supply a new identity. They worked as enablers of an identity transfer to an unborn child, over the course of a series of ceremonies that took place off and on for nearly a year. And when, at the end of the ritual, the head had fulfilled its function as a vector of identity, it no longer had any use and was tossed into the river. When traders picked up on the morbid appetite of the Whites for this kind of object, the heads began to be traded. In the 1970s, some leaders of the Shuar Federation demanded that the *tsantsa* be returned; but they quickly realized that this made little sense. Since the *tsantsa* were not relics, that is, objects that played a fundamental role in the making of local identity, nor were they endowed with magical properties or linked to the presence of a deity, like Christian relics, for example, the demands for restitution were soon dropped. There is thus a wide variety of different situations, each calling for a response appropriate to the specific circumstances; and, with regard to the issue of restitution, moral and legal principles must be considered cautiously.

PC *If I understand you correctly, metropolitan museums may be legitimate sites for these objects, but for this to be entirely consistent, it is not the restitution of foreign objects that we should engage in so much as the wider circulation of the objects that our own civilization has produced?*

PD Or rather a better circulation of the objects produced by all civilizations. One of the points that Anthony Appiah made in the article I just mentioned is that in museums on the African continent, with the paradoxical exception of the former cabinet of curiosities of the Ashanti king, there are almost no objects from Europe, America, or Asia. There are obvious reasons for this, starting with the availability of these works and their price on the art market, which is prohibitive for nations with limited means. But this results in the creation of

186   *The Contemporary World in the Light of Anthropology*

localized heritage sanctuaries that bring together objects that are considered the best representatives of an ethnic or regional identity, but without any confrontation, or comparison, with objects from other regions of the world. Mercifully this is changing slightly. There have been regular exchanges between major developing countries such as Brazil and China. Brazil has sent feather ornaments and other native objects to China, and China has sent in return ancient bronzes and ceramics to Brazil. Circulations of this kind are beginning to develop, but they remain confined to developing countries that already have considerable means. There is an organization called the International Council of Museums (ICOM), which includes many museums from all over the world whose mission should be to facilitate this kind of circulation of objects, and hence the teaching around the world of the diverse ways in which it is inhabited. Unfortunately this does not seem to be one of their priorities, which for the most part remain related to expounding ethical principles. The major ethnographic museums, including the Musée du Quai Branly, now frequently make pieces from their collections available on temporary loan, sometimes for rather long periods, to museums in the countries from which these pieces come. But it is high time that works in the tradition of western art, too, circulated outside Europe and North America—and not only in the luxurious replicas of the major museums erected in places like Abou Dhabi— so that all these objects may be put into mutual perspective.

PC   *We are now coming to the end of our interview, and I would just like to ask you, in conclusion, about an idea that seems to have guided you throughout your career, that of diversity. You have been an observer, and then a thinker, of a double diversity—that of natures and that of cultures—which you have always tried to articulate together. Is this, in the end, the only thing of intrinsic value, the only thing worth defending unconditionally?*

PD   Absolutely! What makes our planet special is that hundreds of millions of years of evolution have made possible a proliferation of forms of life, ways of being, and types of interactions that is absolutely prodigious. And a miniscule part of this very long evolution is marked by the history of human societies, which seems to us already very long and very rich. If there is something admirable and infinitely precious in what might well be the exception in the universe that is Earth, it is precisely this: to have been the support and

The museum 187

condition of such a multiplicity of forms of human and nonhuman existence. Thus, if there is one value to be defended in itself—that is, an absolute value lying outside any utilitarian function, a value that is unique because it is attached to something that may not exist anywhere else and that has proven fragile—this is diversity, in all its manifestations and guises: the diversity of organisms, of environments and landscapes, of modes of life, of ways of doing and communicating, of ways of producing and telling, of ways of coming together and even of destroying one another. The composition of worlds, and the unrivalled role that humans play in it, are also this: from the diversity of elements available to their perception and understanding, by combining these elements in countless ways, humans have increased further still the diversity that early hominids had been given. And they have accomplished this increase not through culture, understood as some luminous graft opposed to natural phenomena, but through the flow of all kinds of innovations, which constitute as many increasingly refined extensions of our human nature, itself in perpetual evolution. In short, they have established a properly human way of being by diffracting the initial puzzle of diversity, by creating an even more complex kaleidoscope of values, institutions, norms, techniques, and images, as well as uncontrollable processes that act in return against the very thing they have contributed to enriching.

Too often, diversity is defended in the name of the support it is said to provide for the perpetuation of life. For example, we are supposed to preserve biodiversity at all costs, since the thousands of animal and plant species that go extinct may have been the sources of molecules that enabled therapeutic breakthroughs, supplied new sources of energy and materials, decontaminated the environment, or offered remarkable nutritional properties. The extinction of these species would thus represent as many missed opportunities to facilitate human life. But, here again, nature is seen as a mere resource, the provider of products and services, a kind of supermarket that is all the more appealing as its shelves are filled with a greater variety of products, and that is in need of protection against vandals if we are to continue to enjoy everything it offers for our consumption. I do not deny that nonhuman organisms could be of great potential use to us, neither do I underestimate the increasingly clear role that the erosion of biodiversity plays in the primary productivity of ecosystems and, ultimately, in compounding the disastrous effects of climate change. But it seems to me that all these

188   *The Contemporary World in the Light of Anthropology*

utilitarian arguments, which may be used to tactical effect against the most aggressive forms of environmental degradation, must nonetheless not be allowed exclusive status, as is now often the case. What we must defend is what we truly hold dear, namely diversity as a value in itself, because living in a world where the forms of life and thought, the languages we speak, and the ways we relate to the world are infinitely varied is a source of joy and a challenge to our intellectual laziness, and because this kind of diversity brings us surprise and awe, gives us the possibility of making our lives into a series of small wonders hanging on threads of chance. A monotone and monochrome world, without unforeseen events or improbable encounters, with nothing new to catch the eye or ear, or tease our curiosity, a world without diversity—that is a nightmare world. I cannot help but think that the decrease in diversity in our ways of producing that was brought about by the standardization of the Industrial Revolution in the early twentieth century has been one of the sources of totalitarian regimes, which were themselves models of hostility to diversity and of standardization of the mind and of ways of being. Charlie Chaplin understood this when he followed *Modern Times* with *The Great Dictator*!

And this critique of utilitarianism also applies to cultural diversity. Its value does not lie only in the fact that, as is often rightly pointed out, every culture is a trove of knowledge, an original experiment in collective life that is a potential source of inspiration; or that, with the disappearance of any one of them—of its language, customs, and institutions—part of the richness of the world is excised, a way of composing it whose recipe is lost forever. The maintenance of cultural diversity—beyond the preservation of heritage that drives us to accumulate testimonies on the variety of practices and works, in the hope of somewhat alleviating the grief caused by their ineluctable loss of significance, beyond the watchword promoted by international organizations that consider the ecumenical combination of diversities as the most fertile ground for perpetual peace—also has an absolute, normative value.

For to exist, for a human being, is to differ.

Notes

Notes to Chapter 1

1 Lévi-Strauss 1969, p. 8.
2 Pouillon 1975, pp. 15–16.
3 Diamond 1974, p. 297.
4 See Jean Pouillon's fine discussion of this question in Pouillon 1975, pp. 29–37.
5 It was subsequently published as "Le Jardin de Colibri: Procès de travail et catégorisations sexuelles chez les Achuar de l'Équateur": see Descola 1983.

Notes to Chapter 2

1 Harris 1974.
2 Chapter 1 in Sahlins 1972 bears this title.
3 Balée 1994.
4 See e.g. Lévy-Bruhl 1923.
5 Godelier 1986.
6 Lévi-Strauss 1964.
7 Descola 1992.
8 Tylor 1871.
9 Bird-David 1999.
10 Leiris 1958, 1948, 2014.
11 Descola 1996; Debaene 2014.
12 See also Barley 1983; Bowen 1954; Maybury-Lewis 1965.
13 Clifford and Marcus 1986.

Notes to Chapter 3

1 See, among others, Sternberg 1905; Bogoras 1904–1909; Hallowell 1981.
2 Haudricourt 1969.
3 Ingold 1998.
4 Racine 1989.
5 von Brandenstein 1982.
6 Granet 1968, p. 297.

190 *Notes*

7 Lévi-Strauss 1969, p. 146. Lévi-Strauss employed this formula to refer to the tangible qualities at work in myths, but it expresses a more general position on the process of understanding.
8 Descola 2012.
9 Mauss 1974, p. 130.
10 On this debate, see Carrithers, Candea, Sykes et al. 2010 and Hallowell 1981.
11 Wagner 1981.
12 These ideas have been developed in Descola 2021.
13 For more on this example, see Descola 2021, pp. 263–296.
14 Lemonnier 1990.
15 Descola 2001.

Notes to Chapter 4

1 Boltanski and Thévenot 2006.
2 Serres 2009.
3 Heidegger 1968.
4 This tangle of local and global levels is the subject of an admirable study by Anna Tsing (see Lowenhaupt Tsing 2015). In it, she provides a transnational and multisite ethnography of the networks of pickers and sellers of matsutake mushrooms.
5 E.g. Lloyd 1996.
6 Le Roy Ladurie 1977; Roche 1981.
7 Sperber 1996.
8 Diamond 2005.
9 Descola, Strathern, Carneiro da Cunha et al. 1998.
10 Hartog 2016.
11 Appiah 2006.

References

Appiah, Anthony Kwame. 2006. "Whose culture is it?" *New York Review of Books*, February 9.

Balée, William. 1994. *Footprints of the Forest: Ka'apor Ethnobotany*. New York: Columbia University Press.

Barley, Nigel. 1983. *The Innocent Anthropologist: Notes from a Mud Hut*. Long Grove, IL: Waveland Press.

Bird-David, Nurit. 1999. "'Animism' revisited: Personhood, environment, and relational epistemology." *Current Anthropology* 40 (Supplement): 67–91.

Bogoras, Waldemar. 1904–1909. *The Chukchee*. New York: E. J. Brill.

Boltanski, Luc, and Laurent Thévenot, 2006. *On Justification: Economies of Worth*. Princeton, NJ: Princeton University Press.

Bowen, Elenore Smith. 1954. *Return to Laughter*. London: Victor Gollancz Ltd.

Carrithers, Michael, Matei Candea, Karen Sykes et al. 2010. "Ontology is just another word for culture: Motion tabled at the 2008 meeting of the Group for Debates in Anthropological Theory, University of Manchester." *Critique of Anthropology* 30(2): 152–200.

Clifford, James, and George Marcus. 1986. *Writing Culture: The Poetics and Politics of Ethnography*. Berkeley: University of California Press.

Debaene, Vincent. 2014. *Far Afield: French Anthropology between Science and Literature*. Chicago, IL: University of Chicago Press.

Descola, Philippe. 1983. "Le Jardin de Colibri: Procès de travail et catégorisations sexuelles chez les Achuar de l'Équateur." *L'Homme* 23(1): 61–89.

Descola, Philippe. 1992. "Societies of nature and the nature of society," in Adam Kuper (ed.), *Conceptualizing Society*. New York: Routledge, pp. 107–126.

192 *References*

Descola, Philippe. 1994. *In the Society of Nature: A Native Ecology in Amazonia.* Cambridge: Cambridge University Press.

Descola, Philippe. 1996. *The Spears of Twilight: Life and Death in the Amazon Jungle.* New York: New Press.

Descola, Philippe. 2001. "The genres of gender: Local models and global paradigms in the comparison of Amazonia and Melanesia," in Thomas Gregor and Donald Tuzin (eds.), *Gender in Amazonia and Melanesia: An Exploration of the Comparative Method.* Berkeley: University of California Press, pp. 91–114.

Descola, Philippe. 2012. "L'Arbre et la grille: Remarques sur la notion de transformation dans l'anthropologie structurale," in Pierre Guenancia and Jean-Pierre Sylvestre (eds.), *Claude Lévi-Strauss et ses contemporains.* Paris: Presses Universitaires de France, pp. 181–194.

Descola, Philippe. 2013. *Beyond Nature and Culture.* Chicago, IL: University of Chicago Press.

Descola, Philippe. 2021. *Les Formes du visible: Une anthropologie de la figuration.* Paris: Seuil.

Descola, Philippe, Marilyn Strathern, Manuela Carneiro da Cunha et al. 1998. "Exploitable knowledge belongs to the creators of it: A debate." *Social Anthropology* 6(1): 109–126.

Diamond, Jared. 2005. *Collapse: How Societies Choose to Fail or Succeed.* New York: Viking Press.

Diamond, Stanley. 1974. *In Search of the Primitive: A Critique of Civilization.* New Brunswick, NJ: Transaction Books.

Godelier, Maurice. 1986. *The Mental and the Material: Thought, Economy, and Society.* London: Verso.

Granet, Marcel. 1968 [1934]. *La Pensée chinoise.* Paris: Albin Michel.

Hallowell, Alfred I. 1981 [1960]. "Ojibwa ontology, behaviour and world view," in Stanley Diamond (ed.), *Culture in History: Essays in Honor of Paul Radin.* New York: Octagon Books, pp. 19–52.

Harris, Marvin. 1974. *Cows, Pigs, Wars and Witches: The Riddles of Culture.* New York: Random House.

Hartog, François, 2016. *Regimes of Historicity: Presentism and the Experience of Time.* New York: Columbia University Press.

Haudricourt, André-Georges. 1969. "Domestication of animals, cultivation of plants, and human relations." *Social Science Information,* 8(3): 163–172.

Heidegger, Martin. 1998. "On the Essence and Concept of φύσις in Aristotle's Physics B, I," in Martin Heidegger, *Pathmarks.* Cambridge: Cambridge University Press, pp. 183–230.

References 193

Ingold, Tim. 1998. "Totemism, animism, and the depiction of animals," in Marketta Seppälä, Jari-Pekka Vanhala, and Linda Weintraub (eds.), *Animal: Anima: Animus*. Pori, Finland: FRAME / Pori Art Museum, pp. 181–207.

Le Roy Ladurie, Emmanuel. 1977. *Les Paysans de Languedoc*. Paris: Flammarion.

Leiris, Michel, 2014. *Phantom Africa*. London: Seagull Books.

Leiris, Michel. 1948. *La Langue secrète des Dogons de Sanga (Soudan français)*. Paris: Institut d'ethnologie.

Leiris, Michel. 1958. *La Possession et ses aspects théâtraux chez les Éthiopiens de Gondar*. Paris: Plon.

Lemonnier, Pierre. 1990. *Guerres et festins: Paix, échanges et compétition dans les Highlands de Nouvelle-Guinée*. Paris: Editions de la Maison des Sciences de l'Homme.

Lévy-Bruhl, Lucien. 1923. *Primitive Mentality*. New York: Macmillan.

Lévi-Strauss, Claude. 1964. *Totemism*. London: Merlin Press.

Lévi-Strauss, Claude. 1969 [1964]. *Mythologiques*, vol. 1: *The Raw and the Cooked*. Chicago, IL: University of Chicago Press.

Lloyd, G. E. R. 1996. *Adversaries and Authorities: Investigations into Ancient Greek and Chinese Science*. Cambridge: Cambridge University Press.

Lowenhaupt Tsing, Anna. 2015. *The Mushroom at the End of the World: On the Possibility of Life in Capitalist Ruins*. Princeton, NJ: Princeton University Press.

Mauss, Marcel. 1974. *Oeuvres 2: Représentations collectives et diversité des civilisations*. Paris: Éditions de minuit.

Maybury-Lewis, David. 1965. *The Savage and the Innocent*. London: Evans Brothers.

Pouillon, Jean. 1975. *Fétiches sans fétichisme*. Paris: François Maspéro.

Racine, Luc. 1989. "Du modèle analogique dans l'analyse des représentations magico-religieuses." *L'Homme* 109: 5–25.

Roche, Daniel. 1981. *Le Peuple de Paris: Essai sur la culture populaire au XVIIIe siècle*. Paris: Aubier.

Sahlins, Marshall. *Stone Age Economics*. New York: Routledge, 1972.

Serres, Michel. 2009. *Écrivains, savants et philosophes font le tour du monde*. Paris: Le Pommier.

Sperber, Dan. 1996. *Explaining Culture: A Naturalistic Approach*. London: Blackwell.

Sternberg, Leo. 1905. "Die Religion der Giljaken." *Archiv für Religionswissenschaft* 8: 244–274.

Tylor, Edward B. 1871. *Primitive Culture: Researches into the*

Development of Mythology, Philosophy, Religion, Language, Art and Custom, 2 vols. London: Murray.

von Brandenstein, Carl Georg. 1982. *Names and Substance of the Australian Subsection System*. Chicago, IL: University of Chicago Press.

Wagner, Roy. 1981 [1975]. *The Invention of Culture*. Chicago, IL: University of Chicago Press.

Index

Aboriginal populations 91, 159–160, 181
Achuar
  and adherence to animist conceptions
    150–151
  and anthropological discourse 164
  cosmology 151–152
  demographic regulation 56
  dreams, role of 59–60, 71
  effects of ecosystem constraints 55, 57
  infant mortality rate 56
  kinship system 63–64
  mechanisms of modes of identification
    151–152
  myths, function of 80
  relationship to environment 33, 44, 57,
    59–60, 62, 74, 161–162
  relationship to nonhumans 33, 59, 60,
    61, 62, 63, 64, 88
  ethnographic study of 19, 33, 35, 43,
    53–54, 56, 57–58, 59–64
  missionaries and 52, 53, 69, 148
  Musée du Quai Branly 176, 181
  shaping of ecosystem 58–59
  symbolic ecology 63
  and time 44, 57, 69, 80, 81, 125
  tourism 163–164
  views on the world of Whites 71–73
Aénts Chicham 51, 52
agrarian techniques
  and approach to environment 57–58,
    89
Amazonia
  author's hypothesis on 66
  captive practices 121
  extent of 50
  forms of exchange 124
  images used in 126, 127

  state of, for research 16–17
  war, interpretations of, in 54–55
Amazonian forest 58
America, northwest coast 122
Amerindians 87
  and the state 20
  absorption of systems of thought
    147–148
  conception of relationship with plants
    and animals 86, 87, 88, 92
  donor animism in 121
  and myth 80
  representation at international levels 76
  suspicion of anthropologists 77
analogism 41, 47, 96, 97–98, 109, 121,
  123, 137, 138, 139, 144, 146
  transition to naturalism 119, 142
  and mnemonic apparatuses 139, 140
analogy, role of 96, 97
Andes 147, 158
anents (chants) 60–62, 164
animal double (*tona*) 96–97
animal husbandry
  and link to political schemas 90
animal totems 94, 123
animism 47, 65–66, 88–89, 90, 91, 92, 98,
  99, 123, 124, 128
  Achuar 135, 137
  Amazonian 92, 125, 126–127
  New Guinea 123
  North America 127
  metamorphosis in 128
  and totemism 89, 90, 91
anthropologists
  advocacy 76, 77
  collaboration with native communities
    78

196 Index

anthropologists (*cont.*)
  as equal to those studied 117
  narrative 82–83
  sense of incongruity 1, 116
anthropology
  attraction to 5–6
  and a broader public 41, 45
  concept of culture 39–40, 111–112
  evolutionary 119, 120–121
  French 83, 99, 111
  imperial perspective 118
  literary techniques in 82–83
  methodological relativism and 113
  and minorities 2
  and monograph writing 45, 46, 83, 84
  and museums 176
  North American 111
  publications 36
  and regional ensembles 170
  relationship to ethnography and
    ethnology 43, 47, 48
  role of 40, 42–43, 101, 104, 125, 169
  and subjectivity 45–46, 84–85
  terminology 98–99
  see also see also Laboratory of
    Social Anthropology; structural
    anthropology
Appiah, Anthony 183
Australia 91, 93, 94, 159
ayahuasca 166

Balée, William 58
Barley, Nigel 83
Barthes, Roland 38
Benveniste, Émile 38
Bernand, Carmen 50
Beyond Nature and Culture 38, 39, 40–41,
    42, 43, 47, 98, 109, 125, 137, 144,
    147, 150
  genesis 86
  theoretical foundation 99–101
biology and ecology 176
Bird-David, Nurit 65
Boas, Franz 84, 111
Bogoras, Waldemar 88, 93
Boltanski, Luc 137
Booty Creek 159
Bororo, the 180
Bourdieu, Pierre 10, 37, 38, 100
  habitus 39
British Columbia 127

Candoshi, the 78
cargo cults, Melanesian 149
chants *see anents*

Chukchee, the 93
Chukotka 122
clan 172
Clastres, Pierre 20–21
Clifford, James 84
cognitive psychology 99
collective existence 111, 113–114
Collège de France 37, 38
compatibility and incompatibility 124,
    147–148, 149
constitution, modern 145
cosmologies 109
  forms of pictorial representation in
    126, 127
  sequencing 119
  stabilization and diffusion 152
  see also ontologies
cultural diversity, threat to 169
cultural hybridization 149
culture as the basis of study 111–112

de Libera, Alain 143
Debaene, Vincent 83
Democritus 138
Descola, Jean 3, 4
Descola, Philippe
  and aboriginal Australia 91
  and anthropological project 40, 46,
    134, 169
  appeal of the particular and abstract 48
  and art historians 128
  and aunt 36
  Catholic University of Quito 22
  combinatorial approach 101
  conceptual reform 116
  and use of images 125
  intellectual influences on 23–25, 26, 27,
    33, 38–40, 99
  and attraction to Amazonia 13, 18–19,
    50
  and choice of anthropology 2, 9–10
  Collège de France 36–37, 38, 40, 46, 51
  and culture 112
  doctoral thesis 26, 33–34, 39, 45
  early exposure to literature 4
  École des Hautes Études en Sciences
    Sociales (EHESS) 34, 35, 88
  École Normale Supérieure 8, 9
  École Pratique des Hautes Études 10, 46
  and ecological determinism 53
  education in England 4–5
  and father 3, 4
  arriving at fieldwork destination in
    Amazonia 52–53
  and fieldwork site choice 14–16, 50

Index

197

and grandfather 4
and humans and nonhumans 46, 86,
88–89, 90
impact of nature on 6–7
impact of writing on
non-anthropologists 41
In the Society of Nature 33, 34, 42,
43, 100
intellectual framework for doctoral
thesis 26, 32–33
interest in travel 3, 5
International Union for Conservation
of Nature and Natural Resources 175
La Fabrique des images (*The Making
of Images*) exhibition 127–128, 180
landscape and environment and 6–7
and Lévi-Strauss 9, 13, 23–24, 27, 31,
32, 34, 35, 38, 51, 65, 91
and Marcel Granet 97
and Michel Foucault 97
Museum of Natural History 56
and naturalism 141
and philosophy 115
and Pierre Bourdieu 100
political activism 7–8, 19–20, 21–23,
133
reflexivity 133
as a relativist 42, 112, 113
reading Marx 8–9
return home from ethnographic work
78
and schemas of practice 39, 40, 100
and structuralism 118
tertiary education 8–10, 13
The Spears of Twilight 35, 36, 42, 43,
44–46
travel to Ecuador 52
University of Nanterre 10
Diamond, Jared 154
discourse representing nature 163
diversity, value of 169, 170, 186–188
domination 15, 20, 117, 120
political response to 171, 173
dreaming, role of 59–60, 71
Durkheim, Émile 31
Dutch painting (17th century) 130

Easter Island 154
ecological discourse 163–164
ecological fundamentalism 175
ecology 162, 175
economies of worth 137
Ecuador 159, 163, 174, 175
El Oriente 175
Elias, Norbert 151

Enlightenment
impact on European life 134
environmental
anthropology 10, 26, 34
determinism 26, 55, 56, 120
movements, native 162
resilience, threat to 155
Eskimo groups 87
ethnobiological classification 25
ethnographic data 84–85
ethnographic objects
scientific treatment 177
ethnographic shock 115
ethnographic study process 35, 45, 46,
66–67, 68–69, 74, 75, 79
ethnographic writing 81–85
influencing museography 178
ethnography 1, 30, 42–43, 44–45, 47, 48,
116
ethnology 42, 43, 44, 47
ethnoscience 26
evangelization 147–148
evolution and art 181–182
evolutionism 173, 178
exaptation 121
exchange, forms of 124, 137

feathers as objects of study and display
180–181
feminisim 22
fieldwork 48, 66, 68–69, 77, 83
equipment for 51
and language 59, 66–67
fieldwork research sites 10, 14
relationship to communities 16–17
influences on choice of 17–18
Foucault, Michel 38, 39
episteme 39–40

geographers 41
Georgescu-Roegen, Nicholas 33
globalization process 149–150
and regional identities 150
Godelier, Maurice 9, 10, 24–25, 33, 34,
56, 65, 176
Goethe, Johann Wolfgang von 105

Hallowell, Irving 88, 111
Harris, Marvin 26
Hartog, François 169
Haudricourt, André-Georges 25, 89
heads, origin and restitution 184–185
Héritier, Françoise 29, 31, 37
as a structuralist 29
heterosubstitution 124

198 Index

historians 4, 34, 36, 41, 45, 46
homosubstitution 124
Human Relations Area Files 30
human diversity, accounting for 111
human nature, dispositions of 46, 94
humans and nonhumans 46, 49,93, 94,
    100, 114, 126–127, 136
  continuity and discontinuity 95, 96,
    98, 131
  coupling 157
  invariants in 47, 107
  see also Achuar
Husserl, Edmund 8–9

ideas, model for replication and diffusion
    of 153
images
  and naturalism 143
  preceding discourse historically 129
  use of in analysis 125–131
Inca ideology 10
Incas 139
indigenous peoples
  knowledge 165–167
  role of struggles 21
individuals, representation of 119
Ingold, Tim 91
intellectuals, role of 174–176
interiority 47, 107
  animal 127, 128
  human 92, 93, 99, 130–131, 146
  nonhuman 66, 80, 95
  and physicality 99–100, 130, 131, 146
International Council of Museums (ICO)
    186
International Plant Medicine
    Corporation 165–166
invariant relationships 105

Jivaros (Ecuador) 50, 148, 174
Jospin, Lionel 176

Ka'apor 58
Kaluli, the 123
Kapawi Lodge 163
Kapawientza River 53
Karikari, Kofi 183
Kasua, the 123
knowledge
  commodification of 166–167
  ownership 165–167
Kunapa clan 159, 160
Kwakwaka'wakw, the 127

Labica, Georges 10

Laboratory of Social Anthropology
    30–31
Lacandon, the 10–11
land, western relationship to 141–142
left and ultraleft thinking 21, 22
Latour, Bruno 108, 135, 143, 144
Leiris, Michel 83
Lemonnier, Pierre 123–124
Leninism 19, 21, 22
Leroi-Gourhan, André 38
Lévi-Strauss, Claude 29, 37, 38
  centennial anniversary 183
  and colleagues 31–32
  criticisms of 28, 42
  and Descola 13, 23–24, 27, 31, 32, 34,
    35, 38, 51, 65, 91, 99
  D'Arcy Thompson 105
  Elementary Structures of Kinship 99,
    105
  and Goethe 105
  Laboratory of Social Anthropology
    30–31, 51
  legacy 32
  myths and mythemes 106, 118
  on nature of structuralism 102
  reciprocity principle 105
  Structuralist School 28–29
  and totemism 65, 91, 95
  transformation in the work of
    104–105
Lévy-Bruhl, Lucien 64
Lloyd, Geoffrey 153

Malaurie, Jean 35
Malaysia 128
Manambu, the 123
Maori heads, origins 184
Marcus, George 84
Marxism 40
  capitalist mode of production 122
  commodity fetishism 79
  and empiricism 25–26
  productive forces 26
  relations of production 26
  and structuralism 25
masks 127, 128, 181
matrimonial alliances 105
matrix of identification 108, 138
  and primacy 108
Mauss, Marcel 31, 37, 109
memory, the art of 140
Mexico, fieldwork in 10–12, 11, 13
  animal double 96
  historical continuities and
    discontinuities 147

Index

mining 158
  protest 158, 172
modernity 135–136
  and empirical study 142, 144
  and nature 145
  as seen by Weber and Durkheim 141
mode of relation 125, 136
modes of identification 40, 98, 100,
    101, 107, 109, 110, 119, 120, 121,
    123,125, 127, 128, 145–146
  images as illustrations of 126
  absorption into 147
  stabilization 96, 151
Momokai 183
Mongolia 122
Montalvo 52
multinaturalism 92
Murdock, G. P. 30
Musée de l'Homme 176, 177
Musée du Quai Branly 176, 177, 183–184
museography, contextualizing 179–180
museums and architecture 179–180
museum objects, circulation 185–186
myths, analysis of 106

nagualism 96
narrative schemes, recurrent 152
natural and social, exhaustion of division
    145
naturalism 47, 91–92, 93, 108, 130, 135,
    136, 138–139, 148
  circulation of 153
  as defined by the author 141, 143–144
  diversity 136–137
  historical existence 142–143
  mediation by specialists 152–153
  systematization 142, 151
  and writing 140
naturalism, modern 42
naturalist mode of identification
  and its constitution 145
  conservation 154–155, 157, 159, 173
  and culture 93, 172
  and nature 91–9
  origins in Europe 119–120
  as a political issue 157, 159
  and preservation of environment 22,
    160
  relationship with 26, 33, 89, 90, 92,
    115–116, 161
  as a resource 187
  socialization of 65
  unification of phenomena under 144
  unintended effects of use of 154–155
  see also political ecology; nonhuman

Nayaka, the 65
New Guinea 123, 124
nonhuman, the
  autonomous 173
  conception of 87
  and humans 25, 46, 87, 93, 123,
    159–160
  as human 123
  as political subjects 171–172
  position in social life 19, 134, 143
  rethinking 134,159–160
Noongar 94, 97
Nouvel, Jean 179

ontologies
  coexistence of, as hybrid form 122–123
  compatibility 147
ontology 108, 109, 110, 111, 139
  conjectural 132
ontological filters 110
ontological mold 93
ontological turn 108, 113

participant observation 67, 68,
    69–70,75–76
Passeron, Jean-Claude 100
patents 165, 166
Pérec, Georges 100
philosophy, history of 39
pictographs 140
Pitt Rivers Museum 177, 178
political, notion of 174
political anthropology 10, 20, 171, 172
political ecology 22–23, 157, 159–160
political schemas, reshaping 158, 173, 174
  and interaction with nonhumans
    158–159, 160, 173
Ponty, Merleau 37, 38
Pouillon, Jean 28–29
predation 54–55
presentism 169
Puyo 52

Quichua 53

reciprocity principle 105
reflexivity 133, 135, 140, 145
  and our own ontology 135
regional identities 150,170
relationship between inner world and
    physical world 47
relativism 112–113, 116
relativism, methodological 113
researcher, impact of working in a
    community on 76

200 Index

restitution of objects 182–185
and comparison 182
Riegl, Aloïs 129
rights 77, 159, 166, 172
property 167
Rivet, Paul 176
Rouen Museum 184

sacred sites 159–160
schemas of practice 100
schematism 99, 100
Schmitt, Carl 141
science, philosophy of 39, 42
self, apprehension of 47
Serres, Michel 137
Severi, Carlo 140
Shakaim (forest spirit) 59
Shaman Pharmaceuticals 165–166
Shuar 55, 56, 155–156, 161, 185
social sciences
concepts 112, 113
in France 31, 38
history of 114
Sperber, Dan 153
Sternberg, Leo 88
structural anthropology 10, 27–28, 102, 104
structural method 102–103
structural ontology 46
structuralism 25, 27, 29, 40, 41, 118
semiology in 103
and the unconscious 103
structuralism and existentialism 29
sumac kawsay (the good life) 164, 165
Surrallés, Alexandre 78
symmetrical anthropology 41, 143
symmetrization 118, 161

Taylor, Anne-Christine 10, 53
Te Papa Museum 184
ter Borch, Gerard (*The Reading Lesson*) 130–131
thermodynamics principle 33

Thévenot, Laurent 137
Thompson, D'Arcy Wentworth 106
time 125–126 *see also* Achuar
tona see animal double
totemic identification 94, 95
totemism 47, 65, 90, 91, 92, 93
Australian 123
classificatory dimension of 95
origins 93
transformation, ecological
nonmodern as inspiration for 168
society's inability to absorb the risk 155–156
technological innovation 156
unintended consequences 154–155, 156
transformation in structural analysis 104–106, 121, 122, 124
tsantsa (Shuar shrunken heads) 185
Tsimshian, the 123
Tupinamba 148
Tzeltal, the 10, 11–12

unity and diversity 136–137
universalism 116–118

variation *see* transformation in structural analysis
Vernant, Jean-Pierre 38
Viveiros de Castro, Eduardo 91
von Brandenstein, Carl Georg 94
von Siebold, Philipp Frantz 178

Wachtel, Nathan 10
Wagner, Roy 112
Wang Chong 138
Warburg, Aby 129
World Wildlife Fund 175
worldview 109–110
writing, role of 139, 140

Yupiit 87, 127, 128

Zuidema, Tom 10